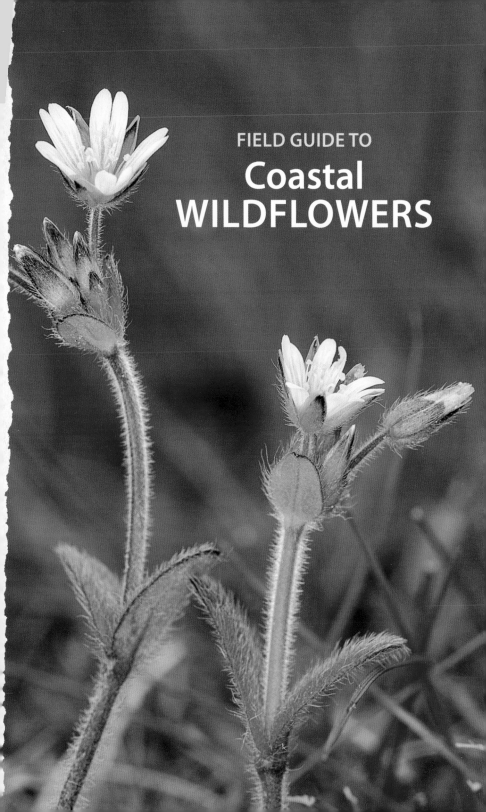

FIELD GUIDE TO
Coastal
WILDFLOWERS

FIELD GUIDE TO
Coastal
WILDFLOWERS
of Britain, Ireland and Northwest Europe

Paul Sterry
and
Andrew Cleave

WILD
NATURE
PRESS

PRINCETON

Published by Princeton University Press,
41 William Street, Princeton, New Jersey 08540
99 Banbury Road, Oxford OX2 6JX

press.princeton.edu

British Library Cataloging-in-Publication Data is available

Library of Congress Control Number 2021952295
ISBN 978-0-691-21815-1
Ebook ISBN 978-0-691-23845-6

Production and design by Julie Dando,
WILDNATUREPRESS Ltd., Plymouth
Printed in Italy

10 9 8 7 6 5 4 3 2 1

Cover: Yellow Horned-poppy *Glaucium flavum*
Back cover: Sea Campion *Silene uniflora*
Page 1: Common Mouse-ear *Cerastium fontanum*
Pages 2–3: Long-headed Clover *Trifolium incarnatum*
ssp. *molinerii*
Right: Sea-kale *Crambe maritima*

CONTENTS

ACKNOWLEDGEMENTS

The authors would like to thank the following people for the support, advice and information they provided. In surname alphabetical order they are:

Ken Adams; Brian Banks; Ian Bennallick; Tony Blunden; Andy Brown; Michael Clark; Andy Clements; Andrew Craggs; Neil Fuller; Peter Gateley; Miranda Gomperts; Mark and Susie Groves; Anne Haden; Gary Hibberd; Bob Hodgson; Chris Jones; Chris Keeling; Simon Leach; Keith and Belinda Lugg; Chris McCarty; Chris Metherell; Tony Mundell; Dawn Nelson; Tristan Norton; Rosemary Parslow; John Poland; Pat O'Reilly; Sue Parker; David Pearman; Martin Rand; Jane Sears; Philip Smith; Roger Smith; James Symonds; Simon Tarrant; Ian Taylor; Kevin Walker; Bob Wardell; Julian Woodman; Dougy Wright; Barry Yates; Mark Yates.

The authors would also like to thank Julie Dando for her input and design expertise; Robert Kirk for his enthusiastic support; and Nigel Redman for his insightful and constructive comments. Their contributions have allowed this book to achieve its full potential.

PHOTOGRAPHIC CREDITS

All the photographs in this book were taken by Andrew Cleave and Paul Sterry with the exception of the following:

Page 30 Machair, Miranda Gomperts; page 37 Anchor, Steve Trewhella/Nature Photographers Ltd; page 66 Early Orache (main picture), Keith Lugg/Nature Photographers Ltd; page 95 Northern Dock, Keith Lugg/Nature Photographers Ltd; page 144 Purple Oxytropis, Laurie Campbell/Nature Photographers Ltd.; page 195 Guernsey Centaury (both pictures), Ignacio Fernandez Villar; page 249 Oxeye Daisy (top picture), Richard Revels/Nature Photographers Ltd; page 282 Irish Marsh-orchid, Simon Tarrant; page 283 Pugsley's Marsh-orchid (top right), Simon Tarrant.

Sea-holly *Eryngium maritimum* growing on the north Norfolk coast.

INTRODUCTION

The British coast has always been important for its island inhabitants. In the past, its greatest significance was as a source of food and place to earn a living, and of course this continues to this day. However, it also acts like a magnet to visitors from inland and there can be few British people who don't visit the coast at least once a year. Since nowhere is said to be more than 70 miles from the sea, the coast's allure is set to increase with the prospect of staycations seeming more attractive than ever before.

Some visitors are attracted by the intrinsic beauty of our rocky coastlines or the sheer scale and lonely isolation of many estuaries and northern beaches. A sense (sadly misplaced these days) that these landscapes and habitats are in some ways untamed and unaffected by man is part of the attraction. Scenery is important of course, but wherever you go on the coast it is impossible to ignore the contribution made by coastal flowers, whatever the time of year. Subliminally or consciously the floral influence is integral to why so many people gravitate towards the sea.

About this book

This book is a celebration of coastal flowers, concentrating on Britain and Ireland. Our southern coasts have floral elements in common with France and further south, while northern shores share species with northern mainland Europe including Scandinavia. Consequently, reference is made to mainland northwest Europe as well, allowing continental readers and British and Irish visitors venturing abroad to benefit from the book's content.

The book's aims are twofold. Firstly, by helping casual visitors identify flowers we hope their appreciation of the natural world will be enhanced. Secondly, by providing an opportunity for seasoned botanists to hone their skills, we hope it will inspire them to make more detailed observations, and submit records of their findings. The bulk of this book deals with the identification of coastal flower species. In addition, the region's main habitat types are discussed in the introduction, and to whet the appetite of enthusiasts the Isles of Scilly (pages 324–327) and northern specialities (pages 328–329) are showcased separately.

When choosing the species for the book we have included both coastal specialities and plants that are common elsewhere but which thrive within sight of the sea. We have used the 4th edition of Clive Stace's definitive *New Flora of the British Isles* (the botanical Bible) to guide us regarding overall classification, currently employed species names and plant status.

Great care has gone into the selection of photographs for this book and in many cases the images have been taken specifically for this project. Preference has been given to photographs that both illustrate key identification features of a given species, and emphasise its beauty. In many instances, additional accompanying photographs illustrate features useful for identification that are not shown clearly by the main image, and leaf cut-outs are included where these help the reader.

The maps provide a general indication of species distributions, with relative geographical abundance or scarcity indicated by intensity of colour. Given the small size at which the maps are printed, the distribution of species with entirely coastal ranges have been exaggerated for ease of reference. The generalised nature of the maps means they are best interpreted with reference to information about location and habitat preferences in the text. When used in this way they can help inform decisions about identification of field discoveries by reference to a given species' range. If the reader wants to plan a trip in order to see specific plants, then the best approach is to study the extremely detailed and interactive maps that can be accessed via the BSBI (Botanical Society of Britain and Ireland) website. Species' status information accompanies each map. B&I is an abbreviation for Britain and Ireland; the NW European range extends from the west coast of France to southern Scandinavia, including the Baltic.

Hoary Stock *Matthiola incana* growing on a crumbling chalk cliff-edge on the Isle of Wight, within inches of a sheer drop to oblivion. Extreme caution is needed when admiring this plant.

Safety first

The coast is a wonderful place for study, exploration and relaxation but it is not without its challenges. There are inherent dangers associated with some areas of shoreline and the sheer power of the sea and tides should always be respected, and never underestimated. The need for a liberal dose of caution cannot be stressed too highly. Maritime terrain and the sea can be unforgiving and a tiny mistake, which inland would be without consequence, can have dire repercussions in the coastal environment. And remember that it is not just you that will be affected if you get into difficulties: somebody will have to come to your rescue, putting themselves, and potentially the lives of others, at risk.

When it comes to cliffs and precipitous coastal slopes, most people have the good sense to keep well away from edges and drops. But remember that invariably the grass or clifftop vegetation will be more slippery, and the soil often more friable, than you expect: a small slip could potentially result in a slide to oblivion. That may sound melodramatic but caution is the watchword when walking on cliffs and steep coastal slopes.

Another threat to safety comes from the sea itself, in the form of rising and falling tides. These days there is no excuse for not knowing the state of the tide at any given location, and at any given time of day: tide timetables can be bought in book form, information is available online, and with apps and websites it is instantly accessible on mobile phones. Remember that in some parts of Britain, on gently-shelving sandy shores for example, it is impossible to out-run the incoming tide.

Cliff bases are often excellent for interesting plants but again caution and common sense are required when it comes to exploration. Cliff faces are constantly eroding and, depending on the substrate, this might involve dramatic rock-falls without warning. An awareness of a habitat's substrate is also vital when exploring saltmarshes. In some locations the ground may appear stable but, without warning, you can find yourself sinking up to your knees in squelchy mud, from which it can be a real challenge to extract yourself.

Respecting natural habitats and a coastal code of conduct

Many coastal habitats are fragile and easily damaged by trampling underfoot, and by more invasive and intrusive forms of leisure activity. Before you start exploring, consider your own physical impact on the environment, and respect any site advice and warnings aimed at minimising the effects of your visit. Sand dunes are a particular case in point, along with seabird colonies. This really is a warning that needs to be heeded, and please trek but don't trample.

Of course, it is important that people continue to visit the coast, and explore, observe and marvel at its wildlife spectacles. Because only with the enthusiasm of people who appreciate coastal flowers, and wildlife generally, is there a chance that wholesale exploitation and disturbance of these precious habitats can be averted. Although individuals can always make a difference, generally a more powerful way of putting forward the conservation message comes from belonging to a wildlife organisation, one that campaigns for wildlife on behalf of its members.

As student naturalists visiting the coast, heed any advice given by custodians of nature reserves in particular, especially when it comes to searching for rare plants. Wherever possible stick to existing paths and avoid the temptation to stray into virgin vegetation. A case in point might be those who search for Dune and Lindisfarne Helleborines, dune specialist orchids found on the northwest and northeast coasts of Britain respectively. With a little homework on the internet and by contacting local botanists it is usually possible to discover precise locations for individual plants whose admiration by enthusiasts will not cause problems of disturbance. Using helleborines as examples, if you can, please avoid the temptation to wander off the beaten track in search of 'your own' specimen – who knows how many non-flowering helleborine spikes, not to mention other species, will be inadvertently trampled as a consequence.

Habitats that are vulnerable to disturbance and damage from visitors are often signposted, with guidelines and routes to follow. Please take care to adhere to any on-site instructions.

GLOSSARY

Achene – one-seeded dry fruit that does not split.

Acute – sharply pointed.

Adpressed – pressed close to the stalk from which the plant part arises.

Aggregate (abbreviation agg.) – group of closely-related species, or micro-species, that for simplicity's sake are treated as a single entity.

Alien – introduced by man from another part of the world.

Alternate – leaf arrangement (not opposite).

Annual – plant that completes its life cycle within 12 months.

Anther – pollen-bearing tip of the stamen.

Appressed (or adpressed) – pressed closely to the relevant part of the plant.

Auricle – pair of lobes at the base of a leaf.

Awn – stiff, bristle-like projection, seen mainly in grass flowers.

Axil – angle between the upper surface or stalk of a leaf and the stem on which it is carried.

Basal – appearing at the base of plant, at ground level.

Basic – soil that is rich in alkaline (mainly calcium) salts.

Beak – projection at the tip of a fruit.

Berry – fleshy, soft-coated fruit containing several seeds.

Biennial – plant that takes two years to complete its life cycle.

Bog – wetland on acid soil, waterlogged by rainfall.

Bract – modified, often scale-like, leaf found at the base of flower stalks in some species.

Bracteole – modified, often scale-like, leaf found at the base of individual flowers in some species.

Bulb – swollen underground structure containing the origins of the following year's leaves and buds.

Bulbil – small, bulb-like structure, produced asexually by some plants and capable of growing into a new plant.

Calcareous – containing calcium, the source typically being chalk or limestone.

Calyx – outer part of a flower, comprising the sepals.

Capsule – dry fruit that splits to liberate its seeds.

Catkin – hanging spike of tiny flowers.

Chlorophyll – green pigment, present in plant leaves and other structures, and essential for photosynthesis.

Clasping – leaf bases that have backward-pointing lobes that wrap around the stem.

Composite – member of the daisy family (Asteraceae).

Compound – leaf that is divided into a number of leaflets.

Cordate – heart-shaped at the base.

Corolla – collective term for the petals.

Cultivar – plant variety created by cultivation.

Deciduous – plant whose leaves fall in autumn.

Decurrent – with the leaf base running down the stem.

Dentate – toothed.

Digitate – resembling the fingers of a splayed hand.

Dioecious – having male and female flowers on separate plants.

Disc floret – one of the inner florets of a composite flower.

Entire – in the context of a leaf, a margin that is untoothed.

Epiphyte – plant that grows on another plant, on which it is not a parasite.

Fen – wetland habitat, waterlogged by ground-water, typically on alkaline soil.

Filament – stalk part of a stamen.

Floret – small flower, part of larger floral arrangement as in composite flowers or umbellifers.

Fruits – seeds of a plant and their associated structures.

Genus (plural genera) – group of closely related species, sharing the same genus name.

Glabrous – smooth, lacking hairs.

Gland – sticky structure at the end of a hair.

Glaucous – blue-grey in colour.

Glume – pair of chaff-like scales at the base of a grass spikelet.

Hybrid – plant derived from the cross-fertilisation of two different species.

Inflorescence – the flowering structure in its entirety, including bracts.

Introduced – not native to the region.

Keel – seen in pea family members: the fused two lower petals, shaped like a boat's keel.

Lanceolate – narrow and lance-shaped.

Lax – open, not dense.

Leaflet – leaf-like segment or lobe of a leaf.

Ligule – membranous flap at the base of a grass leaf, where it joins the stem.

Linear – slender and parallel-sided.

Lip – usually the lower part of an irregular flower such as an orchid.

Lobe – division of a leaf.

Midrib – central vein of a leaf.

Native – occurring naturally in the region and not known to have been introduced.

Node – point on the stem where a leaf arises.

Nut – a dry, one-seeded fruit with a hard outer case.

Nutlet – small nut.

Oblong – leaf whose sides are at least partly parallel-sided.

Obtuse – blunt-tipped (usually in the context of a leaf).

Opposite – (usually leaves) arising in opposite pairs on the stem.

Oval – leaf shape outline.

Ovate – egg-shaped.

Ovary – structure containing a plant's ovules, or immature seeds.

Ovoid – egg-shaped.

Palmate – leaf with finger-like lobes arising from the same point.

Pappus – tuft of hairs on a fruit.

Parasite – plant that derives its nutrition entirely from another living organism.

Pedicel – stalk of an individual flower.

Perennial – plant that lives for more than two years.

Perfoliate – surrounding the stem.

Perianth – collective name for a flower's petals and sepals.

Petals – inner segments of a flower, often colourful.

Petiole – leaf stalk.

Pinnate – leaf division with opposite pairs of leaflets and a terminal one.

Pinnule – secondary division of a pinnate fern frond.

Pod – elongated fruit, often almost cylindrical, seen in pea family members.

Pollen – tiny grains that contain male sex cells, produced by a flower's anthers.

Procumbent – lying on the ground.

Prostrate – growing in a manner pressed tightly to the ground.

Pubescent – with soft, downy hairs.

Ray – one of the stalks of an umbel.

Ray floret – one of the outer florets of a composite flower.

Recurved – curving backwards or downwards.

Reflexed – bent back at an angle of more than 90 degrees.

Rhizome – underground, or ground-level, stem.

Rosette – clustered, radiating arrangement of leaves at ground level.

Saprophyte – plant that lacks chlorophyll and which derives its nutrition from decaying matter.

Sepal – one of the outer, usually less colourful, segments of a flower.

Sessile – lacking a stalk.

Shrub – branched, woody plant.

Species (abbreviation sp., plural spp.) – division within classification that embraces organisms that closely resemble one another and that can interbreed to produce a viable subsequent generation.

Spreading – branching horizontally (in the case of a whole plant) or sticking out at right angles (in the case of hairs).

Stamen – male part of the flower, comprising the anther and filament.

Stigma – receptive surface of the female part of a flower, to which pollen adheres.

Stipule – usually a pair of leaf-like appendages at the base of a leaf.

Stolon – creeping stem.

Style – element of the female part of the flower, sitting on the ovary and supporting the stigma.

Subspecies (abbreviation ssp.) – members of a species that possess significant morphological differences from other groups within the species as a whole; in natural situations, different subspecies are often separated geographically.

Succulent – swollen and fleshy.

Tendril – slender, twining growth used by some plants to aid climbing.

Tepals – both sepals and petals, when the two are indistinguishable.

Tomentose – covered in cottony hairs.

Trifoliate (or trefoil) – leaf with three separate lobes.

Truncate – ending abruptly and squared-off.

Tuber – swollen, usually underground, part of the stem or root.

Tubercle – small swelling.

Umbel – complex, umbrella-shaped inflorescence.

Variety (abbreviation var.) – taxonomic ranking within a species, relating to recognised forms that do not merit being assigned subspecies status.

Whorl – several leaves or branches arising from the same point on a stem.

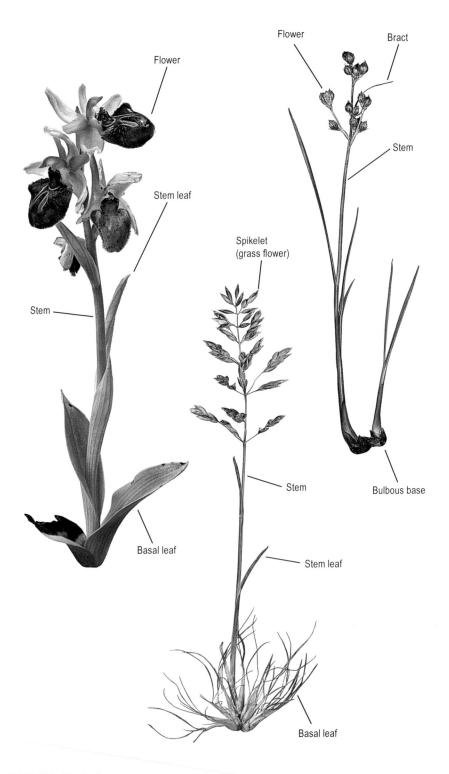

Flower

Flower

Bract

Stem

Stem leaf

Spikelet
(grass flower)

Stem

Stem

Bulbous base

Basal leaf

Stem leaf

Basal leaf

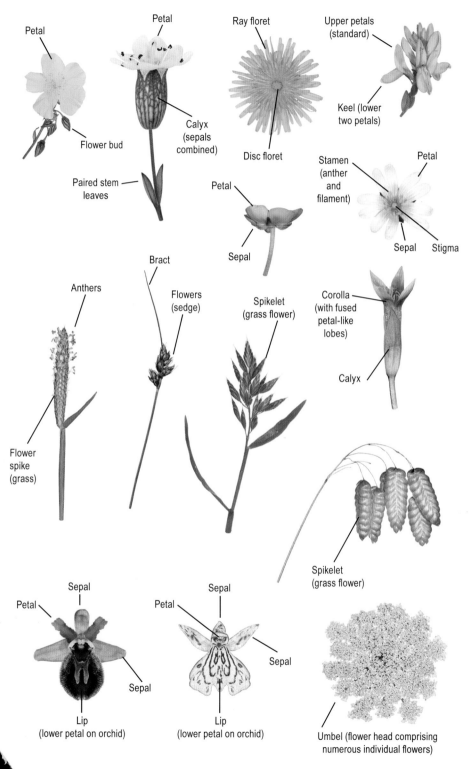

Petal

Petal

Ray floret

Upper petals (standard)

Keel (lower two petals)

Flower bud

Calyx (sepals combined)

Disc floret

Paired stem leaves

Petal

Stamen (anther and filament)

Petal

Sepal

Sepal

Stigma

Bract

Anthers

Flowers (sedge)

Spikelet (grass flower)

Corolla (with fused petal-like lobes)

Calyx

Flower spike (grass)

Spikelet (grass flower)

Sepal

Petal

Sepal

Petal

Sepal

Sepal

Sepal

Lip (lower petal on orchid)

Lip (lower petal on orchid)

Umbel (flower head comprising numerous individual flowers)

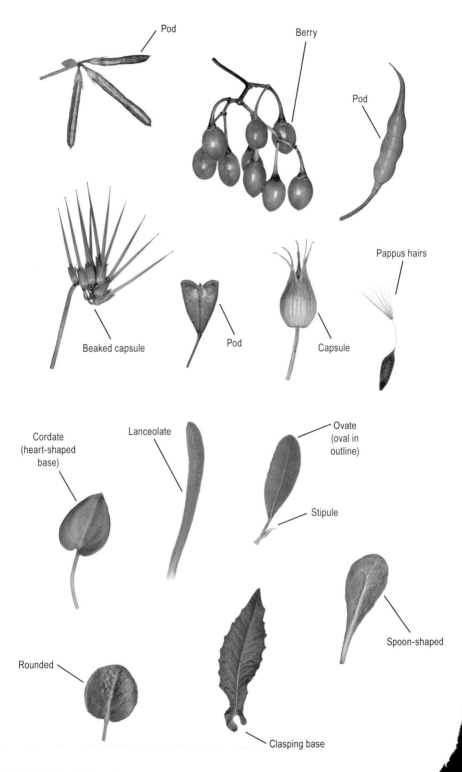

Pod

Berry

Pod

Beaked capsule

Pod

Capsule

Pappus hairs

Cordate (heart-shaped base)

Lanceolate

Ovate (oval in outline)

Stipule

Spoon-shaped

Rounded

Clasping base

Pinnate
(opposite leaflets
and a terminal one)

Finely divided

Toothed margin

Pinnate and spiny

Irregularly lobed

Trifoliate
(three leaflets)

Compound
(divided into
a number of
leaflets)

Stipule

Pinnate

Tendrils

Deeply divided

Leaflet

Tendrils

Opposite pairs
of leaflets

Sandy beaches and dunes

Sand is the name given to fine, granular particles of mineral origin that are smaller than gravel but larger than silt. Coastal sand arises when submerged rocks are eroded, and in some locations fragments of marine mollusc shells are included in the mix. The particles are carried by the sea ultimately falling out of suspension and being deposited on the sea bed or shore. The locations where sand is deposited – as opposed to particles of different size, such as shingle – are determined by the location of suitable submerged rock formations, the nature of tides and currents, and obstacles such as rocky outcrops and headlands.

The ingredients needed for dunes to form are that a beach's intertidal zone be sandy and dry out at low tide, and for there to be consistent onshore winds. Sand particles are blown landwards and accumulate in the shelter of any obstacle, be that tideline debris or vegetation. Pioneer plants such as Sand Couch *Elytrigia arenaria* and Lyme-grass *Leymus arenarius* begin the process of colonisation and subsequently Marram *Ammophila arenaria* plays a crucial part in consolidating the process of stabilising these embryo dunes, and allowing them to grow in stature. With the colonising hard work done, a range of other plants can then become established in the dunes and iconic species include Sea Sandwort *Honckenya peploides*, Prickly Saltwort *Salsola kali*, Sea Mayweed *Tripleurospermum maritimum*, Frosted Orache *Atriplex laciniata*, Sea Rocket *Cakile maritima*, Sea-holly *Eryngium maritimum* and Sea Spurge *Euphorbia paralias*.

Dunes are dynamic systems and their creation and stabilisation are ongoing processes with fresh sand constantly being deposited on the seaward side of the dunes and new dune ridges forming. A succession of increasingly stable sandy habitats progresses inland, the result being that the youngest dunes are nearest the sea, while the oldest dunes are furthest away. In botanical terms, calcareous dunes support greater plant diversity than acid ones; over time, calcium tends to leach out of any dune system and the consequence can be gradation to dune heaths. In all dune systems, you find wet hollows lying between dune ridges and these are known as dune slacks; in calcareous dunes there are botanical parallels with fen habitats and, in most situations, they are good locations to look for orchids.

Marram *Ammophila arenaria* is an important stabilising influence on mobile sand, leading eventually to dune formation.

Sand dune fungi

Sand dunes are challenging environments for life but a few specialist fungi thrive here and nowhere else. Most are found in areas of stabilised sand, including lichen communities on dune heaths and dune slacks colonised by Creeping Willow *Salix repens*. However, a few live amongst Marram, in areas of unstable and shifting sands; the body of the fungus – the mycorrhiza – will be buried deep with only the fruit body near the surface. Interesting species include:

Sandy Mushroom *Agaricus devoniensis*
This mushroom has a cap 6–7cm across that barely makes its presence known above dune heath vegetation; its surface is invariably covered with sand and debris.

Sand Stinkhorn *Phallus hadriani*
You may smell this fungus before you see it: the spores are embedded in a foul-smelling slime that attracts flies; these insects are the stinkhorn's dispersal agents.

Dune Waxcap *Hygrocybe conicoides*
Among the most colourful of dune fungi, this species has a conical, spreading cap that is carried on a stalk 5–7cm long.

Dwarf Earthstar *Geastrum schmidelii*
This small earthstar is just 2–3cm across and has a pleated opening to the spore sac. It is scarce and local in dunes in England and Wales.

Tiny Earthstar *Geastrum minimum*
As its name implies this species is just 2–3cm across, and it has a fibrous opening to the spore sac. It is restricted to a few dunes on the north Norfolk coast.

Winter Stalkball *Tulostoma brumale*
Essentially a tiny puffball borne on a 3cm-tall stalk, the spores are contained within the terminal sac and are puffed out when the fungus is knocked or hit by raindrops.

Green beaches

On the Birkdale coast in northwest England there's an interesting twist to the conventional story of dune formation, one that appears to be unique in the context of Britain and Ireland. Here the pioneer colonisers are saltmarsh plants, specifically saltmarsh-grasses *Puccinellia* (see pages 314–315) rather than classic sandy beach colonisers. Over the last few decades, the grasses have trapped silt and sand and allowed other colonising plants to take root. This habitat, which in botanical terms represents the transition from saltmarsh to sand dune, has been given the name 'Green Beach'. To date, since it was noticed in 1986, the coastline's guardian angel Philip Smith estimates 65 hectares of new habitat have been created by this natural process.

In locations where human trampling does not cause erosion, **Sea Sandwort *Honckenya peploides*** forms carpets on sandy beaches, helping to stabilise the mobile substrate and allowing other plants to become established.

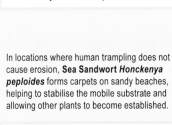

Natterjacks

The Natterjack *Epidalia calamita* is a charming and well-marked little toad that nowadays has its strongholds in sand dunes on the coasts of Norfolk and northwest England. Introductions and re-introductions have been attempted elsewhere, and the species also occurs in a few heathland areas inland. In spring, adults congregate and spawn in seasonal pools in dune slacks. Outside the breeding season, Natterjacks typically burrow and hide during the daytime and are most active after dark. They hibernate during the winter months, typically underground.

Snow Buntings *Plectrophenax nivalis* are found on coasts during the winter months and feed primarily on seeds, often along the strandline of sandy beaches or on bare ground between dune plants.

Sand dune invertebrates

Free-draining ground, shifting substrates and a relative lack of nutrients are among the hurdles to be overcome by creatures that call sand dune habitats home. A few specialist invertebrates have risen to the challenge and many of these are adapted to live there and nowhere else. In reality sand dunes comprise a spectrum of habitats and the natural zonation is reflected in their wildlife. Some species favour areas of mobile sand while more stable substrate is ideal for solitary bees and wasps to make burrows in which their larvae can develop. Here are two interesting examples:

Northern Dune Tiger-beetle *Cicindela hybrida*
Restricted mainly to dunes in northwest England, this beetle is an active predator of other invertebrates which it captures and dispatches with its fearsome (by insect standards) mandibles. It is a sun-loving creature, most active on warm days. It sometimes takes to the wing and flies short distances, a behaviour that can make it extremely difficult to follow. Look for Northern Dune Tiger-beetles along sheltered sandy tracks.

Bee Wolf *Philanthus triangulum*
By wasp standards, this species is colourful and distinctive. Although solitary in terms of its life-cycle, where conditions suit it lives in the insect equivalent of 'towns'. It favours stable sandy slopes and each wasp excavates its own nest chamber in the soil. These are stocked with paralysed honey bees and leaf-cutter bees, on which the wasp lays its eggs and on which its larvae feed. Once rare, the Bee Wolf is now widespread on dunes in southern England.

Shingle

Although we all recognise the word 'shingle' it is not a precise geological definition. Nor is it a particle size, and it is not a specific rock type. It is a broadly encompassing term, comprising pebbles and cobbles that range in size from roughly 3–20cm, depending on the location. Anything larger is best referred to as a boulder. Pebbles and cobbles form as a result of erosion of rocks, or strata containing rocks, from nearby cliffs or submerged deposits. All have their edges rounded by attrition, caused by wave action and currents. Depending on rock type, they vary considerably in shape: those that are granite tend to be egg-shaped or rounded, smooth but with a granular texture; eroded flints retain an irregular, jagged appearance; and shale cobbles are flat.

Cobbles and pebbles (and indeed sand, gravel and other particles) are moved around by the sea and beaches form by longshore drift, a marine process caused by wave action. Waves are driven by prevailing winds and in most locations the wind direction, and hence that of the waves, is oblique to the shoreline. There is more energy in the breaking wave (the swash, which breaks obliquely up the beach) than the backwash which runs directly down the beach. As a result, not only do more particles that are carried by the sea get deposited than are washed away (because of the energy difference) but also those that remain mobile move slowly but inexorably in the direction of the prevailing winds and waves.

It has been estimated that 25–40% of the coast of England and Wales has a shingle element. However, most are limited in extent, constrained by natural geography, ruined by development, or wrecked by shingle extraction, both on land and in the marine environment. Areas sufficiently extensive to allow vegetation to colonise are relatively rare, and ones that are protected are even rarer. In terms of size and significance, Dungeness in Kent wins the rosette and comprises 2,000 hectares of shingle. Chesil Beach is, however, arguably the most visually stunning, its virtues easily appreciated when viewed from the Isle of Portland, which it connects to mainland Dorset.

Chesil Beach in Dorset, arguably our most impressive shingle beach.

Sea Pea *Lathyrus japonicus* thrives on coastal shingle and depends on the sea for its survival: its seeds are dispersed by marine currents.

Shingle beaches tend to be steep and their porous structure dissipates most of the energy of the waves, making them a natural defence against coastal erosion. However, the one thing they cannot combat is rising sea levels and in certain circumstances this is leading to their erosion.

Shingle is a challenging environment for any plant or animal, being by its very nature unstable, incredibly free-draining and lacking anything that resembles conventional soil. But a few plant species are adapted and hardy enough to survive here. Indeed, specialists such as Sea-holly *Eryngium maritimum*, Yellow Horned-poppy *Glaucium flavum* and Sea-kale *Crambe maritima* are seldom found anywhere else.

Shingle invertebrates

Surprisingly, a number of invertebrates manage to live among the pebbles that comprise a shingle beach and most feed on the debris that accumulates in the interstices close to the high tide mark. Among their number are the following:

Scaly Cricket *Pseudomogoplistes squamiger*
This mainly nocturnal insect lives just above the strand-line spending the daytime hidden among the shingle interstices. It emerges after dark to feed on organic matter and its stronghold is Chesil Beach in Dorset. The species may well be overlooked elsewhere.

Looping Snail *Truncatella subcylindrica*
This delicate snail favours muddy gravel on the landward side of shingle ridges and it cannot tolerate disturbance, being extremely fragile. Its muscular foot allows it to shuffle along like a looper caterpillar or leech and its main range is southern England.

Moths of stabilised shingle habitats

Human activity is the most significant factor in deciding the fate of any shingle system. This can take the form of marine extraction (which affects deposition locally and natural shingle expansion), extraction on land, human disturbance (trampling), wholesale habitat destruction (building works) and water extraction (which affects the availability and salinity of ground water). However, left to its own devices, over time shingle is colonised by plants and becomes increasingly stable on the landward side of any formation. As the landscape becomes increasingly vegetated (albeit sparsely) a number of specialist invertebrates call stabilised shingle home and among their moth species are the following:

Bright Wave *Idaea ochrata*
Restricted to shingle beaches and the margins of sandy golf courses, this rare species is confined in Britain and Ireland to Kent. Its larval foodplants – Smooth Tare *Vicia tetrasperma* and Hare's-foot Clover *Trifolium arvense* – are not especially coastal so other factors must explain its habitat-specific occurrence in our region.

Sussex Emerald *Thalera fimbrialis*
This colourful and attractive moth is a real rarity. Its main stronghold is Dungeness (in Kent) although it appears to have returned to its namesake county, occurring now at Rye Harbour. The foodplant is Wild Carrot *Daucus carota*.

Shingle and nesting birds

In the absence of human activity, the likelihood is that shingle beaches around the coast of Britain would be thronged with nesting birds during the summer months, not to mention having better stabilised vegetation on the landward side. As it is, nesting terns, gulls and waders have a hard time and are in essence excluded from all but the most heavily protected areas.

An **Oystercatcher** *Haematopus ostralegus* incubating its eggs on a protected shingle beach. The eggs themselves are remarkably well camouflaged for this habitat.

Many coastal plants such as **Sea-kale** *Crambe maritima* are tough and resilient, and happily colonise locations where shingle has been built up as a sea defence.

Estuaries and saltmarshes

Estuaries form where rivers meet the sea, and where the energy is removed from the flow suspended mud is deposited. Over time mudflats are consolidated in suitable spots by invertebrate communities, then colonised by vegetation leading to the formation of saltmarshes. Saltmarshes are subject to both tidal exposure and river influences. Conditions are brackish overall but saltmarsh surface exposure ranges from near-freshwater during and after heavy rain, to pure seawater during extreme tides. That's a challenging environment for any plant.

Saltmarsh on the Hampshire coast, with a carpet of **Sea-purslane** *Atriplex portulacoides* and drifts of **Common Sea-lavender** *Limonium vulgare*.

During the winter months, most estuaries are positively dreary in botanical terms, studded with a mosaic of bedraggled-looking vegetation and very little else. But in the summer months, they come to life thanks to the specialist, salt-tolerant plants that colonise and stabilise the oozing mud. Able to cope with twice-daily inundation by sea water, these saltmarsh plants include species of glasswort *Salicornia* and sea-lavender *Limonium*, as well as Sea-purslane *Atriplex portulacoides* and Annual Sea-blite *Suaeda maritima*.

As mentioned, mudflats and saltmarshes are tidal habitats, subject to inundation by seawater twice a day. Location above the low water mark influences the period of time any given spot is exposed to air or immersed in sea water, leading to zonation among the invertebrates living in the mud. But higher up the shore it is also evident in the plant life too. Zonation is a familiar concept on a rocky shore where more obvious vertical tidal range is reflected in visually-defined bands of different seaweed species. However, zonation is also evident in the floral makeup of saltmarshes although here the effects of tidal range are more horizontal than vertical in nature. Consequently, a tidal range of say 5m on a saltmarsh may extend across hundreds of metres of habitat.

In the summer months, saltmarshes are colourful habitats. Here, on the north Norfolk coast, **Common Sea-lavender** *Limonium vulgare* takes pride of place.

Saltmarsh floral zonation is well illustrated among the glassworts *Salicornia*, represented in Britain and Ireland by six or seven species (or taxa groups) depending on which botanical authority you follow. Each species is adapted to different periods of inundation by the tide, some in essence occupying the equivalent of the splash zone, only occasionally being subjected to seawater although their root systems permeate salt-laden substrate. Others occur in lower zones and are immersed in seawater for much longer periods each day.

During the winter months, saltmarsh vegetation is an important dietary component for visiting wildfowl, such as these **Brent Geese** *Branta bernicla*.

Cliffs

Combining spectacular scenery and floral abundance, our cliffs are glorious, especially those in the west and north of the region. In terms of sheer majesty, they are among Britain's botanical highlights, and are world-class flowering spectacles by any standard. Pretty in pink, Thrift *Armeria maritima* is usually the undeniable star of the show but a supporting cast of Sea Carrot *Daucus carota*, Sea Campion *Silene uniflora* and various species of sea-spurrey add botanical diversity and provide colourful counterpoint to the scene. At their best these majestic maritime rockeries, while created by nature, are worthy of any stately home or botanical garden.

In geological terms, sea cliffs are coastal rock formations that are eroded at the base by waves. The appearance of the cutting edge – the cliff face – is largely determined by the substrate that is being eroded, with its stature dictated by its height above sea level. Erosion of harder rocks tends to produce vertical or near-vertical cliff faces while softer substrates typically erode in a more haphazard manner, crumbling, slipping and sliding unpredictably.

For a cliff plant to survive it must be able to tolerate – indeed thrive - by being battered by the wind and exposed to salt spray. In addition, the species of plants that colonise sea cliffs are influenced by the chemical nature of the rock substrate, which ranges from calcareous in the case of chalk cliffs to acidic with granite cliffs. Furthermore, a plant's ability to colonise is also affected by erosion – the fact that the White Cliffs of Dover are white is a testament in part to the fact that they erode faster than most plants can colonise.

If a cliff's geology allows for long-lasting ledges and crevices to be created through erosion, then so much the better for colonising plants. They provide niches in which plants can gain a foothold and establish their anchoring root systems. An added benefit is that ledges on steep cliffs are often out of reach of grazing animals.

There can be few more colourful coastal locations than the cliffs of Grosnez on Jersey, which are carpeted with the coastal, prostrate form of **Broom *Cytisus scoparius* ssp. *maritimus***.

A cliff's geographical aspect and location will also influence the plant species that colonise its slopes. North facing slopes will be shadier than ones facing south, which has twin consequences – less sunlight for photosynthesis but reduced desiccation in the summer months. With cliffs that are in areas of high rainfall, such as western and northern Britain, the effects of salt spray are diluted by comparison with cliffs in the southeast, which receive much less rainfall.

Seabird cliffs

In a few special locations where rock type and subsequent erosion create ledges, boulder fields and grassy slopes inaccessible to mammalian predators, thriving seabird colonies develop. An inevitable consequence of spending time on land while nesting is the accumulation of droppings, and the rocks are usually splattered white and adorned with guano, the name given to bird excrement.

With a diet of fish and other seafood, it is hardly surprising that seabird guano is nutrient-rich, particularly when it comes to nitrogen and ammonia. The concentration of these natural fertilisers does not suit all plant life but certain species thrive in and around seabird colonies. For example, Buck's-horn Plantain *Plantago coronopus* can be positively luxuriant in its growth form, as can Common Scurvygrass *Cochlearia officinalis* and Common Sorrel *Rumex acetosa*.

Where conditions suit them, **Kittiwakes *Rissa tridactyla*** nest in large colonies on coastal cliffs.

Landslips and undercliffs

The undercliffs and landslips on the south coast of the Isle of Wight harbour rich botanical treasures.

If a given cliff formation is pre-disposed to landslips and slumps then at its base a jumble of sediments will form, referred to as the undercliff. Depending on the strata above, undercliff composition may include rocks and boulders of varying sizes, as well as clay. Inland from the cliff itself the soil's water table and makeup often combine to create freshwater seepages that contribute to the decay of the cliff face – erosion from within – and the likelihood of landslips.

Because of the way they form and their continuous evolution, undercliffs are by their nature unstable. However, this very instability suits a range of plants and animals, among them some rare invertebrates that are found nowhere else in Britain and Ireland. These include the following:

Glanville Fritillary *Melitaea cinxia*
Restricted mainly to undercliffs on the southern coast of the Isle of Wight, this attractive butterfly flies in May and June. Its larvae feed on the leaves of Sea Plantain *Plantago maritima*.

Cepero's Ground-hopper *Tetrix ceperoi*
This relative of grasshoppers and crickets is unobtrusive and easily overlooked. It lives around the margins of freshwater seepages on undercliffs in southern Britain.

Clifftop moths

Although many moth species are catholic in terms of their larval foodplants, a few are more selective and favour clifftop coastal flowers. Their range is restricted by their coastal plant associations. Here are a few of note:

Thrift Clearwing
Pyropteron muscaeformis
This day-flying species resembles a small buzzing fly and is seldom seen away from areas where Thrift *Armeria maritima* carpets the ground; its larvae feed on the plant's roots.

Devonshire Wainscot
Leucania putrescens
As its name suggests, this is a West Country species associated with sea cliffs where its larvae feed on coastal grasses.

Black-banded
Polymixis xanthomista
With a larval diet of Thrift *Armeria maritima* this species is restricted to coasts of southwest England and Wales. It seldom strays away from the coast.

Barrett's Marbled Coronet *Conisania andalusica*
The larvae of this species feed on the roots of Sea Campion *Silene uniflora* and Rock Sea-spurrey *Spergularia rupicola*. It is restricted to coasts of southwest England.

If you visit exposed coastal locations in the west for flowers, keep your eyes and ears open for **Choughs *Pyrrhocorax pyrrhocorax***. These aerobatic and vocal members of the crow family favour short cliff-top vegetation, which they probe with their bills for invertebrates.

Machair

Machair is the name (Gaelic in origin) for windswept, flower-rich, low-lying coastal grasslands found in scattered locations around northern Britain and Ireland. The habitat is in part an unintended consequence of traditional, low-intensity agriculture. The Outer Hebridean islands of North Uist, South Uist, Barra and Tiree boast the best examples and greatest extent but machair is also found on other Hebridean islands, on Orkney and Shetland, as well as the west and north coasts of Ireland. Today, it is one of the rarest and most precious habitats in Europe.

Typically, machair forms on wind-blown sand, whose content is partly shell fragments, in the lee of dunes that form at the top of the beach. The soil on which the grassland grows is both free-draining and to varying degrees calcareous. As well as being influenced by climate – specifically the wind – some of the best machair is affected by human activity and its survival reliant in part on continued traditional farming methods, which include seasonal grazing and cutting for hay. In terms of floral display, machair grasslands often grade into neighbouring arable farmland, and some farmed fields are fertilised by the spreading of seaweed from the shore.

Dune Pansy *Viola tricolor* ssp. *curtisii*

Harebell *Campanula rotundifolia*

Common Bird's-foot-trefoil *Lotus corniculatus*

Hebridean Spotted-orchid *Dactylorhiza fuchsii* var. *hebridensis*

Machair grassland hosts a seasonal array of plants starting with **Primrose *Primula vulgaris*** in spring as seen here on North Uist in the Outer Hebrides, followed by a succession of other grassland species.

In floral terms it is not unusual species that make machair grasslands so special, it is the sheer abundance of a select band of plants that are widespread elsewhere in the region but seldom seen in such profusion. Classic machair species include Red Clover *Trifolium pratense*, Common Bird's-foot-trefoil *Lotus corniculatus*, Dune Pansy *Viola tricolor* ssp. *curtisii*, Harebell *Campanula rotundifolia*, Daisy *Bellis perennis* and Yarrow *Achillea millefolium*, with damper ground supporting several species of orchids. Of course, there are a few machair specialities and these include Irish Lady's-tresses *Spiranthes romanzoffiana* and Hebridean Spotted-orchid *Dactylorhiza fuchsii* var. *hebridensis*.

Great Yellow Bumblebee

The impressive **Great Yellow Bumblebee, *Bombus distinguendus*** is one of the rarest British bumblebee species, and nowadays almost exclusively restricted to machair grassland. Flower-rich sites are important for feeding of course, but so are locations for overwintering, namely dry, sheltered grass tussocks such as those that sit at the margins between machair and dune.

Corncrake

Here and there, at the margins of pools and in wet hollows, damp-loving vegetation dominates with stands of Yellow Iris *Iris pseudacorus*, and grassland studded with the flowers of Ragged-robin *Lychnis flos-cuculi* and Silverweed *Potentilla anserina*. Such locations are ideal for the **Corncrake *Crex crex***, a summer visitor that now has its remaining strongholds in machair habitats. Once widespread across much of Britain and Ireland, the species has been extirpated elsewhere by modern farming practices, which destroy suitable habitat and virtually eliminate the insects and other invertebrates on which the bird feeds.

Maritime heath

In lowland southern Britain, heathland communities of plants develop on acid, free-draining soils and the most characteristic component species are members of the heather family (hence the habitat's name) and gorse species. Heathland is also a feature of many stretches of coast in western Britain, especially where the underlying rock is granite. Heather, Bell Heather, Common Gorse and Western Gorse are the dominant species in coastal heathland and the habitat is at its most colourful in floral terms from midsummer to early autumn. Because of its proximity to and the influence exerted on it by the sea, communities growing on the coast are referred to by botanists as 'maritime heath'.

Maritime heath vegetation is typically no more than knee-high, the plants 'pruned' by the wind and inhibited by salt spray. In particularly exposed locations, the vegetation is known as 'waved heath', the habitat having a rippled appearance that echoes waves on the sea. These botanical 'waves' are mostly a feature of Heather and Bell Heather and are caused when the side of a plant facing the prevailing wind and salt spray (typically facing west) is killed off, while growth continues on the sheltered (typically east-facing) side.

The dominant component plants with classic maritime heath habitats are usually Heather and Bell Heather, which form dense vegetation when undamaged by human trampling; the relative impenetrability on foot is at least partly guaranteed by low-growing intermingled Western Gorse. Here and there the dense sward is studded by clumps or isolated plants of Wild Thyme *Thymus drucei*, Bird's-foot-trefoil *Lotus corniculatus*, Kidney-vetch *Anthyllis vulneraria*, Tormentil *Potentilla erecta*, Yorkshire-fog *Holcus lanatus* and Sheep's-fescue *Festuca ovina*. In a few locations, maritime specialities such as Spring Squill *Scilla verna*, Autumn Squill *Scilla autumnalis*, Thrift *Armeria maritima* and Sea Campion *Silene uniflora* make seasonal appearances.

Red-barbed Ant

The **Red-barbed Ant** *Formica rufibarbis* is one of Britain and Ireland's rarest insects. It occurs on Surrey heaths where it is extremely vulnerable but a more resilient population lives on maritime heath on St Martin's in the Isles of Scilly. Its nests are not especially obvious, sited either underground or under stones, usually amongst heathland vegetation.

Emperor Moth larva

Although the **Emperor Moth** *Saturnia pavonia* is widespread on heaths and moors, it is a particular favourite on maritime heaths. Not so much the day-flying adults, which are on the wing in March and April, but more so the plump and intensely green larvae, which arouse curiosity and interest among visitors in the summer months. In coastal locations, their primary foodplant is Heather *Calluna vulgaris*.

Manmade

Manmade structures are familiar coastal features these days and they take many forms. For as long as there have been seafarers, people have built harbours and docks. Other commercial activities have played a part too, such as salt pans built to extract salt through evaporation. In addition, sea defences in various guises have long been used to combat high tides and to claim land from the sea for agriculture. Increasingly, the role that sea walls fulfil today is one of protection from increased flooding risk due to rising sea levels, itself the consequence of climate change.

Common Sea-lavender *Limonium vulgare* (above) and **Rock Samphire** *Crithmum maritimum* (above right) growing on a Hampshire sea wall.

Harbours and sea defences create artificial 'hard landscaping' for colonising plants. Rocky shore plants like these 'new' habitats but by and large the species that colonise sea walls mirror the habitat on the seaward side. Consequently, if the habitat in question is saltmarsh then plants such as Sea Aster *Tripolium pannonicum*, Golden Samphire *Limbarda crithmoides*, and Common Sea-lavender *Limonium vulgare* will benefit, with Slender Hare's-ear *Bupleurum tenuissimum* and Sea Clover *Trifolium squamosum* growing on the top or the landward side of the bank. When shingle is dumped in an attempt to combat coastal erosion then plants that thrive on this substrate will appear, including Yellow-horned Poppy *Glaucium flavum* and Rock Samphire *Crithmum maritimum*.

Bristly Oxtongue *Helminthotheca echioides* growing on a recently-created sea wall.

Manmade lagoons such as this one at Pennington in Hampshire support important colonies of brackish-tolerant aquatic and marginal plants.

CONSERVATION

Almost all the pressures that coastal habitats and their plant communities face result from the impacts of humans on the environment. There is direct pressure from the sheer numbers of people that visit the coast or want to live there. Other impacts are subtler and less evident, including insidious pollution and water abstraction for example. And then there's the big one – climate change and consequent rising sea levels.

Seaside tourism is big business. Evidence that, given the opportunity, a large proportion of the population gravitates to the coast for recreation and relaxation was manifest after the easing of lockdown measures in early summer 2020. With unprecedented visitor numbers heading to the coast, human environmental impact manifested itself as soil erosion, vegetation trampling and general mis-use of coastal habitats. Predictably the hordes were attracted mostly to sand and shingle habitats and iconic landmarks, and these suffered the worst effects.

If post-lockdown staycation fever has taught us anything it is that unbridled visitor pressure on maritime habitats should be discouraged. As authors, throughout our travels and in conversation with conservation-minded guardians of our coastal habitats, the people we have met and talked to have had one thing in common: a sense of despair when faced with battalions of members of the public descending on fragile coastal habitats and treating them as playgrounds. Destinations for themselves and sometimes for out-of-control dogs.

In theory, reducing human pressure while allowing people to experience our coastal splendours is an achievable goal, by informing, educating and enlightening the public. Part of the process involves the ability to recognise and understand the complexity and fragility of life on the coast and we hope that, in some small way, this book will contribute to this ambition. We all need to recognise that with the privilege of having thousands of miles of wonderful coast for us to explore comes responsibility.

The tip of Portland Bill in Dorset is an extremely popular tourist destination visited by tens of thousands of people each year. Until relatively recently their trampling feet laid bare the entire site but an inspired project to rope off areas of ground has reaped rewards. As can be seen in this photograph, the erosive effect of human trampling is plain to see as is the power of nature to recover. In just a few years, roped-off areas have returned to their former floral glory.

Even seemingly trivial actions can have disproportionately devastating consequences. Take, for example, yacht anchors – dropped in calm bays, and in numbers, they destroy fragile eelgrass beds, along with the specialist animals that call this vulnerable habitat home.

Human impact on the coastal environment is sometimes more profound than just a matter of feet on the ground. Every new house or car park or visitor attraction means the loss of natural habitat. In addition, for some the coast is a resource to be exploited in a more wholesale manner. Take for example the coastal and marine extraction of shingle and sand. Above sea level, it removes coastal habitats in one fell swoop. Below the water, entire marine habitats are destroyed and furthermore, and equally profoundly, it removes material destined to become the natural coastal barriers of the future: without marine sand and shingle, the deposition of material that leads to beach formation is affected.

Humans also have an impact on marine water quality and nowadays pollution of the sea to a greater or lesser degree is a given and tacitly accepted even if it is not acceptable. In addition, how we use and abuse freshwater can also be an issue for the marine environment: nutrient enrichment through run-off of agricultural fertilisers (and even overflowing septic tanks in holiday areas) affects plant and animal growth in estuaries in particular. Furthermore, freshwater abstraction impacts water availability and salinity in sensitive coastal habitats such as stabilised shingle communities and coastal lagoons.

Arguably the biggest problem, and the one that we, as individuals, are least able to influence is rising sea levels, primarily the self-inflicted consequence of climate change. In general, the approach to the problem has been two-pronged. In certain locations, where land is available, so-called 'managed retreat' has been adopted – letting nature take its course, with sea incursion and coastal habitats moving slowly but inexorably inland. The other approach is to combat the effects of rising water levels through the construction of barriers of one kind or another. The most familiar are sea walls. Although, to a degree, they protect habitats on the landward side, there are adverse consequences for plants, animals and habitats on the marine side.

All marine habitats are influenced by tides and intertidal plants and animals are found in zones, their precise location dictated by their ability to tolerate different degrees of exposure to air and inundation by seawater. Zonation is strikingly apparent among seaweeds on the rocky shore but also evident among saltmarsh plants. At one extreme there are species that require prolonged immersion, while at the other are plants that favour only brief inundation by seawater. It is the latter group – the upper-shore species – that are most vulnerable to rising sea levels. In the absence of an immovable object such as a sea wall, saltmarsh habitats and their zones would move slowly and surely inland as sea levels rise. Put a sea wall in the way of this natural progression and sooner or later the upper zones will have nowhere to go and will disappear.

When it comes to sand dune systems, it may seem strange to say it but human inaction is having far-reaching consequences for these vulnerable habitats. Until relatively recently received wisdom had it that dune erosion was the enemy, and indeed that is true when it comes to wholesale destruction caused by, for example, sand extraction or quadbike and scrambling activities. However, recently there has been a re-evaluation and a recognition (prompted in the main by scrub-encroachment) that some form of vegetation management is needed for dune flora to survive.

Looking at the bigger ecological picture, dunes are succession habitats, intermediate in the progression from colonisation of bare sand by specialist plants that leads ultimately to the formation of woodland. In the past, most dune systems were far more open than they are today, maintained by human intervention in the form of grazing animals and scrub clearance for, for example, fuel. If we value the specialist communities associated with dunes, which are found nowhere else, above generalist scrub and woodland habitats that are widespread elsewhere, then some form of informed, targeted and enlightened 'gardening on a grand scale' needs to take place. In the absence of that, most of the dune systems we have visited are facing problems with scrub encroachment, along with the proliferation of invasive non-native species. The list includes Broad-leaved Everlasting-pea *Lathyrus latifolius*, Traveller's-joy *Clematis vitalba* and Sea-buckthorn *Hippophae rhamnoides* on the Sefton coast, Pirri-pirri-bur *Acaena novae-zelandiae* at Lindisfarne National Nature Reserve, and (to the authors' eyes at least) Burnet Rose *Rosa spinosissima* and Rough Star-thistle *Centaurea aspera* on the dunes at St Ouen's Bay on Jersey.

Fortunately for our coasts, all of the above problems are widely recognised even if they are not always addressed satisfactorily. Natural England is the statutory body responsible for nature conservation in England, with sister organisations in Wales (Natural Resources Wales), Scotland (NatureScot), Northern Ireland (Northern Ireland Environment Agency) and the Republic of Ireland (the National Parks and Wildlife Service). Landowners also play a vital role and these range from well-intentioned individuals to organisations such as the National Trust, National Trust for Scotland, National Trust for Ireland, the county Wildlife Trusts and the Royal Society for the Protection of Birds. What most of these organisations lack is adequate funding needed to carry out the required work. What you, the reader, can do is to lobby on behalf of funding for statutory bodies, join conservation organisations and volunteer if assistance is ever needed with conservation land management.

The cardinal rule with successful conservation is that if you don't know what you've got, how can you conserve it or know whether any actions you take are reaping biodiversity rewards or doing further damage? Consequently, recording, surveying and monitoring is the key to success and the Botanical Society of Britain and Ireland (BSBI) plays a key role when it comes to understanding our coastal plants. Its expert teams and recorders are the gold standard when it comes to botanical recording and their informed and skilled advice is put to good use with habitat management.

The coast acts like a magnet for people, especially in spring and summer when flowering is most prolific. Some stretches of coastline can withstand visitor pressure. However, many of our finest botanical hotspots, such as stabilised shingle and sand dunes habitats, have vegetation that is fragile, vulnerable, and easily damaged by trampling.

Good news stories

In many situations successful conservation relies on the passion and commitment of individuals, both those employed by conservation organisations who are willing to go beyond the call of duty to help endangered plants, and private individuals who see it as their mission in life. While working on this book it has been our privilege to meet some of these people. Here are a couple of good news stories.

Pedunculate Sea-purslane *Atriplex pedunculata*

Pedunculate Sea-purslane has a chequered past but a future with some promise. Declared extinct in 1937, then rediscovered in 1987, it has had a couple of false starts when it comes to returning from the brink. However, thanks to hands-on efforts involving seed collection, cultivation and translocation its future seems reasonably secure although it is currently confined to just one site on the Essex coast. Here it grows on the landward side of a sea wall, in a remnant of saltmarsh; to be precise, the margins of a previously meandering creek and adjacent saline grassland.

In late September 2020 we were fortunate enough to be able to join Natural England's Neil Fuller and Chris Keeling on their annual count of the species, on a private site in Essex. Numbers fluctuate from year to year, as is the way with annual plant species, but 2020 had produced a bumper crop numbering in the thousands. Neil and Chris, along with the farming landowner, are to be congratulated on their enthusiasm for this enigmatic plant.

Globally, Pedunculate Sea-purslane has a patchy range and is restricted to sheltered shores in northwest Europe, its stronghold being saltmarshes on the Danish coast. There is a theory that seeds of the plant may have been transported by wildfowl – Brent Geese for example – migrating from mainland Europe to Essex.

Stinking Hawk's-beard *Crepis foetida*

Despite its uninviting English name, Stinking Hawk's-beard is an attractive plant, which in Britain and Ireland is associated with stabilised shingle habitats. In the past it was best known as a resident of Dungeness until it became extinct in 1980. Enthusiasts maintained a cultivated seed bank and it has been re-introduced there and at Rye Harbour Nature Reserve, the latter a wonderful environment managed most successfully for wildlife by the Sussex Wildlife Trust. At Rye, its current guardian angels – warden Barry Yates and ecologist Brian Banks – look out for its well-being. Long may their good work and enthusiasm continue. Elsewhere in the world, Stinking Hawk's-beard is not exclusively coastal and is widespread in Europe; it has also been introduced accidently and become naturalised in parts of the USA and Australia.

Sea-buckthorn *Hippophae rhamnoides*

HEIGHT To 3m.

ECOLOGY & NATURAL HISTORY
Branched, thorny shrub that forms
dense stands. These are most
striking and obvious in autumn
when festooned with bright orange
berries that are food for migrant
thrushes and other birds.
Trunks of mature bushes host
the bracket fungus *Fomitiporia
hippophaeicola*.

HABITAT Native to stabilised
coastal sand dunes but also
widely planted.

FLOWERS Tiny and greenish,
with male and female flowers
on separate plants, March to
April.

FRUITS Bright orange berries,
on female plants only.

LEAVES Narrow and greyish
green.

Bracket fungus *Fomitiporia hippophaeicola*.

B&I STATUS Native to east
coasts but planted elsewhere,
and an invasive threat in
many dune locations where
it comes to dominate unless
controlled.
NW EUROPEAN STATUS
Widespread on coasts;
occasionally planted.

Wild Privet *Ligustrum vulgare*

HEIGHT To 3m.
ECOLOGY & NATURAL HISTORY
Much-branched, semi-evergreen
shrub that has downy young twigs.
Colonises dunes and forms dense
stands in places. Its leaves are food
for larvae of the Privet Hawk-moth
Sphinx ligustri, its flowers are visited
by pollinating insects and its fruits
are food for migrant birds such as
thrushes in autumn.
HABITAT Stable dunes and
calcareous ground elsewhere.
FLOWERS 4–5mm across,
creamy white, fragrant
and 4-petalled; they are
borne in terminal spikes,
May to June.
FRUITS Shiny, globular
and poisonous (to
humans), ripening black
in the autumn; borne in
clusters.
LEAVES Shiny, untoothed, oval
and opposite.

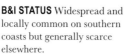

B&I STATUS Widespread and
locally common on southern
coasts but generally scarce
elsewhere.
NW EUROPEAN STATUS
Widespread in NW France;
patchy distribution or
planted elsewhere.

Privet Hawk-moth larva *Sphinx ligustri*.

Grey Willow *Salix cinerea*

HEIGHT To 6m.

ECOLOGY & NATURAL HISTORY Large shrub or small tree with downy, grey twigs. A classic scrub species, its flowers are visited by spring-flying moths, and its leaves are food for the larvae of numerous moth species, as well as other insects. If left to its own devices, Grey Willow will occasionally form extensive thickets that in some locations need to be controlled if low-growing classic dune flora is to thrive.

HABITAT Typical species of stable dunes and coastal scrub.

FLOWERS Ovoid catkins appear in spring on separate-sex trees: females are yellower than males.

FRUITS Plumed seeds.

LEAVES Oblong, pointed and short-stalked. Upper surface is matt, lower surface is downy and grey in spring, acquiring rusty hairs by autumn in some forms.

B&I STATUS Common on coasts; widespread elsewhere and not exclusively coastal.

NW EUROPEAN STATUS Widespread, north to S Sweden.

upper   under

Creeping Willow *Salix repens*

HEIGHT To 1.5m.
ECOLOGY & NATURAL HISTORY Low-growing, creeping shrub with downy young twigs. The roots form mycorrhizal associations with a range of fungal species, and the resulting enhanced nutrient uptake allows the plant to colonise impoverished dune soils.
HABITAT Grows in coastal dune slacks.
FLOWERS Ovoid catkins.
FRUITS Plumed seeds.
LEAVES Ovate, usually untoothed, to 4cm long; hairless above, with silky hairs below.

upper

under

B&I STATUS Widespread and locally common.
NW EUROPEAN STATUS Widespread but local, north to S Norway and coastal central Sweden.

Blackthorn *Prunus spinosa*

HEIGHT To 5m.

ECOLOGY & NATURAL HISTORY Thorny shrub that often forms dense thickets. Given half a chance, Blackthorn forms impenetrable scrub which acts as a refuge for nesting birds and tired migrants. Its flowers are popular with pollinating insects. The mouth-puckering fruits are eaten, when fully ripe, by birds and make an excellent tipple in the form of Sloe Gin. The stony seeds are stashed by Bank Voles as a winter food supply.

HABITAT Grows on a wide range of soil types and common in coastal hedgerows and scrub, and on sea cliffs.

FLOWERS 14–18mm across with 5 white petals; they appear before the leaves, March to April.

FRUITS (referred to as sloes) are purplish with a powdery bloom, and resemble tiny plums.

LEAVES Oval, 2–4cm long and with toothed margins.

B&I STATUS Common on coasts; widespread elsewhere and not exclusively coastal.

NW EUROPEAN STATUS Widespread, north to coastal S Norway and S Sweden.

Hawthorn *Crataegus monogyna*

HEIGHT To 12m.

ECOLOGY & NATURAL HISTORY Thorny shrub or small tree that forms dense thickets. The flowers (so-called May Blossom) are a magnet for pollinating insects, its fruits are food for birds including migrant thrushes, and its leaves are eaten by the larvae of a range of moths.

HABITAT Component of coastal hedgerows and scrub, dunes and sea cliffs.

FLOWERS 15–25mm across with 5 white petals; borne in clusters, May to June.

FRUITS Ripen to form clusters of bright red berries.

LEAVES Shiny, roughly oval and divided into 3–7 pairs of lobes.

B&I STATUS Common on coasts; widespread elsewhere and not exclusively coastal.

NW EUROPEAN STATUS Widespread, north to coastal S Norway and S Sweden.

Cotoneasters *Cotoneaster* and *Chaenopetalum* species

HEIGHT To 50cm.

ECOLOGY & NATURAL HISTORY Recent reclassification splits this variable group of evergreen shrubs into two genera, all members of which have branches that divide and spread in a flat plane. For simplicity, the group can be sorted into species with white flowers (genus *Chaenopetalum*) e.g. Entire-leaved Cotoneaster *C. integrifolius* and Small-leaved Cotoneaster *C. microphyllos*, and those with pink or red flowers (genus *Cotoneaster*) e.g. Wall Cotoneaster *C. horizontalis*. Wild Cotoneaster *C. cambricus* (just a handful of plants now grow on Great Orme Head in Wales) is sometimes regarded as native. Garden-escape cotoneasters are a smothering threat to native flora. On a plus-note, their flowers are a good nectar-source for bees. Judging by their persistence, the berries are unattractive to migrant birds.

HABITAT Cliffs and rocky coasts, mainly on calcareous soils; similar rocky ground inland too.

FLOWERS White or pink (depending on genus), May to July.

FRUITS Bright red, spherical berries.

LEAVES 5–15mm long, depending on species, glossy above and hairless below.

B&I STATUS Widely grown in gardens and occasionally naturalised; can become an invasive problem for native wildlife.

NW EUROPEAN STATUS Occasional.

ROSACEAE – Roses and allies

Butterfly-bush *Buddleja davidii*

HEIGHT To 4m.

ECOLOGY & NATURAL HISTORY Robust shrubby perennial with long, arching branches. The flowers are hugely popular with a few butterfly species and other pollinating insects. However, it is a shockingly invasive shrub capable of completely crowding-out native plants in the absence of control. Its benefits to insects (which have other sources of nectar) should be weighed carefully against its negative impact in the wild on native flora.

HABITAT Grows on coasts, and cliffs, and waste and disturbed ground.

FLOWERS 3–4mm across, 4-lobed and pinkish purple; borne in long spikes, June to September.

FRUITS Capsules with winged seeds.

LEAVES Long, narrow and darker above than below.

B&I STATUS Popular as a garden plant but also widely naturalised.

NW EUROPEAN STATUS Widely naturalised.

Elder *Sambucus nigra*

HEIGHT To 10m.

ECOLOGY & NATURAL HISTORY
Deciduous shrub or small tree with
spreading, out-curved main branches and
corky bark. A component of coastal scrub
whose fragrant flowers are a magnet for
pollinating insects and whose berries
are food for birds, including migrant
warblers and thrushes.

HABITAT Grows in coastal scrub and
hedgerows, thriving best on chalky and
nitrogen-enriched soils.

FLOWERS 5mm across and creamy
white; borne in flat-topped clusters,
10–20cm across, June to July.

FRUITS Blackish
purple berries,
borne in clusters.

LEAVES
Unpleasant-
smelling and
divided into
5–7 leaflets.

B&I STATUS Common on
coasts; widespread elsewhere
and not exclusively coastal.

NW EUROPEAN STATUS
Widespread as far north
as Denmark; coastal in S
Norway and S Sweden.

Tamarisk *Tamarix gallica*

HEIGHT To 8m.

ECOLOGY & NATURAL HISTORY
Forms a straggly, windswept tree, which is deciduous and very twiggy. It is tolerant of salt spray hence its primary use as a coastal windbreak. Tamarisk has limited appeal to native wildlife; it is the larval foodplant of a few southern European moths but none that occur regularly in Britain and Ireland.

HABITAT Wide range of coastal habitats.

FLOWERS Minute, pink and 5-petalled flowers; borne in long sprays, May to June.

FRUITS Beaked capsules contain cottony seeds that are wind-dispersed.

LEAVES Greenish blue and scale-like.

B&I STATUS Introduced to Britain and Ireland and sometimes naturalised; native to the Middle East and widely planted around the Mediterranean.

NW EUROPEAN STATUS Planted on coasts of NW France.

Duke of Argyll's Teaplant *Lycium barbarum*

HEIGHT To 1.5m.

ECOLOGY & NATURAL HISTORY
Deciduous perennial with spiny and greyish white, woody stems; these often root where they droop and touch the ground.

HABITAT Grows on disturbed ground and in hedgerows near the coast.

FLOWERS 8–10mm long, purplish and 5-lobed, with projecting, yellow anthers; borne in groups of 1–3 flowers that arise from leaf axils, June to September.

FRUITS Egg-shaped, red berries.

LEAVES Lanceolate and grey-green.

B&I STATUS Introduced from China and naturalised, especially near the sea.
NW EUROPEAN STATUS Widely naturalised.

The superficially similar **Chinese Teaplant *Lycium chinense*** has subtle overlapping differences from *L. barbarum* (e.g. some flowers are marginally larger). It is not considered further here and readers should refer to Stace for more information.

SOLANACEAE – Nightshades, potato and allies

Traveller's-joy *Clematis vitalba*

HEIGHT To 20m.

ECOLOGY & NATURAL HISTORY
Scrambling perennial that takes on the appearance of a shrub when it smothers other plants by late summer.

HABITAT Calcareous dunes and other base-rich soils.

FLOWERS Creamy-white, with prominent stamens; borne in clusters, July to August.

FRUITS Comprise clusters of seeds with woolly, whitish plumes, hence plant's alternative name of Old Man's Beard.

LEAVES Divided into 3–5 leaflets.

B&I STATUS Locally common, mainly in the south.
NW EUROPEAN STATUS Locally common.

COASTAL OAKS

Our two native *Quercus* species – Pendunculate and Sessile Oaks – are not exclusively coastal and are widespread deciduous trees throughout the region, each with subtly different distributions and ecological requirements. They are included here because of their significance to wildlife, coastal and otherwise, and to aid separation from a third species, the introduced Holm Oak, which is something of a coastal speciality. The latter adds to the arboreal mix and thrives in locations where it has been planted and seeded itself. The three species can be identified and distinguished from one another using the leaves and acorns, as well as other characters.

Holm Oak *Quercus ilex*

HEIGHT To 28m.

ECOLOGY & NATURAL HISTORY
A broadly-domed tree whose crown is often very dense and twiggy. It has dark, shallow-fissured bark that cracks to form squarish scales. In some situations, Holm Oak regenerates prolifically and the shade cast by its permanent canopy and the dense carpet of fallen leaves excludes native flora. It has to be controlled where it becomes a threat to native wildlife and habitats.

HABITAT Grows on a wide range of free-draining coastal soils and tolerates salt spray and strong winds.

FLOWERS Male catkins appear in spring, their golden colour contrasting with silvery new leaves and darker twigs.

FRUITS Acorns, up to 2cm long, that sit deeply in cups covered with rows of small hairy scales.

LEAVES Variable and usually ovate to oblong with a pointed tip and a rounded base on mature trees; on young trees they are holly-like. All leaves are dark glossy above, paler and downy below with raised veins, borne on 1–2cm-long, hairy petioles.

B&I STATUS Native of S Europe, planted in coastal Britain and Ireland as a shelter-belt tree. Naturalised occasionally.

NW EUROPEAN STATUS Occasional near coasts of NW France.

Trees and shrubs

Pedunculate Oak *Quercus robur*

HEIGHT To 36m.

ECOLOGY & NATURAL HISTORY A large, spreading, deciduous tree with a dense crown of heavy branches. The bark is grey and fissured and shoots and buds are hairless. Pedunculate Oak is one of the most ecologically important species in Britain and Ireland and its significance to native wildlife cannot be over-stated; it is food for innumerable invertebrates and others that feed on them.

HABITAT A wide range of soil types but thrives on heavy clay.

FLOWERS Male and female catkins are produced just as the first flush of leaves appears in spring. Male catkins die off after pollination by which time its leaves are fully open.

FRUITS Acorns, borne on long stalks in roughly scaled cups, in groups of 1–3.

LEAVES Deeply lobed with 2 auricles at the base; borne on very short stalks (5mm or less).

B&I STATUS Widespread and common.

NW EUROPEAN STATUS Widespread as far north as S Norway and S Sweden.

Sessile Oak *Quercus petraea*

HEIGHT To 40m.

ECOLOGY & NATURAL HISTORY Sturdy deciduous tree with a domed shape. The grey-brown bark has deep fissures and the trunk tends to be more upright than Pedunculate Oak. Coastal Sessile Oak woodlands are often rich in epiphytic mosses, liverworts and lichens; hole-nesting birds, notably Pied Flycatchers and Redstarts, are associated with this habitat, feeding on the abundant insect life.

HABITAT Thrives on poor soils, often on rocky ground and coastal slopes, particularly in western Britain.

FLOWERS Pendulous green male catkins appear in May and fall off as leaves open fully.

FRUITS Acorns are long and egg-shaped, stalkless, and sit directly on the twig in small clusters.

LEAVES Lobed, flattened, dark green and hairless above, paler below with hairs along the veins; on yellow stalks, 1–2.5cm long, and lacking auricles at the base, distinguishing them from those of Pedunculate Oak.

B&I STATUS Common and widespread in western parts of Britain. Forms dense stands on some west-coast slopes.

NW EUROPEAN STATUS Widespread in NW France; scarcer and planted north to S Norway and S Sweden.

Monterey Pine *Pinus radiata*

HEIGHT To 45m.
ECOLOGY & NATURAL HISTORY Large,
variable pine with fissured and grey
bark that blackens with age. Slender
and conical when growing vigorously,
becoming more domed and flat-topped
on a long bole with age. Main branches
sometimes droop low enough to touch the
ground.
HABITAT Grows on a wide range of soil
types and tolerates salt-spray.
FLOWERS Male flowers grow in dense
clusters near ends of twigs, releasing
pollen in spring. Female flowers (cones)
grow in clusters of 3–5 around tips of
shoots.
FRUITS Female flowers ripen to large,
solid woody cones, to 15cm long and
9cm across, with a characteristic
asymmetrical shape. Cone scales are
thick and woody with rounded outer
edges; they conceal black, winged seeds.
LEAVES Bright green needles in bunches
of 3; each needle is thin and straight, to
15cm long, with a finely toothed margin
and sharp-pointed tip.

B&I STATUS Widely planted in mild
areas as a shelter-belt tree or for
ornament, growing well next to the
sea. Native to a small area around
Monterey, California, plus Guadalupe
Island and Baja California, Mexico.
NW EUROPEAN STATUS Planted
occasionally but not especially hardy.

Trees and shrubs

Cabbage-palm *Cordyline australis*

HEIGHT To 13m.

ECOLOGY & NATURAL HISTORY A superficially palm-like evergreen with ridged and furrowed bark. Trees of flowering age have a bare, forked trunk with a crown of foliage on top of each fork. The fruits are popular with birds, notably Starlings and thrushes.

HABITAT Planted on a wide range of coastal soils to create the illusion of sub-tropical conditions in resorts.

FLOWERS Appear in midsummer in large spikes, to 1.2m long comprising numerous small, fragrant, creamy-white flowers, each about 1cm across, with 6 lobes and 6 stamens.

FRUITS Small rounded bluish white berries about 6mm across containing several black seeds.

LEAVES Long, spear-like and parallel-veined, to 90cm long and 8cm wide. Upper leaves are mostly erect, but lower leaves hang down to cover top of trunk.

B&I STATUS Native of New Zealand, planted here for ornament. It survives quite far north, as long as there is some protection from severe cold.

NW EUROPEAN STATUS Planted occasionally.

Hairy Buttercup *Ranunculus sardous*

HEIGHT To 40cm.
ECOLOGY & NATURAL HISTORY Hairy annual that is the most coastally-restricted of our widespread *Ranunculus* species. It often grows on disturbed soils and ground trampled by grazing animals.
HABITAT Coastal grassland and tracks.
FLOWERS 15–25mm across with 5 pale yellow petals and reflexed sepals, May to October.
FRUITS Have a green border inside which the surface is usually warty.
LEAVES Divided into 3 lobes and mainly basal.

B&I STATUS Local, mainly in the south and east, favouring coastal grassland.
NW EUROPEAN STATUS Local north to Netherlands; scarce north to S Sweden.

Creeping Buttercup *Ranunculus repens*

HEIGHT To 50cm.
ECOLOGY & NATURAL HISTORY Perennial, whose long, rooting runners aid its spread.
HABITAT A familiar lawn species, Creeping Buttercup favours a range of coastal grassland habitats, particularly on disturbed ground and damp and seasonally flooding sites such as dune slacks.
FLOWERS 20–30mm across with 5 yellow petals and upright sepals; borne on furrowed stalks, May to August.
FRUITS Borne in rounded heads.
LEAVES Hairy and divided into 3 lobes; the middle lobe is stalked.

B&I STATUS Widespread and common.
NW EUROPEAN STATUS Widespread throughout.

Meadow Buttercup *Ranunculus acris*

HEIGHT To 1m.
ECOLOGY & NATURAL HISTORY Downy perennial that is an indicator of undisturbed (unploughed and unsprayed) land. It does well in damp coastal meadows and dune grassland.
HABITAT Damp grassland habitats.
FLOWERS 18–25mm across with 5 shiny, yellow petals and upright sepals; carried on long, unfurrowed stalks, April to October.
FRUITS Hook-tipped and borne in a rounded head.
LEAVES Rounded and divided into 3–7 lobes; upper leaves are unstalked.

B&I STATUS Widespread and abundant throughout.
NW EUROPEAN STATUS Widespread throughout.

Bulbous Buttercup *Ranunculus bulbosus*

HEIGHT To 40cm.
ECOLOGY & NATURAL HISTORY Hairy perennial with a diagnostic swollen stem base. The flowers are magnets for a wide range of pollinating insects.
HABITAT Dry grassland, including dunes and coastal meadows, favouring free-draining neutral or calcareous soils.
FLOWERS 20–30mm across with 5 bright yellow petals and reflexed sepals; borne on furrowed stalks, March to July.
FRUITS Smooth.
LEAVES Divided into 3 lobes, each of which is stalked.

B&I STATUS Widespread and often abundant.
NW EUROPEAN STATUS Widespread north to S Sweden.

Small-flowered Buttercup *Ranunculus parviflorus*

HEIGHT To 30cm.
ECOLOGY & NATURAL HISTORY
Sprawling, hairy annual that does best
on disturbed and trampled ground,
beside coastal paths and where Rabbits
have scuffed the soil.
HABITAT Dry, bare ground, often
on sandy soils that are neutral to
calcareous.
FLOWERS 3–5mm across with pale
yellow petals; borne on furrowed stalks,
often arising from the fork of a branch,
May to July.
FRUITS Roughly hairy.
LEAVES Rounded and lobed basal
leaves; stem leaves are narrowly lobed.

B&I STATUS Local on coasts
of S Ireland, S England and
S Wales; distribution is much
patchier inland.
NW EUROPEAN STATUS Local
in NW France.

Rough-fruited Buttercup *Ranunculus muricatus*

HEIGHT To 30cm.
ECOLOGY & NATURAL HISTORY
Clump-forming annual that benefits
from soil disturbance, particularly
favouring bulb fields in Britain
and Ireland. The flowers
are popular with small
pollinating insects.
HABITAT Cultivated
bulb fields.
FLOWERS Yellow and
12–15mm across, April to June.
FRUITS Prickly, borne in
spiky-looking heads.
LEAVES Basal leaves are
lobed, the lobes unstalked.

B&I STATUS Native to S Europe
and Mediterranean region,
introduced and established
locally on Isles of Scilly. Very
occasional in Cornwall as well.
NW EUROPEAN STATUS Absent.

**Jersey Buttercup *Ranunculus
paludosus*** grows to 50cm in
winter-wet hollows that bake dry
in summer. It has basal tubers,
flowers 3–5cm across on long
stalks and spiky-headed fruits.
Leaves, evident only in winter, are
fan-shaped at base and stalked
and divided on stem. Seldom
seen on Jersey now and very
local and scarce in NW France.

Brackish Water-crowfoot *Ranunculus baudotii*

HEIGHT Submerged and floating water plant.
ECOLOGY & NATURAL HISTORY Aquatic annual or perennial. Of all the water-crowfoots, this is the most coastal and saline-tolerant species.
HABITAT Favours brackish pools, ditches and channels near the coast, and pools in dune slacks.
FLOWERS 12–18mm across with 5 white petals, April to August.
FRUITS Borne in rounded, long-stalked heads.
LEAVES Comprise deeply lobed floating leaves and thread-like submerged ones that do not collapse out of water.

B&I STATUS Local around the coast.
NW EUROPEAN STATUS Coastal, north to central Sweden.

Celery-leaved Buttercup *Ranunculus sceleratus*

HEIGHT To 50cm.
ECOLOGY & NATURAL HISTORY Yellowish green annual with hollow stems.
HABITAT Favours pool margins, and muddy hollows in coastal grazing marshes. Tolerates nutrient enrichment and saline conditions.
FLOWERS 5–10mm across with pale yellow petals; borne in clusters, May to September.
FRUITS Comprise elongated heads.
LEAVES Celery-like, basal leaves are divided into 3 lobes, stem leaves are less divided.

B&I STATUS Locally common in the south.
NW EUROPEAN STATUS Locally common.

Yellow Horned-poppy *Glaucium flavum*

HEIGHT To 50cm.

ECOLOGY & NATURAL HISTORY Blue-grey, clump-forming short-lived perennial. When in flower, it is one of the most distinctive beach plants.

HABITAT Shingle beaches are its favoured habitat; occasionally also on broken ground at the base of sea cliffs.

FLOWERS 6–9cm across with overlapping yellow petals, June to September.

FRUITS Elongated, curved and tusk-like capsules up to 30cm long; these are the eponymous 'horns'.

LEAVES Pinnately divided, the clasping upper ones having shallow, toothed lobes.

B&I STATUS Locally common on most suitable coasts although absent from most of Scotland.

NW EUROPEAN STATUS Local in NW France; occasional further north to S Sweden.

FUMITORIES

Fumitories belong to the genus *Fumaria* and comprise a group of rather superficially similar plants identified by flower shape, size and colour and leaf shape. They are plants of disturbed ground and arable fields. Some species have distinctly coastal distributions but our two widespread members – Common Fumitory and Common Ramping-fumitory – are also at their most showy on coasts where farming methods, particularly the application of herbicides, tends to be more traditional and (usually unintentionally) wildlife-friendly.

Common Fumitory *Fumaria officinalis*

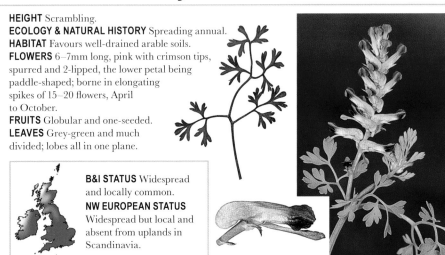

HEIGHT Scrambling.
ECOLOGY & NATURAL HISTORY Spreading annual.
HABITAT Favours well-drained arable soils.
FLOWERS 6–7mm long, pink with crimson tips, spurred and 2-lipped, the lower petal being paddle-shaped; borne in elongating spikes of 15–20 flowers, April to October.
FRUITS Globular and one-seeded.
LEAVES Grey-green and much divided; lobes all in one plane.

B&I STATUS Widespread and locally common.
NW EUROPEAN STATUS Widespread but local and absent from uplands in Scandinavia.

Common Ramping-fumitory *Fumaria muralis*

HEIGHT Scrambling.
ECOLOGY & NATURAL HISTORY Spreading or upright annual.
HABITAT Arable land, banks and walls.
FLOWERS 9–11mm long and pinkish purple with dark tips, the lower petal almost parallel-sided (not paddle-shaped) with erect margins; borne in spikes of 12–15 flowers, April to October.
FRUITS Globular and one-seeded.
LEAVES Much divided, with lobes not in one plane.

B&I STATUS Widespread and fairly common.
NW EUROPEAN STATUS Widespread but local north to Belgium; occasional further north to Denmark.

Western Ramping-fumitory *Fumaria occidentalis*

HEIGHT Scrambling.
ECOLOGY & NATURAL HISTORY Similar to Common Ramping-fumitory but with larger flowers.
HABITAT Disturbed and cultivated ground.
FLOWERS 12–14mm long, white and intensely purple-tipped at first, flushing pink with age; borne in spikes of 12–15 flowers, May to October.
FRUITS Globular and one-seeded.
LEAVES Much-divided, very similar to Common Ramping-fumitory given the overall variability of both species.

B&I STATUS Locally common on Isles of Scilly and also grows, very locally, in Cornwall.
NW EUROPEAN STATUS Absent.

Tall Ramping-fumitory *Fumaria bastardii*

HEIGHT Scrambling.
ECOLOGY & NATURAL HISTORY Robust upright annual.
HABITAT Arable fields and waste ground, especially near the sea.
FLOWERS 9–11mm long, pink with a purple tip, the lower petal parallel-sided (not paddle-shaped); borne in spikes of 15–25 flowers, April to October.
FRUITS Globular and one-seeded.
LEAVES Much-divided, and very similar to Common Ramping-fumitory given the overall variability of both species.

B&I STATUS Widespread and fairly common only in western Britain and Ireland.
NW EUROPEAN STATUS Very local in NW France.

Common Nettle *Urtica dioica*

HEIGHT To 1m.
ECOLOGY & NATURAL HISTORY The familiar stinging nettle. It is a perennial whose leaves are the foodplant for the larvae of a number of butterflies, including Peacock *Aglais io*, Small Tortoiseshell *Aglais urticae* and Red Admiral *Vanessa atalanta*, plus several moth larvae too.
HABITAT Does best on nitrogen-enriched and disturbed soils.
FLOWERS Pendulous catkins; borne on separate-sex plants, June to October.
FRUITS Resemble the flowers superficially.
LEAVES Oval, pointed-tipped, toothed and borne in opposite pairs; 8cm long and longer than stalks.

Red Admiral

B&I STATUS Widespread and common.
NW EUROPEAN STATUS Widespread.

Small Nettle *Urtica urens*

HEIGHT To 50cm.
ECOLOGY & NATURAL HISTORY Upright plant, similar to Common Nettle but smaller and annual. On the basis of personal experience, its sting is more intense than that of its cousin. Its leaves are eaten by a similar range of butterfly and moth larvae as Common Nettle.
HABITAT Grows on disturbed ground and in tilled arable fields, doing best on free-draining sandy soils.
FLOWERS Pendulous catkins, male and female on same plant, June to September.
FRUITS Similar to female flowers.
LEAVES Oval, pointed-tipped and toothed; to 4cm long.

B&I STATUS Widespread and locally common.
NW EUROPEAN STATUS Widespread but becoming local in north and absent from uplands in Scandinavia.

Pellitory-of-the-wall *Parietaria judaica*

HEIGHT To 50cm.
ECOLOGY & NATURAL HISTORY Spreading, downy perennial with reddish stems.
HABITAT Colonises cliffs, walls, roadsides and rocky ground.
FLOWERS Borne in clusters at leaf bases, June to October.
FRUITS Clustered at leaf bases.
LEAVES Oval, up to 5cm long and long-stalked.

B&I STATUS Widespread in England, Wales and Ireland; commonest in coastal areas and in the southwest.
NW EUROPEAN STATUS Local in NW France only.

Pellitory-of-the-wall leaves are food for the larvae of a miniscule micromoth called **Cosmopterix pulchrimella**; they are small enough to be able to 'mine' inside the leaf itself.

URTICACEAE – Nettles and allies

Hottentot-fig *Carpobrotus edulis*

HEIGHT Creeping, forming a mat up to 1m deep.
ECOLOGY & NATURAL HISTORY Exotic looking fleshy perennial, introduced from South Africa. On some coasts it forms carpets and smothers native vegetation; in many areas it is controlled and removed to aid native biodiversity.
HABITAT Coastal cliffs and banks.
FLOWERS Usually yellow, sometimes purple, 7–10cm across and many-petalled, May to July.
FRUITS Swollen and succulent.
LEAVES Dark green, succulent, narrowly 3-sided and 6–7cm long.

B&I STATUS Naturalised in the southwest.
NW EUROPEAN STATUS NW France only.

Spear-leaved Orache *Atriplex prostrata*

HEIGHT To 60cm but sometimes straggly and near-prostrate.
ECOLOGY & NATURAL HISTORY Variable annual.
HABITAT Coastal ground including just above the strandline. Also widespread inland on disturbed ground.
FLOWERS Small, greenish and borne in leafy spikes, July to September.
FRUITS Have triangular bracteoles that are fused along half their length.
LEAVES Toothed, the upper ones rather lanceolate, at least some of the lower ones with backward facing lobes.

B&I STATUS Widespread and locally common in suitable habitats except in the far north; occasional inland.
NW EUROPEAN STATUS Widespread but coastal in Scandinavia.

Atriplex species have separate-sex flowers, and fruits that are enclosed by enlarged bracteoles, which only become apparent as the fruits ripen in late summer.

Babington's Orache *Atriplex glabriuscula*

HEIGHT Prostrate.
ECOLOGY & NATURAL HISTORY A spreading, mealy annual. Stems are usually reddish and whole plant often turns red in autumn. The floating seeds are dispersed by tides and currents.
HABITAT Restricted to stabilised shingle and sandy beaches close to the strandline; less frequently grows on bare, coastal ground.
FLOWERS Borne in leafy spikes, July to September.
FRUITS Diamond-shaped, maturing red, glistening silvery white.
LEAVES Triangular or diamond-shaped with basal lobes projecting at right angles; they are fleshy and snap easily.

under

upper

B&I STATUS Locally common.
NW EUROPEAN STATUS Locally common on coasts from N France to S Norway and S France.

Kattegat Orache *Atriplex x gustafssoniana*

HEIGHT To 70cm but often straggly and near-prostrate.
ECOLOGY & NATURAL HISTORY Naturally-occurring hybrid between Spear-leaved (*A. prostrata*) and Long-stalked (*A. longipes*) Oraches. Often grows in the absence of the latter parent species, and is usually much more common and widespread. Easiest to identify in September when fruits are ripe.
HABITAT Upper reaches of salt-marshes, often tangled amongst patches of Spear-leaved Orache and just below the lowest point where trees can grow.
FLOWERS Both solitary and borne in compact clusters.

leaves

FRUITS Variable, but typically diamond-shaped or recalling a bricklayer's trowel, up to 7mm long. Mostly unstalked (especially clusters) but most plants have a few stalked fruits, stalks up to 7mm long.
LEAVES Variable, with some narrowly-diamond shaped (rather like Long-stalked) and others akin to Spear-leaved.

leaf

Long-stalked Orache
Atriplex longipes
is superficially similar to Kattegat Orache and grows in similar habitats. However, its fruit's bracteoles are larger (to 25mm), more consistently shaped like a bricklayer's trowel, with stalks up to 25mm. Easiest to identify in September when fruits are ripe.

fruit

B&I STATUS Widespread and local, but easily overlooked and probably under-recorded.
NW EUROPEAN STATUS Local and coastal, north to S Scandinavia.

fruit

Grass-leaved Orache *Atriplex littoralis*

HEIGHT To 1m.
ECOLOGY & NATURAL HISTORY Upright annual that forms dense stands in suitable locations.
HABITAT Saltmarsh strandlines, estuary margins, sea walls, bare coastal ground.
FLOWERS Small, greenish and borne in spikes with small leaves, July to September.
FRUITS Greenish, toothed and warty.
LEAVES Long and narrow, sometimes with shallow teeth.

B&I STATUS Locally common.
NW EUROPEAN STATUS Locally common on coasts from N France to S Norway and S Sweden.

Common Orache *Atriplex patula*

HEIGHT To 70cm but sometimes straggly and near-prostrate.

ECOLOGY & NATURAL HISTORY Upright annual whose stems are often tinged red. The saline-tolerant (halophytic) nature of the species has allowed it to spread inland, colonising roads that are salt-treated in winter to combat ice.

HABITAT Thrives best on beaches and in saltmarshes but also occurs on waste and bare ground near the sea.

FLOWERS Borne in rather short spikes, July to September.

FRUITS Triangular and surrounded by green bracts.

LEAVES Oval to diamond-shaped; upper ones gently lobed, lower ones with forward-projecting lobes but still tapering towards base.

B&I STATUS Widespread and common except in north.
NW EUROPEAN STATUS Widespread and common, becoming scarce further north.

Early Orache *Atriplex praecox* is a northern speciality, probably overlooked and under-recorded in NW and N Scotland, Shetland and Orkney. It grows on sheltered beaches, just above the strandline and above the highest seaweed zone. Its leaves are typically deep maroon and rather diamond-shaped in outline. The English name is unhelpful since it does not flower noticeably earlier than Common Orache.

Frosted Orache *Atriplex laciniata*

HEIGHT Usually prostrate.

ECOLOGY & NATURAL HISTORY Distinctive silvery grey plant with stems that are usually flushed with pink. The buoyant seeds are spread by tides and currents.

HABITAT Characteristic plant of strandlines on sandy and shingle beaches.

FLOWERS Whitish and borne in clusters, July to September.

FRUITS Diamond-shaped and toothed.

LEAVES Fleshy, mealy, toothed and diamond-shaped.

B&I STATUS Widespread and locally common but exclusively coastal.
NW EUROPEAN STATUS Local and coastal, north to S Norway and S Sweden.

Sea-purslane *Atriplex portulacoides*

HEIGHT To 1m.

ECOLOGY & NATURAL HISTORY
Spreading, mealy perennial that sometimes forms rounded clumps.

HABITAT Entirely coastal, and restricted to drier reaches of saltmarshes, sometimes forming extensive stands beside creeks and pools.

FLOWERS Yellowish and borne in spikes, July to October.

FRUITS Lobed and unstalked.

LEAVES Grey-green and oval at the plant's base but narrow further up the stem.

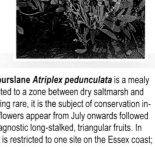

Pedunculate Sea-purslane *Atriplex pedunculata* is a mealy annual that is restricted to a zone between dry saltmarsh and saline grassland; being rare, it is the subject of conservation interest. Its yellowish flowers appear from July onwards followed by distinctive and diagnostic long-stalked, triangular fruits. In Britain and Ireland it is restricted to one site on the Essex coast; elsewhere it is found, locally, from northern France to the Baltic with its main European stronghold on the Danish coast.

fruit

leaf

B&I STATUS Widespread and locally common.

NW EUROPEAN STATUS Locally common from NW France to NW Germany.

Stinking Goosefoot *Chenopodium vulvaria*

HEIGHT To 25cm but usually prostrate.
ECOLOGY & NATURAL HISTORY Spreading, mealy annual that smells strongly of rotting fish.
HABITAT Favours slightly disturbed, often nitrogen-enriched soils, mainly near coasts.
FLOWERS Green, mealy and borne in clusters, July to September.
FRUITS Similar to flowers.
LEAVES Green, mealy and particularly foul-smelling.

Chenopodium species have hermaphrodite flowers that are tiny and appear in clusters; their fruits look superficially similar to the flowers.

B&I STATUS Rare and very local, mainly in the south. A mainly S European species, Britain is almost the northernmost limit of its range. Its occurrence here is likely to be the result of accidental introductions by man and its decline associated with changes in agricultural practices. It has been introduced to other parts of the world (USA, Australia and New Zealand) and in some locations it is considered invasive.
NW EUROPEAN STATUS Widespread but generally scarce, and typically accidental in appearance, from NW France to the Baltic states.

Saltmarsh Goosefoot *Chenopodiastrum chenopodioides*

HEIGHT To 30cm.
ECOLOGY & NATURAL HISTORY Recalls Red Goosefoot, which occurs in same habitats, but shorter and less robust. Mature plants recognisable by their red-tinged appearance. Declines have been attributed to habitat loss and degradation (eg. drainage for agriculture). Previously known as *Chenopodium chenopodioides*.
HABITAT Grows around the drying muddy margins of saltmarsh creeks and pools, and cattle-poached brackish mud on coastal grazing marshes.
FLOWERS Reddish green and borne in clusters, July to September.
FRUITS Rounded, red and borne in clusters.
LEAVES Rounded to diamond-shaped, superficially similar to those of Red Goosefoot but mature leaves are always red below.

B&I STATUS Rare and declining with a stronghold in the Thames estuary, particularly N Kent.
NW EUROPEAN STATUS Very local on coasts from NW France to S Baltic.

Red Goosefoot *Chenopodiastrum rubrum*

HEIGHT To 60cm.
ECOLOGY & NATURAL HISTORY Variable upright annual, whose stems often turn red in old or parched specimens. Previously known as *Chenopodium rubrum*.
HABITAT Favouring manure-enriched soils, typically the margins of drying pools (including brackish ones) and cattle-trampled mud on grazing meadows.
FLOWERS Small and numerous, borne in upright, leafy spikes, July to September.
FRUITS Spherical and enclosed by 2–4 sepals.
LEAVES Shiny, diamond-shaped and toothed.

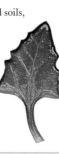

B&I STATUS Widespread and common in S England; scarce elsewhere.
NW EUROPEAN STATUS Local and coastal, north to S Norway and S Sweden.

Oak-leaved Goosefoot *Oxybasis glauca*

HEIGHT Low-growing, stems to 30cm long.
ECOLOGY & NATURAL HISTORY Spreading and usually prostrate annual whose leaves remain green. An ephemeral plant of nutrient-rich soils. Previously known as *Chenopodium glaucum*.
HABITAT Margins of dung heaps or around drinking troughs, drying margins of pools on coastal grazing marshes.
FLOWERS Green and borne in clusters.
FRUITS Spherical, similar to flowers and ripening to reveal black seeds.
LEAVES Variable in shape; a few upper leaves may be entire but most are shaped like narrow oak leaves. Upperside green, but underside coated mealy-white.

UK STATUS Fickle in appearance and often disappearing from a precise location as quickly as it appeared. Mainly introduced but possibly native at some coastal sites.
NW EUROPEAN STATUS Local and coastal, north to S Norway and S Sweden.

upper   under

Sea Beet *Beta vulgaris* ssp. *maritima*

HEIGHT To 1m.
ECOLOGY & NATURAL HISTORY Sprawling, clump-forming exclusively coastal perennial.
HABITAT Grows on cliffs, shingle beaches, saltmarsh strandlines and other coastal habitats. Thrives particularly well in nutrient-rich soils such as seabird colonies.
FLOWERS Green and borne in dense, leafy spikes, July–September.
FRUITS Spiky; often stick together in a clump.
LEAVES Dark green, glossy and leathery with reddish stems; shape varies from oval to triangular.

B&I STATUS Locally common.
NW EUROPEAN STATUS Locally common on coasts of NW France and Belgium; scarce north to S Sweden.

GLASSWORTS

Glassworts are classic saltmarsh plants that play a vital role in the ecology of this habitat, amongst other things helping stabilise mudflats. They belong to the goosefoot family (Chenopodiaceae) and have a fanciful resemblance to miniature Saguaro cacti; fused leaves create what appear to be their swollen stems and branches. They comprise two genera in Britain and Ireland: annual plants in the genus *Salicornia* (eight or so 'species'), and perennial *Sarcocornia*, represented by a single species. All are extreme halophytes that tolerate (and indeed depend on) periodic inundation by seawater and they grow in the saltiest of mud.

Identifying glassworts

Glassworts are tricky to identify and don't be disappointed if you fail to reach a conclusion with certain specimens. It is best to leave identification until September, when reasonably definitive colours have been acquired and the plants' fruits and flowers are fully formed. Each species has its favourite zone on the saltmarsh shore. You will also need a hand lens to examine the relative sizes of the flowers or fruits, structures that sit at the base of terminal segments, partly sheathed by the scale-like tip of the segment below; the angle of this tip is reasonably diagnostic for each species. Overall size is not particularly useful; most species range from 15–40cm in height although *Sarcocornia perennis* and *Salicornia disarticulata* seldom exceed 25cm. For those who want the challenge, here's an illustrated guide to all but two of the rarest 'species'. For a more detailed account, consult Stace or the Plant Crib, which align with Francis Rose's earlier clarification of the group.

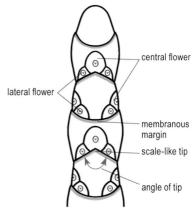

Glassworts are so-called because, after burning, their ashes are a source of soda ash, used in times past in glass-making. *Salicornia* plants are edible and, confusingly, often referred to as 'Samphire' when grown commercially.

Perennial Glasswort (p. 73)

One-flowered Glasswort (p. 73)

Common Glasswort (p. 74)

Purple Glasswort (p. 74)

Perennial Glasswort *Sarcocornia perennis*

Mature plants are branched, woody at the base and form patches with age. They spread by runners although this feature is little use with plants in their first year of life. Ripe flowering spikes are blunt-ended and turn orange. The 3 flowers are of equal size and the segments appear 'swollen'. Restricted to drier, upper reaches of saltmarshes.

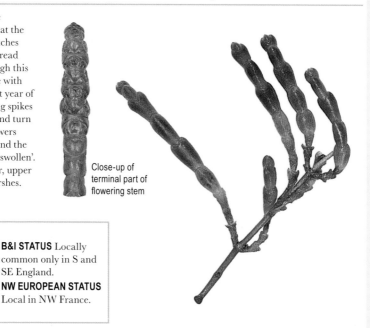

Close-up of terminal part of flowering stem

B&I STATUS Locally common only in S and SE England.
NW EUROPEAN STATUS Local in NW France.

One-flowered Glasswort *Salicornia disarticulata*

The only British glasswort with 1 flower per segment; all others have 3. As a note of caution, with young specimens of some 3-flowered species only a single flower may be visible. *S. disarticulata* is branched, and has a dense-looking terminal 'spike' that matures orange-red. It is restricted to dry, upper levels of saltmarshes. Formerly known as *Salicornia pusilla*.

Close-up of terminal part of flowering stem

B&I STATUS Locally common in S Britain and Ireland, and perhaps declining.
NW EUROPEAN STATUS Local in NW France only.

The remaining annual *Salicornia* glasswort species, covered in these two pages, are typically grouped into two species aggregates, ones where fertile spikes are 'beaded' in outline (*Salicornia europaea* agg.) and those whose fertile spikes are more-or-less cylindrical (*Salicornia procumbens* agg.).

As a word of warning, don't expect these features to be obvious in all specimens – glassworts are frustratingly variable.

'Beaded' group *Salicornia europaea* aggregate

Common Glasswort *Salicornia europaea*

Upright and usually much-branched, yellowish green when mature with a matt surface. Grows on the middle to upper levels of saltmarshes, and muddy shingle. Central flower is larger than laterals, and scale-like tip forms an angle of around 90° with a pale membranous margin roughly 0.1mm wide.

Similar **Glaucous Glasswort *Salicornia obscura*** is grey-green (like it has a thin coating of silt), the scale-like tip forming an angle of around 150°. Rare and hard to determine with certainty.

B&I STATUS Widespread and locally common, except in far north.
NW EUROPEAN STATUS Local and coastal, north to S Scandinavia.

Close-up of terminal part of flowering stem

Purple Glasswort *Salicornia ramosissima*

Glossy, dark green at first but maturing deep reddish purple. Grows on the middle to upper levels of saltmarshes. Central flower is larger than laterals, and scale-like tip forms an angle of around 110–120° with a membranous margin roughly 0.2mm wide.

B&I STATUS Widespread and locally common, especially in S and E Britain.
NW EUROPEAN STATUS Local from NW France to S Baltic.

Close-up of terminal part of flowering stem

Long-spiked Glasswort *Salicornia dolichostachya*

Often prostrate, yellowish green, maturing pale brown. Lower branches ('spikes') are almost as long as the main stem. Mudflats and lowest levels of saltmarshes. Flowers are similar in size, and the scale-like tip forms a very shallow angle.

Close-up of terminal part of flowering stem

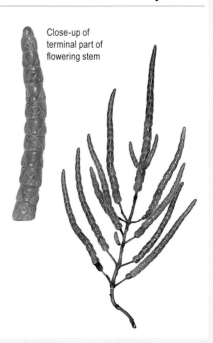

B&I STATUS Widespread and locally common, especially in S and E Britain.
NW EUROPEAN STATUS Local from NW France to S Baltic.

Yellow Glasswort *Salicornia fragilis*

Upright and yellowish green, maturing pale brown, its lower branches ('spikes') relatively short and unbranched. Mudflats and lowest levels of saltmarshes, often forming dense stands. Flowers are a similar size, and the scale-like tip forms a very shallow angle.

Similar **Shiny Glasswort *Salicornia emerici* (*nitens*)** is shiny and yellow-green maturing orange. Side branches are short, slender and unbranched. Rare and hard to determine with certainty.

B&I STATUS Widespread but local, least so in S and E Britain.
NW EUROPEAN STATUS Local, north to S Baltic.

Close-up of terminal part of flowering stem

Annual Sea-blite *Suaeda maritima*

HEIGHT To 50cm.
ECOLOGY & NATURAL HISTORY
Much-branched annual. Forms
small clumps that vary from
yellowish green to reddish.
HABITAT Grows in saltmarshes,
often alongside Sea-purslane.
FLOWERS Tiny and green; 1–3
appear in axils of upper leaves,
August to October.
FRUITS Contain dark, flattish
seeds.
LEAVES Succulent, cylindrical
and pointed.

B&I STATUS Widespread
and locally common on
all suitable coasts.
NW EUROPEAN STATUS
Local, from NW France
to S Scandinavia.

Shrubby Sea-blite *Suaeda vera*

HEIGHT To 1m.
ECOLOGY & NATURAL HISTORY
Much-branched, evergreen
perennial with woody stems.
HABITAT Restricted to coastal
shingle and upper saltmarshes.
FLOWERS Tiny and yellowish
green; 1–3 appear in leaf axils,
June to October.
FRUITS Contain rounded, black
seeds.
LEAVES Succulent, bluish green,
blunt and almost semi-circular in
cross-section.

B&I STATUS Locally
common in SE
England.
NW EUROPEAN STATUS
NW France only.

Prickly Saltwort *Salsola kali*

HEIGHT To 50cm.
ECOLOGY & NATURAL HISTORY Spiky-looking, prickly annual that can form extensive patches.
HABITAT Grows on sandy beaches, usually growing near the strandline in a fairly well-demarcated zone. Occasionally found beside regularly salted roads inland.
FLOWERS Tiny and yellowish, appearing at leaf bases, July to October.
FRUITS Similar to the flowers.
LEAVES Swollen, flattened-cylindrical, fleshy-looking and spiny-tipped.

B&I STATUS Locally common.
NW EUROPEAN STATUS Local, from NW France to S Scandinavia.

Springbeauty *Claytonia perfoliata*

HEIGHT To 30cm.
ECOLOGY & NATURAL HISTORY
Introduced from North America for
horticulture at the end of the 18th
Century and first observed growing
wild in the mid-19th Century.
Previously known as *Montia perfoliata*.
HABITAT Favours dry, sandy soil.
FLOWERS White, 5-petalled and 5mm
across; borne in loose spikes, April to
July.
FRUITS Capsules.
LEAVES Oval and stalked at the base;
flowering stems bear fused pairs of
perfoliate leaves.

B&I STATUS Widespread and locally
abundant, doing particularly well
near the sea.
NW EUROPEAN STATUS Local, from
NW France to S Scandinavia.

PORTULACACEAE – Purslanes and relatives

Sea Sandwort *Honckenya peploides*

HEIGHT Prostrate.
ECOLOGY & NATURAL HISTORY
Mat-forming perennial that
spreads by means of stolons. It is
one of the pioneer colonising plants
that helps stabilise mobile shore
substrates, leading to the formation
of stable dunes on sandy shores.
HABITAT Coastal shingle and
sandy beaches.
FLOWERS Greenish white and 6–8mm
across, May to August. Petals are slightly
shorter than sepals.
FRUITS Yellowish green and pea-like.
LEAVES Oval and fleshy; in opposite pairs
on creeping stems.

B&I STATUS Locally
common on suitable
habitats on most coasts.
NW EUROPEAN STATUS
Widespread on coasts but
scarce in Scandinavia.

Common Chickweed *Stellaria media*

HEIGHT To 30cm, but sometimes prostrate.
ECOLOGY & NATURAL HISTORY Annual or short-lived perennial whose stems are hairy in lines on alternate sides between leaf nodes.
HABITAT Disturbed ground, including coastal strandlines.
FLOWERS White, 5-petalled and 5–10mm across, flowering year-round; 3–8 stamens.
FRUITS Capsules on long, drooping stalks.
LEAVES Oval, fresh green and in opposite pairs; upper ones unstalked.

B&I STATUS Widespread and common.
NW EUROPEAN STATUS Widespread.

Sea Mouse-ear *Cerastium diffusum*

HEIGHT To 30cm, but sometimes prostrate.
ECOLOGY & NATURAL HISTORY Low annual that is covered in sticky hairs.
HABITAT Grows on sandy ground, mainly near the sea.
FLOWERS White and 3–6mm across, usually with 4 sepals and petals and 4 stamens, April to July.
FRUITS Capsules.
LEAVES Ovate and dark green; bracts do not have transparent margins.

Similar **Little Mouse-ear *Cerastium semidecandrum*** usually has 5 petals and sepals and 5 stamens, bracts pale with a green centre; flowers April to May and grows in similar habitats.

B&I STATUS Locally common near the coast but scarce inland.
NW EUROPEAN STATUS Local, from NW France to S Scandinavia.

Common Mouse-ear *Cerastium fontanum*

HEIGHT To 30cm.
ECOLOGY & NATURAL HISTORY Mat-forming hairy perennial with prostrate non-flowering shoots and upright flowering ones.
HABITAT Disturbed ground, including sand dunes, shingle and tracksides.
FLOWERS White, 5–7mm across with 5 deeply notched petals and 10 stamens, April to October.
FRUITS Capsules.
LEAVES Grey-green and borne in opposite pairs.

B&I STATUS Widespread and common throughout.
NW EUROPEAN STATUS Widespread.

Similar **Sticky Mouse-ear *Cerastium glomeratum*** is upright with sticky hairs, flowers with 5 petals and 10 stamens, sepals with hairs extending beyond tip; flowers April to September and grows in similar habitats.

Field Mouse-ear *Cerastium arvense*

HEIGHT To 30cm.
ECOLOGY & NATURAL HISTORY Spreading, downy perennial that sometimes forms sizeable patches.
HABITAT Dry, free-draining ground, including calcareous sand dunes and shingle.
FLOWERS White, 12–20mm across, with 5 deeply notched petals and 5 styles, April to August.
FRUITS Capsules.
LEAVES Ovate and paired.

Similar **Snow-in-summer *Cerastium tomentosum*** is a garden escape with white woolly leaves and stems.

Greater Stitchwort *Stellaria holostea* is a woodland plant that sometimes occurs near coasts, and flowers April to June. It has long, slender leaves and flowers with 3 styles.

B&I STATUS Local, mainly in E England.
NW EUROPEAN STATUS Local, from N France to S Scandinavia.

Sea Pearlwort *Sagina maritima*

HEIGHT To 8cm.
ECOLOGY & NATURAL HISTORY
Wiry, fleshy annual.
HABITAT Favours bare,
dry ground, almost
always within sight
of the sea.
FLOWERS Have 4
greenish sepals and
either 4 minute white
petals or no petals,
May to September.
FRUITS Capsules.
LEAVES Fleshy and blunt
with only a minute terminal
bristle.

B&I STATUS Widespread but
local and almost entirely
coastal.
NW EUROPEAN STATUS
Local on coasts, from NW
France to S Scandinavia.

Similar **Annual
Pearlwort** *Sagina
apetala* has
leaves that taper
to a fine point,
and typically no
petals, May to
September;
occurs on coasts
but also wide-
spread inland.

Procumbent Pearlwort *Sagina procumbens*

HEIGHT Prostrate.
**ECOLOGY & NATURAL
HISTORY** Creeping
perennial that forms mats
comprising a central rosette
with radiating shoots that root
at intervals giving rise to
erect flowering stems.
HABITAT Damp, bare
ground on cliffs, beside
tracks and disturbed ground
inland.
FLOWERS Green, petal-less and borne
on side shoots, May to September.
FRUITS Capsules.
LEAVES Narrow, bristle-tipped and hairless.

B&I STATUS Widespread and
common.
NW EUROPEAN STATUS
Widespread and common
throughout.

Knotted Pearlwort *Sagina nodosa*

HEIGHT To 12cm.
ECOLOGY & NATURAL HISTORY Wiry
perennial; stems look 'knotted' due to the
clustered arrangement of its leaves.
HABITAT Damp, sandy soils, particularly
dune slacks on coasts.
FLOWERS White, 5-petalled (petals twice
as long as sepals) and 7–10mm across,
with 5 styles, July to September.
FRUITS Capsules.
LEAVES Short and clustered.

B&I STATUS
Widespread but
local.
**NW EUROPEAN
STATUS**
Widespread but
local.

Similar **Heath Pearlwort *Sagina subulata***
has rosettes of narrow leaves, flowers 5–7mm
across with sepals as long as petals, May
to July. Grows on dry, sandy soils including
cliffs and heaths, mostly in W Britain and near
coasts.

Upright Chickweed *Moenchia erecta*

HEIGHT To 8cm.
ECOLOGY & NATURAL HISTORY Tiny, upright
annual whose flowers only open in bright
sunshine.
HABITAT Short, dry grassland, typically on
gravelly or sandy soils including dune slacks
and clifftop grassland.
FLOWERS White with 4 petals, and sepals
that are white-edged and longer than the
petals, April to June.
FRUITS Capsules.
LEAVES Waxy grey-green, stiff and narrow.

B&I STATUS Local in
England and Wales only.
NW EUROPEAN STATUS
Local, NW France only.

Lesser Sea-spurrey *Spergularia marina*

HEIGHT Prostrate.

ECOLOGY & NATURAL HISTORY Straggling, often stickily hairy annual. Since the 1980s it has spread inland, growing on verges and central reservations of salt-treated roads and motorways.

HABITAT Favours the drier, grassy upper margins of saltmarshes.

FLOWERS Deep pink and 6–8mm across, the 5 petals shorter than the sepals, May to August.

FRUITS Capsules.

LEAVES Narrow, fleshy and pointed; in opposite pairs on trailing stems.

Similar **Greek Sea-spurrey** *Spergularia bocconei* is a stickily hairy annual or biennial of bare, sandy ground near the sea, often beside tracks. Its tiny pink flowers are just 2mm across, petals shorter than sepals. This doubtfully native rarity is confined mainly to coastal paths in Cornwall.

B&I STATUS Widespread and locally common around the coast, increasingly inland too beside roads.

NW EUROPEAN STATUS Widespread but local on suitable coasts.

Sand Spurrey *Spergularia rubra*

HEIGHT Prostrate.
ECOLOGY & NATURAL HISTORY
Straggling, stickily hairy
annual or biennial.
HABITAT Grows in dry, sandy
ground, on the coast favouring
sand dunes and stabilised
shingle.
FLOWERS Pink and 3-5mm
across, the 5 petals shorter than
the sepals, May to September.
FRUITS Capsules.
LEAVES Grey-green, narrow
and bristle-tipped; borne in
whorls with silvery, lanceolate
stipules.

B&I STATUS Widespread
and locally common.
NW EUROPEAN STATUS
Local, from NW France
to S Scandinavia.

Greater Sea-spurrey *Spergularia media*

HEIGHT To 10cm.
ECOLOGY & NATURAL
HISTORY Robust, fleshy
perennial.
HABITAT Drier, upper
reaches of saltmarshes.
FLOWERS Pinkish white and
7–12mm across, the 5 petals
longer than the sepals,
June to September.
FRUITS Capsules.
LEAVES Fleshy, bristle-tipped
and semi-circular in cross
section.

B&I STATUS Widespread
and common around
coasts.
NW EUROPEAN STATUS
Local, from NW France
to S Scandinavia.

Rock Sea-spurrey *Spergularia rupicola*

HEIGHT To 20cm.
ECOLOGY & NATURAL HISTORY
Stickily hairy perennial, often
with purplish stems. Sometimes
forms clumps with woody bases.
HABITAT Found on cliffs, walls
and rocky places near the sea.
FLOWERS Pink, 5-petalled
(petals and sepals equal) and
8–10mm across with yellow
anthers, June to September.
FRUITS Capsules.
LEAVES Narrow, flattened and
fleshy; borne in whorls.

B&I STATUS
Locally common
in the west.
**NW EUROPEAN
STATUS** NW
France only.

Four-leaved Allseed *Polycarpon tetraphyllum*

HEIGHT To 12cm.
ECOLOGY & NATURAL HISTORY Straggly, much-branched annual.
HABITAT Favours sandy soils and grows in field margins and even in cracks in paving.
FLOWERS White and 2–3mm across, in tight, much-branched heads, June to August.
FRUITS Capsules.
LEAVES Narrow-ovate, the lower ones appearing as whorls of 4.

B&I STATUS Locally common on Isles of Scilly, rare elsewhere in West Country and Channel Islands.
NW EUROPEAN STATUS Local and scarce, mainly NW France.

Similar **Allseed** *Radiola linoides* (family Linaceae–Flaxes) grows to 5cm and only flourishes in short, grazed turf, mainly near coasts in W Britain. Minute white flowers are just 1–2mm across, July to August.

Fringed Rupturewort *Herniaria ciliolata*

HEIGHT Prostrate.
ECOLOGY & NATURAL HISTORY Spreading, evergreen perennial with woody, hairy stems.
HABITAT Grows on sandy and rocky ground.
FLOWERS 2mm across and yellowish green; borne in clusters, June to July.
FRUITS Capsules.
LEAVES Ovate and fringed with hairs.

B&I STATUS Restricted to Cornwall's Lizard Peninsula, and fairly easy to find at Kynance Cove, and Channel Islands.
NW EUROPEAN STATUS NW France only.

Strapwort *Corrigiola litoralis*

HEIGHT Prostrate.
ECOLOGY & NATURAL HISTORY Low-growing, spreading plant that by late summer sometimes forms a dense mat.
HABITAT Grows on the drying margins of coastal freshwater.
FLOWERS Tiny, whitish and borne in clusters, June to September.
FRUITS Capsules.
LEAVES Greyish green, strap-like and blunt-tipped.

B&I STATUS Rare, and confined as a native species to Slapton Ley in S Devon, and successfully re-introduced to Loe Pool in Cornwall. Ephemeral, appearing in good numbers in some years but absent in others.
NW EUROPEAN STATUS Widespread but local, NW France to S Sweden.

Red Campion *Silene dioica*

HEIGHT To 1m.
ECOLOGY & NATURAL HISTORY
Hairy biennial or perennial. Hybridises with White Campion, showing characters of both and usually pinkish flowers.
HABITAT Cliffs, coastal grassland, shingle, hedgerows, grassy banks and wayside places generally.
FLOWERS Reddish pink and 20–30mm across; male flowers are smaller than females and borne on separate plants, March to October.
FRUITS Reveal 10 reflexed teeth when ripe.
LEAVES Hairy and borne in opposite pairs.

B&I STATUS Widespread and common.
NW EUROPEAN STATUS Widespread and common except in north.

Shetland Red Campion *Silene dioica* ssp. *zetlandica* is similar but with larger and deeper pink flowers; it is confined to the Shetland Isles. Some authorities do not recognise its ssp. status.

Sea Campion *Silene uniflora*

HEIGHT To 20cm.
ECOLOGY & NATURAL HISTORY Cushion-forming perennial. In suitable locations, forms dense carpets of vegetation topped by an array of flowers borne on similar-length stalks. The larvae of the moths Netted Pug *Eupithecia venosata* and Marbled Coronet *Hadena confusa* feed on the seeds.
HABITAT Confined to coastal habitats, notably cliffs and shingle beaches.
FLOWERS White and 20–25mm across, with overlapping petals; borne on upright stems, June to August.
FRUITS Capsules.
LEAVES Grey-green, waxy and fleshy.

White Campion *Silene latifolia*

HEIGHT To 1m.
ECOLOGY & NATURAL HISTORY Hairy, branched perennial. Sometimes hybridises with Red Campion.
HABITAT Disturbed, free-draining ground and grassy habitats.
FLOWERS White, 5-petalled and 25–30mm across; male flowers and smaller female flowers on separate plants, May to October.
FRUITS Have erect teeth.
LEAVES Oval and borne in opposite pairs.

B&I STATUS Widespread and common.
NW EUROPEAN STATUS Widespread, NW France to S Scandinavia.

Similar **White Sticky Catchfly** *Silene viscosa* has sticky stems and white flowers similar to White Campion, borne in open spikes; grows on shores, mainly around the Baltic.

Marbled Coronet *Hadena confusa*

B&I STATUS Widespread and locally common around the coast.
NW EUROPEAN STATUS Widespread on suitable coasts from NW France to Scandinavia.

Netted Pug *Eupithecia venosata*

Sand Catchfly *Silene conica*

HEIGHT To 35cm.
ECOLOGY & NATURAL HISTORY
Upright, stickily hairy and greyish green annual.
HABITAT Grows in dunes and sandy shingle.
FLOWERS 4–5mm across with 5 notched and pinkish petals; sometimes borne in clusters, May to July.
FRUITS Form within inflated, flagon-shaped capsules.
LEAVES Narrow and downy.

B&I STATUS Local and scarce, restricted mainly to coastal SE England.
NW EUROPEAN STATUS Local, NW France to Netherlands; locally naturalised around S Baltic.

Small-flowered Catchfly *Silene gallica*

HEIGHT To 40cm.
ECOLOGY & NATURAL HISTORY
Stickily hairy annual.
HABITAT Arable land and disturbed ground, favouring coastal locations and sandy soils.
FLOWERS 10–12mm across, pinkish or white and some-times flushed red at the base; in 1-sided spikes, June to October.
FRUITS Form inside inflated capsules.
LEAVES Hairy, upper ones narrower than basal ones.

B&I STATUS Widespread but local and generally scarce.
NW EUROPEAN STATUS NW France only.

Var. *quinquevulnera*

Nottingham Catchfly *Silene nutans*

HEIGHT To 50cm.
ECOLOGY & NATURAL HISTORY Slightly downy and sticky perennial. Flowers are pollinated at night by moths. By day, when petals are tightly inrolled, the plant has the straggly appearance of a robust grass; it is easiest to spot when viewed from ground level, and on overcast days when the petals may unfurl slightly.
HABITAT Calcareous grassland and shingle beaches.
FLOWERS Nodding and 17mm across; pinkish white petals are in-rolled during daytime but roll back at dusk, May to July.
FRUITS Capsules.
LEAVES Oval, the lower ones stalked while stem leaves are unstalked.

at night

B&I STATUS Local and scattered.
NW EUROPEAN STATUS Scattered and local, N France to S Scandinavia.

Nottingham Catchfly is the sole larval foodplant for the **White Spot *Hadena albimacula*** moth, and south coast shingle expanses are its stronghold. The larvae feed on seeds and seed capsules by night and hide among the pebbles during the day.

Childing Pink *Petrorhagia nanteuilii*

HEIGHT To 40cm.
ECOLOGY & NATURAL HISTORY Slender annual with greyish leaves and stem.
HABITAT Grows on stabilised coastal shingle.
FLOWERS 6–8mm across and terminal, July to September.
FRUITS Capsules.
LEAVES Grey-green, narrow and mainly basal.

Similar **Jersey Pink *Dianthus gallicus*** has flowers up to 1.5cm across comprising 5 pale pink petals with frilly margins. Grows in damp dune slacks. Rare and local in western Europe, established on Jersey (sometimes regarded as introduced there) and recently discovered on south Hampshire/Dorset coast.

B&I STATUS More widespread in the past; nowadays it is only reliably seen at Pagham Harbour in Sussex, where it is very locally common, and near Shoreham; also found on Jersey.
NW EUROPEAN STATUS Rare and local, NW France only.

Fringed Pink *Dianthus superbus* has petals with dissected, frilly margins and grows in free-draining soils; widespread but absent from Britain and Ireland.

Sea Knotgrass *Polygonum maritimum*

HEIGHT Prostrate.
ECOLOGY & NATURAL HISTORY Creeping perennial that has a woody base.
HABITAT Grows on sand and shingle beaches, on strandline of highest spring tides.
FLOWERS Pinkish and arising in the leaf axils, July to September.
FRUITS Nut-like, as long as or slightly longer than perianth.
LEAVES Grey-green and rolled-under at the margins; stipules silvery with 6–12 branched veins, upper ones at least as long as internodes.

B&I STATUS Very local, at scattered locations on south coast, from Cornwall to Sussex, and Channel Islands.
NW EUROPEAN STATUS NW France only.

Ray's Knotgrass *Polygonum oxyspermum* ssp. *raii*

HEIGHT Prostrate.
ECOLOGY & NATURAL HISTORY Mat-forming annual.
HABITAT Undisturbed coastal sand and shingle beaches, on strandline of highest spring tides.
FLOWERS Pinkish white and arising in the leaf axils, August to September.

FRUITS Nut-like and protruding well beyond the withering perianth.
LEAVES Grey-green oval, leathery and alternate, sometimes with slightly in-rolled margins; stipules with 4–6 unbranched veins, all shorter than internodes.

B&I STATUS Local and commonest in the west.
NW EUROPEAN STATUS Scattered and local, NW France to S Scandinavia.

Knotgrass *Polygonum aviculare*

HEIGHT To 1m, but often prostrate when growing in coastal habitats.
ECOLOGY & NATURAL HISTORY Much-branched annual.
HABITAT Bare soil and open ground, including seashores.
FLOWERS Pale pink and arising in leaf axils, June to October.
FRUITS Nut-like and enclosed by withering perianth.
LEAVES Grey-green, oval, leathery and alternate with a silvery basal sheath; main stem leaves are larger than those on side branches.

B&I STATUS Widespread and common.
NW EUROPEAN STATUS Widespread and common throughout.

Similar **Northern Knotgrass *Polygonum boreale*** is the northern counterpart of Knotgrass, replacing that species in N Scotland, the northern isles and Outer Hebrides. The leaf petiole is longer than the stipule (shorter in Knotgrass) and the nut-like fruit is proportionately larger.

Equal-leaved Knotgrass *Polygonum depressum*

HEIGHT Prostrate.
ECOLOGY & NATURAL HISTORY Mat-forming annual, superficially similar to Knotgrass.
HABITAT Bare soil, tracks and paths; tolerates trampling.
FLOWERS Pale pink and arising in leaf axils, June to October.
FRUITS Nut-like and enclosed by withering perianth.
LEAVES Grey-green, oval and equal in size on main stem and side branches (cf. Knotgrass).

B&I STATUS Widespread and common.
NW EUROPEAN STATUS Widespread and common throughout.

Common Sorrel *Rumex acetosa*

HEIGHT To 60cm.
ECOLOGY & NATURAL HISTORY Variable,
usually upright perennial. The whole plant
often turns red as it goes over. Subspecies
hibernicus grows locally on dunes and machair
on west coasts; it is downy and fleshier that its
inland counterpart subspecies.
HABITAT Grows in a wide range of
unimproved grassy habitats, including
stabilised shingle and coastal meadows.
FLOWERS Reddish and borne in slender
spikes, May to July.
FRUITS Glossy and nut-like
with a small tubercle.
LEAVES Deep green, arrow-shaped and narrow, the
basal lobes pointing backwards; taste mildly of vinegar.

B&I STATUS Widespread
and common.
NW EUROPEAN STATUS
Widespread and common
throughout.

Sheep's Sorrel *Rumex acetosella*

HEIGHT To 25cm.
ECOLOGY & NATURAL HISTORY Short,
upright perennial. In suitable habitats,
forms open swards that appear as
conspicuously red patches when flowers and
fruits mature red.
HABITAT Grows on well-drained acid soils,
including shingle beaches and short coastal
grassland.
FLOWERS Greenish and borne in loose,
slender spikes, May to August.
FRUITS Glossy and nut-like.
LEAVES Arrow-shaped, the basal lobes
pointing forwards; upper leaves clasp
the stem.

B&I STATUS Widespread
and common in suitable
habitats.
NW EUROPEAN STATUS
Widespread.

The insect in the picture above is a sawfly larva. These differ from
superficially similar moth caterpillars in the number of pairs of sucker-
like false legs behind the front three pairs of true legs; moths have no
more than four pairs, whereas sawflies have five or more pairs.

Curled Dock *Rumex crispus*

HEIGHT To 1m.
ECOLOGY & NATURAL HISTORY
Upright perennial. The subspecies
littoreus is entirely coastal.
HABITAT Rough meadows and
disturbed ground; ssp. *littoreus* grows
in sand dunes, on shingle and along
strandlines on beaches.
FLOWERS Flattened and oval; borne
in dense, leafless spikes that do not
spread away from the stem, June to
October.
FRUITS Oval and untoothed, usually
with a single tubercle.
LEAVES Narrow, up to 25cm long
and with wavy edges.

fruit

B&I STATUS Widespread
and common.
NW EUROPEAN STATUS
NW France to coastal
S Scandinavia.

Northern Dock *Rumex longifolius*

HEIGHT To 1m.
ECOLOGY & NATURAL HISTORY
Upright perennial of disturbed
ground. Superficially similar to
Curled Dock.
HABITAT Grows on cliffs and
beaches and inland beside rivers
and roads.
FLOWERS Pale green, borne in
narrow spikes, July to September.
FRUITS Heart-shaped and lacking
teeth and tubercles.
LEAVES Up to 80cm long, broader
than those of Curled Dock with a
heart-shaped (not tapering) base.

fruit

B&I STATUS Locally
common in the eastern
half of Scotland.
NW EUROPEAN STATUS
Widespread in
Scandinavia.

Fiddle Dock *Rumex pulcher*

HEIGHT To 30cm.
ECOLOGY & NATURAL HISTORY
Upright to spreading perennial with
branches spreading at right angles.
HABITAT Favours well-drained soil,
especially near the coast in fields
that are grazed and trampled.
FLOWERS Borne on spikes in widely
separated whorls, June to August.
FRUITS Toothed and have 3
tubercles.
LEAVES Up to 10cm, 'waisted' and
violin-shaped.

fruit

B&I STATUS Local, and
restricted to S England and
S Wales.
NW EUROPEAN STATUS Very
local, NW France only.

Wildflowers

Broad-leaved Dock *Rumex obtusifolius*

HEIGHT To 1m.
ECOLOGY & NATURAL HISTORY Familiar upright perennial.
HABITAT Coastal field margins and disturbed meadows; widespread inland.
FLOWERS Borne in loose spikes that are leafy at the base, June to August.
FRUITS Have prominent teeth and 1 tubercle.
LEAVES Broadly oval, heart-shaped at the base and up to 25cm long.

B&I STATUS Widespread and extremely common throughout.
NW EUROPEAN STATUS NW France to S Scandinavia.

Clustered Dock *Rumex conglomeratus*

HEIGHT To 1m.
ECOLOGY & NATURAL HISTORY Upright perennial with a zigzag stem and spreading branches.
HABITAT Grows in damp meadows and beside tracks.
FLOWERS Borne in leafy spikes.
FRUITS Small, untoothed, with 3 elongated, narrow tubercles, June to August.
LEAVES Oval; basal ones are heart-shaped at base and often slightly 'waisted'.

B&I STATUS Mostly common but rare in Scotland.
NW EUROPEAN STATUS Widespread NW France to Denmark; occasional elsewhere.

Shore Dock *Rumex rupestris*

HEIGHT To 1m

ECOLOGY & NATURAL HISTORY Superficially similar to Clustered Dock (see p. 97) but the whorled inflorescence is leafy only at the base, June to July. A threatened species that is the subject of recovery projects.

HABITAT Rocky and shingle shores, particularly at the base of unstable cliffs and eroding shore banks; invariably grows at freshwater seepages on the shoreline.

FLOWERS Borne in dense whorls that are tightly packed on long spikes.

FRUITS All three tubercles are much larger (relative to tepals) than in Clustered Dock and are extremely swollen, which presumably aids buoyancy – marine currents are thought to aid the species' dispersal.

LEAVES Greyish and blunt.

B&I STATUS Most reliably found on S Devon and Cornwall coasts, but also occurs in S Wales, the Channel Islands and Isles of Scilly.

NW EUROPEAN STATUS Rare, NW France only.

fruit

Golden Dock *Rumex maritimus*

HEIGHT To 70cm

ECOLOGY & NATURAL HISTORY
Annual or biennial that turns golden-yellow in fruit.

HABITAT Muddy freshwater and brackish margins.

FLOWERS Borne in dense, widely separated whorls, June to August.

FRUITS Have 3 tubercles and teeth longer than valves. The dense clusters of fruits turn a striking golden-orange colour as they mature, at which time the reason for the plant's common name becomes obvious.

LEAVES Lanceolate.

fruit

B&I STATUS Widespread but local, mainly in the south.

NW EUROPEAN STATUS Very local, NW France to S Scandinavia.

Thrift *Armeria maritima*

HEIGHT To 20cm

ECOLOGY & NATURAL HISTORY Attractive, cushion-forming perennial. The sole foodplant for the larvae of the Thrift Clearwing *Pyropteron muscaeformis* (see p. 29), an atypical day-flying moth that is locally common in western Britain.

HABITAT Often carpets suitable coastal cliffs. Sometimes also grows in saltmarshes.

FLOWERS Pink and borne in dense, globular heads, 15–25mm across, that are carried on slender stalks, April to July.

FRUITS Capsules.

LEAVES Dark green, long and narrow.

Wildflowers

B&I STATUS Widespread and locally abundant, particularly in W Britain. **NW EUROPEAN STATUS** Locally common NW France to Denmark; local in coastal Norway and S Sweden.

Similar **Jersey Thrift** *Armeria arenaria* grows to 30cm tall, has far fewer, but broader, leaves than Thrift and its pink flower heads borne on more slender stalks, May to July. It grows on dry ground and, in our region, is restricted to coastal dunes on Jersey and cliffs of SE Dorset.

Common Sea-lavender *Limonium vulgare*

HEIGHT To 30cm
ECOLOGY & NATURAL HISTORY
Distinctive, hairless perennial that
is woody at the base. It is easily
overlooked when not in flower; its
blooms are extremely attractive to
pollinating insects.
HABITAT Entirely restricted to
saltmarshes and tolerates tidal
inundation.
FLOWERS 6–7mm long and pinkish
lilac; they are borne in branched,
flat-topped dense heads on arching
sprays that branch from *above* the
middle of the stem (cf. Lax-flowered),
July to September.
FRUITS Capsules.
LEAVES Spoon-shaped with long
stalks.

B&I STATUS Widespread and
locally common in S and SE
England but scarce or absent
elsewhere.
NW EUROPEAN STATUS
Local, NW France to S Baltic
coasts.

Common Sea-lavender

Lax-flowered Sea-lavender *Limonium humile*

HEIGHT To to 25cm.
ECOLOGY & NATURAL HISTORY
Similar to Common Sea-lavender alongside which it often grows but with subtle differences in appearance of flower heads and leaves. To confuse matters, the two species hybridise.
HABITAT Restricted to saltmarshes.
FLOWERS 6–7mm long and pinkish lilac; borne in open, lax clusters with well-spaced flowers; sprays branch from *below* the middle of the stem, July to September.
FRUITS Capsules.
LEAVES Narrow and long-stalked.

B&I STATUS Local in England, Wales, and S Scotland; widespread and fairly common on Irish coasts where Common Sea-lavender is absent.
NW EUROPEAN STATUS Very local, NW France and SW Sweden.

Rock Sea-lavenders *Limonium binervosum* agg.

HEIGHT To 30cm.

ECOLOGY & NATURAL HISTORY This complex group of hairless perennials comprises a mix of 'species' and 'subspecies' that have evolved in isolation, and are separated geographically and by habitat preference including soil and rock type. Their classification is bafflingly confusing for the beginner: some authors treat the group as a single 'aggregate' entity but here we have chosen to follow Stace's classification breakdown. Given the variability within each taxon, identification is a task that is beyond the scope of this book and the key in Stace should be referred to. But for the benefit of botanists who relish the challenge we have used geographical location and habitat as pointers for identification.

Tip! To be sure you are looking at a Rock Sea-lavender and not one of the look-alike species you need to scrutinise the leaves, and specifically the veins (easiest to observe back-lit): only Rock Sea-lavenders have 1–3 veins that originate separately at the base. Two extremely rare Channel Island species have 5–7 leaf veins that originate at the base (see box); all other species have leaves with pinnate veins.

HABITAT Habitats favoured by the species/subspecies include coastal cliffs and rocks, stabilised shingle beaches, sand dunes and saltmarshes.

FLOWERS 6–7mm long and pinkish lilac; borne in clusters on sprays that branch from below the middle, July to August; flower density varies considerably.

FRUITS Capsules.

LEAVES Narrow spoon-shaped with winged stalks; those of all species/subspecies have leaves with 1–3 veins.

Limonium binervosum ssp. *anglicum*

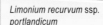

Limonium recurvum ssp. *portlandicum*

B&I STATUS Very locally common on coasts, each species/subspecies typically having a restricted range.

NW EUROPEAN STATUS Very local, NW France.

Limonium procerum ssp. *procerum*

GROUP MEMBERS:

1. *Limonium binervosum* group – ROCK SEA-LAVENDERS
  A. *Limonium binervosum* ssp. *binervosum* Sussex and south Kent; saltmarshes and chalk cliffs.
  B. *Limonium binervosum* ssp. *cantianum* North Kent; saltmarshes and chalk cliffs.
  C. *Limonium binervosum* ssp. *anglicum* Norfolk and Lincolnshire; saltmarshes.
  D. *Limonium binervosum* ssp. *saxonicum* Essex and Suffolk; saltmarshes.
  E. *Limonium binervosum* ssp. *mutatum* Devon; rocky cliffs.
  F. *Limonium binervosum* ssp. *sarniense* Channel Islands; rocky cliffs.

2. *Limonium paradoxum* – ST DAVID'S HEAD SEA-LAVENDER St David's Head, Wales; rocky cliffs.

3. *Limonium procerum* group – TALL SEA-LAVENDERS
  G. *Limonium procerum* ssp. *procerum* Western Britain; saltmarshes and cliffs.
  H. *Limonium procerum* ssp. *devoniense* South Devon; cliffs.
  I. *Limonium procerum* ssp. *cambrense* Pembrokeshire, Wales; cliffs.

4. *Limonium britannicum* group – WESTERN SEA-LAVENDERS
  J. *Limonium britannicum* ssp. *britannicum*
  Southwest England; cliffs and rocky coast.
  K. *Limonium britannicum* ssp. *coombense*
  Southwest England; cliffs.
  L. *Limonium britannicum* ssp. *transcanalils*
  Southwest England and Wales; saltmarshes,
  shingle and cliffs.
  M. *Limonium britannicum* ssp. *celticum* Northwest
  England and Wales; saltmarshes and cliffs.

5. *Limonium parvum* – SMALL SEA-LAVENDER
Saddle Point, west Wales; cliffs.

6. *Limonium loganicum* – LOGAN'S SEA-LAVENDER
Land's End, Cornwall; rocky cliffs.

7. *Limonium transwallianum* – GILTAR SEA-LAVENDER
Giltar Point, West Wales; cliffs.

8. *Limonium dodartiforme* – PURBECK SEA-LAVENDER
Dorset; shingle and cliffs.

9. *Limonium recurvum* group – IRISH SEA-LAVENDERS
  N. *Limonium recurvum* ssp. *recurvum* Portland,
  Dorset (tip of island); cliffs.
  O. *Limonium recurvum* ssp. *portlandicum*
  Portland (other than tip), elsewhere in Dorset, and
  Ireland; saltmarshes and cliffs.
  P. *Limonium recurvum* ssp. *pseudotranswallianum*
  Ireland; cliffs.
  Q. *Limonium recurvum* ssp. *humile* Northwest
  Britain and Ireland; cliffs.

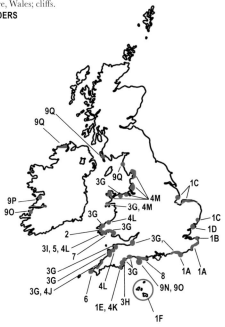

Two Channel Island specialities have leaves with 5–7 veins that arise at the base of the petiole. **Broad-leaved Sea-lavender** *Limonium auriculae-ursifolium* is robust (Height: to 40cm) with broad leaves; it grows in rock crevices on Jersey. **Alderney Sea-lavender** *Limonium normannicum* is shorter (Height: to 20cm) with dense flower spikes and leaves; it is restricted to Alderney and Jersey.

Limonium procerum
ssp. *procerum*

Alderney
Sea-lavender

Alderney Sea-lavender

Rottingdean Sea-lavender *Limonium hyblaeum*

HEIGHT To 30cm.
ECOLOGY & NATURAL HISTORY
Upright perennial that recalls a
species of rock sea-lavender but
whose leaves have pinnate veins.
Native to Sicily. Cultivated in
gardens but also naturalised and
intentionally planted.
HABITAT Chalk cliffs and sea walls.
FLOWERS 5–6mm long and bluish
lilac, in upright spikes, July to
August.
FRUITS Capsules.
LEAVES Deciduous, spoon-shaped
and often tinged red; borne in a tight,
saxifrage-like basal rosette.

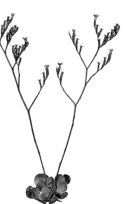

B&I STATUS Non-native, sometimes
naturalised as a garden-escape but also
planted. Found on chalk cliffs at Rottingdean
and Seaford Head in Sussex, and in profusion
planted on sea defences at West Bay, Dorset.
NW EUROPEAN STATUS Planted and
naturalised occasionally.

Matted Sea-lavender *Limonium bellidifolium*

HEIGHT To 25cm.
ECOLOGY & NATURAL HISTORY Recalls
Common Sea-lavender but with subtle
differences in appearance of flower heads
and leaves; plant branches from near base.
HABITAT Restricted to saltmarshes.
FLOWERS 5–6mm
long and pale
pinkish lilac; in
arching sprays
with many
non-flowering
shoots below,
July to
August.
FRUITS
Capsules.
LEAVES
Spoon-shaped and
mainly basal; wither
before flowering shoots
appear.

B&I STATUS Locally common only
on N Norfolk coast.
NW EUROPEAN STATUS A mainly
Mediterranean species, mostly
absent from mainland NW Europe.

Common Mallow *Malva sylvestris*

HEIGHT To 1.5m.
ECOLOGY & NATURAL HISTORY Upright or spreading perennial.
HABITAT Grassy verges and disturbed ground, sometimes near sea cliffs or just above beach strandlines.
FLOWERS 25–40mm across with 5 purple-veined pink petals, much longer than sepals; in clusters from leaf axils, June to October.
FRUITS Round, flat capsules.
LEAVES Basal leaves are rounded, while stem leaves are 5-lobed.

B&I STATUS Widespread and common in S Britain; scarce elsewhere.
NW EUROPEAN STATUS Widespread, north to Denmark; occasional S Sweden.

Dwarf Mallow *Malva neglecta*

HEIGHT To 40cm.
ECOLOGY & NATURAL HISTORY Upright or spreading perennial.
HABITAT Grows beside coastal tracks and occasionally on strandlines; also found on disturbed and waste ground with low vegetation, on coasts and inland.
FLOWERS 1–2cm across with purple-veined and notched pale lilac petals; borne in clusters along stems, June to September.
FRUITS Round, flat capsules.
LEAVES Rounded with shallow lobes.

UK STATUS Widespread and locally common in the south but scarce elsewhere.
NW EUROPEAN STATUS Widespread, north to Denmark; occasional S Scandinavia.

Tree-mallow *Malva arborea*

HEIGHT To 3m.
ECOLOGY & NATURAL HISTORY Imposing woody biennial, covered in starry hairs. Frost-intolerant and thrives in nutrient-rich soils. Previously known as *Lavatera arborea*.
HABITAT Favours rocky ground near the coast, often near seabird colonies and roosts.
FLOWERS 3–5cm across with dark-veined pinkish purple petals; borne in terminal clusters, June to September.
FRUITS Round, flat capsules.
LEAVES 5–7 lobed.

B&I STATUS Locally common on west coasts of Britain and S and W Ireland.
NW EUROPEAN STATUS NW France only.

Smaller Tree-mallow *Malva multiflora*

HEIGHT To 1m.
ECOLOGY & NATURAL HISTORY Annual or biennial with a hairy stem. Previously known as *Lavatera cretica*.
HABITAT Margins of coastal arable fields and tracks.
FLOWERS 2–3cm across with pink, slightly waxy-looking petals, July to October.
FRUITS Disc-shaped.
LEAVES Downy, with 5–7 lobes.

B&I STATUS Thought to have been introduced to Britain in mid-18th Century although possibly native in southwest. Nowadays only reliably found on Isles of Scilly and Channel Islands; sporadic and occasional elsewhere.
NW EUROPEAN STATUS A Mediterranean/Atlantic coast species; NW France only.

Marsh-mallow *Althaea officinalis*

HEIGHT To 2m.
ECOLOGY & NATURAL HISTORY
Attractive, downy perennial with
starry hairs; very soft to touch.
HABITAT Found in coastal wetlands
and often on the upper reaches of
saltmarshes.
FLOWERS 35–40mm across and
pale pink, August to September.
FRUITS Rounded flat capsules.
LEAVES Triangular with
shallow lobes.

B&I STATUS Locally
common on south coasts
of Britain and Ireland.
NW EUROPEAN STATUS
Very local and scattered,
north to S Sweden.

MALVACEAE – Mallows and relatives

Perforate St John's-wort *Hypericum perforatum*

HEIGHT To 80cm.
ECOLOGY & NATURAL HISTORY Upright,
hairless perennial with 2-lined stems.
HABITAT Grows in dry dune grassland, and
similar habitats inland, usually on calcareous
soils.
FLOWERS 2cm across, the deep yellow
petals often with black marginal spots,
June to September.
FRUITS Dry capsules.
LEAVES Oval with translucent
spots; borne in opposite pairs.

stem

Several other *Hypericum* species
occur in our region. Although none
could be said to be exclusively
coastal, a couple are occasional
floral components of dune slacks
and coastal grassland. **Imperforate
St John's-wort *H. maculatum*** has
square stems and leaves that lack
translucent dots; it grows in damp
soils. **Square-stemmed St John's-
wort *H. tetrapterum*** has square
stems that are winged at the angles
and leaves with translucent dots; it
also grows in damp soils.

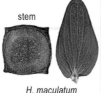

stem

H. maculatum

stem

H. tetrapterum

B&I STATUS
Widespread, more
common in the south.
**NW EUROPEAN
STATUS** Widespread
and locally common.

Common Rock-rose *Helianthemum nummularium*

HEIGHT To 40cm.
ECOLOGY & NATURAL HISTORY Attractive, branched undershrub. Flowers are popular with pollinating insects; leaves are among the larval foodplants of Brown Argus *Aricia agestis* butterfly.
HABITAT Grows in dry grassland including sand dunes, mostly on calcareous soils.
FLOWERS 2.5cm across with 5 crinkly yellow petals, June to September; petals are easily dislodged.
FRUITS Capsules.
LEAVES Narrow-oval, downy white below and paired; margins slightly in-rolled.

B&I STATUS Widespread and locally common in SE and E England but scarce further north and west.
NW EUROPEAN STATUS Very locally common but patchy, north to S Sweden.

Hoary Rock-rose *Helianthemum oelandicum*

HEIGHT To 40cm.
ECOLOGY & NATURAL HISTORY Branched, spreading and variably hairy shrubby perennial.
HABITAT Grows in dry, grassy places, mostly on coastal limestone.
FLOWERS 10–15mm across with 5 crinkly, yellow petals, May to July.
FRUITS Dry capsules.
LEAVES Very narrow and greyish white below.

B&I STATUS Extremely local in N England, Wales; locally very common in W Ireland.
NW EUROPEAN STATUS Very local, north to S Scandinavia (scientific name derives from Swedish island of Öland).

White Rock-rose *Helianthemum apenninum*

HEIGHT To 40cm.
ECOLOGY & NATURAL HISTORY
Attractive, branched and spreading
shrubby perennial.
HABITAT Grows in dry, coastal
grassland on limestone.
FLOWERS 2.5cm across with 5 crinkly,
white petals, May to July.
FRUITS Capsules.
LEAVES Narrow-oval, downy white above
and below, with in-rolled margins.

B&I STATUS Local,
restricted to coastal areas
of S Devon (Berry Head)
and N Somerset (Brean
Down).
NW EUROPEAN STATUS
A mainly Mediterranean/
mountain species, the
British populations
represent the northern limit
of its range; rare in NW
France only.

Spotted Rock-rose *Tuberaria guttata*

HEIGHT To 30cm.
ECOLOGY & NATURAL HISTORY Hairy
annual, easily overlooked when not in
flower.
HABITAT Grows in dry, coastal grassland
on thin, free-draining soils overlying
hard rocks.
FLOWERS 1–2cm across and yellow with
a red spot at each petal base, April to
August. Petals are easily dislodged
and usually fall of their own
accord by midday.
FRUITS Capsules.
LEAVES
Narrowly
oval, in
a basal
rosette and
in opposite
pairs on the
stem.

B&I STATUS Rare and local,
confined to Anglesey, W Ireland and
the Channel Islands.
NW EUROPEAN STATUS A typical
Mediterranean/Atlantic coast
species; NW France only.

Dwarf Pansy *Viola kitaibeliana*

HEIGHT To 10cm.
ECOLOGY & NATURAL HISTORY Low-growing annual, recognisable as a member of the violet family but miniature in all respects.
HABITAT Grows in short coastal turf and bare, disturbed ground on sandy ground.
FLOWERS 5mm long, typically creamy white with a yellow centre but often variably tinged purple, April to May.
FRUITS Egg-shaped.
LEAVES Ovate.

B&I STATUS Rare and restricted to Isles of Scilly (Bryher) and Channel Islands (Guernsey and Jersey).
NW EUROPEAN STATUS NW France only.

Dune Pansy *Viola tricolor* ssp. *curtisii*

HEIGHT To 12cm.
ECOLOGY & NATURAL HISTORY *Viola tricolor* occurs as two subspecies in Britain and Ireland: annual ssp. *tricolor* (Heartsease); and perennial ssp. *curtisii* (Dune Pansy).
HABITAT Ssp. *curtisii* is restricted to dry coastal grassland, especially sand dunes; ssp. *tricolor* is widespread in cultivated ground, including coastal areas.
FLOWERS 15–25mm across; variably yellow, white and violet but more often yellow and white in ssp. *curtisii*, April to August.
FRUITS Egg-shaped.
LEAVES Lancelolate with leaf-like stipules.

tricolor

curtisii

B&I STATUS Ssp. *curtisii* is restricted to coastal habitats mainly in W Britain.
NW EUROPEAN STATUS Widespread.

Similar **Heath Dog-violet *Viola canina*** is the other violet species most likely to be found in coastal habitats. It has uniformly blue flowers, 15–20mm across, and a dull yellowish spur; it grows in grassy coastal heaths and dunes.

Wildflowers

Sea-heath *Frankenia laevis*

HEIGHT Prostrate.
ECOLOGY & NATURAL HISTORY Branched, mat-forming and woody perennial.
HABITAT Restricted to the drier, upper reaches of saltmarshes.
FLOWERS 5mm across with 5 pink and crinkly petals, June to August.
FRUITS Capsules.
LEAVES Small and narrow with in-rolled margins; densely packed and opposite on side shoots.

B&I STATUS Local, from Dorset to Norfolk only.
NW EUROPEAN STATUS NW France only.

FRANKENIACEAE – Sea-heaths

Wallflower *Erysimum cheiri*

HEIGHT To 60cm.
ECOLOGY & NATURAL HISTORY Showy perennial with a woody base to the stems and branched hairs.
HABITAT Grows on cliffs and old walls, especially on calcareous substrates.
FLOWERS 2–3cm across with 4 orange-yellow petals; borne in terminal clusters, March to June.
FRUITS Flattened pods up to 7cm long.
LEAVES Narrow and untoothed.

B&I STATUS Introduced but widely naturalised as a garden escape, established here for several centuries.
NW EUROPEAN STATUS Widespread but local, mainly NW France to N Germany.

Hoary Stock *Matthiola incana*

HEIGHT To 80cm.
ECOLOGY & NATURAL HISTORY
Downy, greyish annual or
perennial with a woody base
to the stem. The flowers are
popular with pollinating insects.
HABITAT Grows on sea cliffs,
stabilised shingle and other
habitats.
FLOWERS Fragrant and
25–50mm across, with 4 white
to purple petals, April to July.
FRUITS Cylindrical pods up to
13cm long.
LEAVES Narrow and
untoothed.

B&I STATUS Scarce and
local on coasts; doubtfully
native and best treated as a
long-established naturalised
species.
NW EUROPEAN STATUS
Absent.

Sea Stock *Matthiola sinuata*

HEIGHT To 80cm.
**ECOLOGY & NATURAL
HISTORY** Downy, grey-
green biennial or short-
lived perennial, the base
of which is not woody.
HABITAT Grows on coastal
dunes and sea cliffs.
FLOWERS Fragrant and
25–50mm across, with
4 pinkish petals, June to
August.
FRUITS Narrow and
elongated pods.
LEAVES Narrow with
toothed or lobed margins.

B&I STATUS Native and
perhaps introduced in
places; easiest to find in
S Wales and N Devon.
NW EUROPEAN STATUS
NW France only.

Common Whitlowgrass *Erophila verna*

HEIGHT To 20cm.
ECOLOGY & NATURAL HISTORY
Variable, hairy annual.
HABITAT Grows on sand dunes,
stabilised shingle and calcareous
cliffs; also found inland
on dry, bare ground.
FLOWERS 3–6mm
across with 4 deeply
notched whitish petals,
March to May.
FRUITS Elliptical pods,
borne on long stalks.
LEAVES Narrow and toothed;
form a basal rosette from the centre
of which the flowering stalk arises.

B&I STATUS Common
and widespread
throughout, and locally
common on coasts.
NW EUROPEAN STATUS
Widespread, north to
S Scandinavia.

Similar **Yellow Whitlowgrass** *Draba aizoides* is a compact
perennial that forms clumps up to 12cm tall. The yellow
flowers appear from
March to May. It grows on
limestone walls and cliffs
and is a long-established,
presumed introduction
on the Gower Peninsula
in S Wales; it is absent
from elsewhere in NW
Europe.

Shepherd's-purse *Capsella bursa-pastoris*

HEIGHT To 35cm.
ECOLOGY & NATURAL HISTORY
Distinctive upright annual.
HABITAT Grows beside coastal
tracks and wayside ground; also
favours arable fields and gardens
inland.
FLOWERS 2–3mm across with 4
white petals; in terminal clusters,
and in flower year-round.
FRUITS Green, triangular and
notched.
LEAVES Vary from lobed to entire;
upper ones are usually toothed and
clasp the stem.

fruit

B&I STATUS Widespread
and rather common
throughout.
NW EUROPEAN STATUS
Widespread.

Common Scurvygrass *Cochlearia officinalis*

HEIGHT To 50cm.
ECOLOGY & NATURAL HISTORY
Biennial or perennial. Common
name derives from its use as a
cure for scurvy, a disease caused
by vitamin C (ascorbic acid)
deficiency – the leaves are a
good source.
HABITAT Grows on saltmarshes,
coastal walls and cliffs (and on
mountains inland); colonises
salt-treated roadside verges
inland.
FLOWERS 8–10mm across with
4 white petals, April to October.
FRUITS Rounded to ovoid,
4–7mm long and longer than
stalk.
LEAVES Kidney-shaped basal
leaves more than 2cm long, and
clasping, arrow-shaped ones
on stem.

B&I STATUS Locally
common.
NW EUROPEAN STATUS
Widespread on coasts,
north to N Norway and
S Sweden.

Danish Scurvygrass *Cochlearia danica*

HEIGHT To 20cm.
ECOLOGY & NATURAL HISTORY
Compact, often prostrate, annual.
HABITAT Grows on sandy soils, shingle and walls, mainly around the coast; also flourishes alongside salt-treated roads and motorway verges and central reservations.
FLOWERS 4–6mm across with 4 white petals, January to August.
FRUITS Ovoid pods, 6mm long.
LEAVES Comprise long-stalked heart-shaped basal leaves and stalked, ivy-shaped stem leaves.

B&I STATUS Widespread and common around most coasts.
NW EUROPEAN STATUS Widespread on coasts, north to S Scandinavia.

English Scurvygrass *Cochlearia anglica*

HEIGHT To 35cm.
ECOLOGY & NATURAL HISTORY
Straggly biennial or perennial.
HABITAT Grows in estuaries and coastal mudflats; appears not to colonise salt-treated roadside verges inland.
FLOWERS 10–14mm across with 4 white petals, April to July.
FRUITS Elliptical and 10–15mm long.
LEAVES Basal leaves are long-stalked and narrow, tapering gradually to the base; stem leaves clasp the stem.

B&I STATUS Locally common around most coasts in suitable habitats.
NW EUROPEAN STATUS Widespread and locally common.

basal leaf

Hutchinsia *Hornungia petraea*

HEIGHT To 15cm.
ECOLOGY & NATURAL HISTORY
Delicate, usually branching
annual that is easily overlooked.
HABITAT Restricted to
calcareous rocks and soils; on
the coast, associated with
stable sand dunes and rocky
outcrops.
FLOWERS 1mm across with 4
whitish petals, March to May.
FRUITS Flattened, elliptical
pods.
LEAVES Pinnately divided;
basal ones are stalked and form a
rosette; stems leaves are unstalked.

B&I STATUS Local and scarce;
S Wales sites are the best
coastal locations.
NW EUROPEAN STATUS
Scattered and extremely local,
from NW France to S Sweden.

Shepherd's Cress *Teesdalia nudicaulis*

HEIGHT To 25cm.
ECOLOGY & NATURAL HISTORY
Unobtrusive tufted, often
hairless annual.
HABITAT Grows on bare, sandy
ground and shingle.
FLOWERS 2mm across with
4 white petals, 2 of which are
much shorter than the other 2,
April to June.
FRUITS Heart-shaped
and notched pods.
LEAVES Pinnately
lobed and appear
mainly as a basal
rosette.

fruit

B&I STATUS Locally
common only in the
south; rare elsewhere.
NW EUROPEAN STATUS
Widespread but local,
north to S Scandinavia.

Smith's Pepperwort *Lepidium heterophyllum*

HEIGHT To 40cm.
ECOLOGY & NATURAL HISTORY Grey-green, hairy and branched perennial.
HABITAT Grows on dry, bare and acidic soils and shingle.
FLOWERS 2–3mm across with 4 white petals and violet anthers; borne in dense heads, May to August.
FRUITS Oval and smooth pods.
LEAVES Comprise oval, untoothed basal leaves and arrow-shaped, clasping ones on stem.

Similar **Narrow-leaved Pepperwort** *Lepidium ruderale* is much-branched and grows on disturbed ground near the sea. Flowers are minute and greenish, usually missing petals, June to August. Fruits are small, elliptical and leaves comprise pinnately lobed basal leaves and untoothed ones on stem.

B&I STATUS Locally common, especially in the south and west.
NW EUROPEAN STATUS Introduced and widespread.

Hoary Cress *Lepidium draba*

HEIGHT To 60cm.
ECOLOGY & NATURAL HISTORY Variable, often hairless perennial.
HABITAT Grows on disturbed ground, particularly near the sea.
FLOWERS Small and white; borne in large, frothy terminal clusters, May to June.
FRUITS Heart-shaped and inflated.
LEAVES Grey-green and variably toothed; stem leaves are clasping, basal leaves soon wither.

B&I STATUS Introduced; now locally common in the south and occasional elsewhere.
NW EUROPEAN STATUS Widespread and occasional, especially on coasts.

Dittander *Lepidium latifolium*

HEIGHT To 1.5m.
ECOLOGY & NATURAL HISTORY Historically, its leaves were used to make peppery-tasting sauces and in the treatment of leprosy. Cultivated forms are sometimes grown in gardens.
HABITAT Grows on the banks of saltmarsh creeks and ditches, and in saline grassland.
FLOWERS Small and white with a very subtle pink tinge; borne in large clusters, July and August.
FRUITS Flat and rounded in outline.
LEAVES Oval and subtly toothed; basal leaves long-stalked, stem leaves very short-stalked.

B&I STATUS Native in E and SE England, naturalised as a garden escape elsewhere.
NW EUROPEAN STATUS Widespread and occasional, especially on coasts.

Swine-cress *Lepidium coronopus*

HEIGHT Prostrate.
ECOLOGY & NATURAL HISTORY Creeping annual or biennial.
HABITAT Disturbed and waste ground, often near the sea. Tolerates trampling and often found near gateways.
FLOWERS 2–3mm across and white; in compact clusters, June to September.
FRUITS Knobbly and flattened pods.
LEAVES Pinnately divided and toothed, some-times forming a dense mat on the ground.

Similar **Lesser Swine-cress** *Lepidum didymum* has petals that are minute or absent and pods that are shorter than stalks (longer than stalks in *L. coronopus*). Introduced from S America but now widespread on disturbed ground, mainly in the south.

B&I STATUS Common in S and E England but scarce elsewhere.
NW EUROPEAN STATUS Widespread but local, north to S Sweden.

Wildflowers

Lundy Cabbage *Coincya wrightii*

HEIGHT To 90cm.

ECOLOGY & NATURAL HISTORY Upright perennial that is unique to its namesake island. Two species of beetles – Lundy Cabbage Flea Beetle *Psylliodes luridipennis* and Lundy Cabbage Weevil *Ceutorhynchus contractus pallipes* – feed on it and also occur nowhere else in the world.

HABITAT Grows on broken and rocky ground within sight of the sea.

FLOWERS Comprise 4 yellow petals, borne in heads, May to July.

FRUITS Elongated pods.

LEAVES Lobed and toothed.

Above: Lundy Cabbage Flea Beetle *Psylliodes luridipennis*

Right: Lundy Cabbage Weevil *Ceutorhynchus contractus pallipes*

B&I STATUS Endemic to Lundy and grows only on the east side, with densest concentrations either side of the road that leads from the landing bay to the village.

NW EUROPEAN STATUS Not found elsewhere in Europe.

Wild Cabbage *Brassica oleracea* var. *oleracea*

HEIGHT To 1.25m.
ECOLOGY & NATURAL HISTORY
Tough perennial. The wild ancestor
of cultivated varieties including Savoy
Cabbage, Broccoli, Cauliflower and
Brussels Sprouts.
HABITAT Coastal chalk cliffs
and near seabird colonies.
FLOWERS 25–35mm
across; borne in
elongated heads,
April to August.
FRUITS Cylindrical
pods, up to 8cm long.
LEAVES Grey-green;
the lower ones are
large, fleshy and often
ravaged by the larvae
of the Large White
Pieris brassicae butterfly.

Isle of Man Cabbage *Coincya monensis* ssp. *monensis*

HEIGHT To 30cm.
ECOLOGY & NATURAL HISTORY Straggly endemic
and almost exclusively coastal, growing within
sight of the sea. Suffers when human trampling
causes excessive dune erosion but moderate erosion
maintains the open setting the plant likes. The plant
owes the current revival in its fortunes on the Sefton
coast to the perseverance of local conservationists.
HABITAT Grows just above the strandline and on open
sand dunes.
FLOWERS Comprise 4 yellow petals, borne in heads,
May to July.
FRUITS Elongated pods.
LEAVES Pinnately divided, mostly forming a basal
clump or rosette.

B&I STATUS Local in NW England and
Isle of Man, with sites in S Wales and
SW Scotland. The Sefton coast is the
species' stronghold.
NW EUROPEAN STATUS Not found
elsewhere in Europe; superficially similar
subspecies *C. m. cheiranthos* (Wallflower
Cabbage) is established locally.

Brussels Sprout

Savoy Cabbage

Cauliflower

Broccoli

Large White *Pieris brassicae* larvae

Similar **Perennial Wall-rocket**
Diplotaxis tenuifolia grows to
70cm tall on disturbed ground near
the sea, mainly S Britain. Flowers
are 15–25mm
across, pods
are cylindrical
and slender,
and leaves
and narrowly
pinnately
lobed.

Black Mustard *Brassica nigra*

HEIGHT To 2m.

ECOLOGY & NATURAL HISTORY Robust and upright, greyish annual.

HABITAT Often found on sea cliffs, shingle, riverbanks and on waste ground near farms. In some places, such as west Cornwall, it is visually dominant for a month or so on cliffs and along coastal roadside verges.

FLOWERS 12–15mm across with 4 yellow petals, May to August. Borne in heads, themselves carried in three-dimensional 'candelabras'.

FRUITS Elongated pods pressed close to the stem at first, then parallel to the stem when ripe.

LEAVES Stalked, the lower ones pinnately lobed and bristly.

B&I STATUS Locally common in England and Wales; rather scarce elsewhere.

NW EUROPEAN STATUS Widespread but local, north to S Scandinavia.

Sea Radish *Raphanus raphanistrum* ssp. *maritimus*

HEIGHT To 60cm.
ECOLOGY & NATURAL HISTORY Robust, roughly hairy biennial or short-lived perennial. Wild relative of cultivated radish.
HABITAT Grows on stabilised shingle, sand dunes and coastal grassland.
FLOWERS Yellow and 4-petalled, May to July. White-flowered plants are relicts of cultivation.
FRUITS Pods with up to 5 beaded segments.
LEAVES Comprise pinnate lower leaves and narrow, entire upper ones.

B&I STATUS Locally common only in south and southwest.
NW EUROPEAN STATUS Widespread but local.

Sea-kale *Crambe maritima*

HEIGHT To 50cm.
ECOLOGY & NATURAL HISTORY
Robust perennial that forms
domed and expansive clumps.
The seeds can be distributed by
the sea, colonising new areas.
The flowers are popular with
pollinating insects.
HABITAT Shingle and sandy
beaches.
FLOWERS 6–12mm across with
4 whitish petals; in flat-topped
clusters, June to August.
FRUITS Ovoid, one-seeded pods.
LEAVES Fleshy with wavy
margins; the lowers ones 25cm
long and long-stalked.

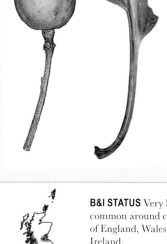

B&I STATUS Very locally
common around coasts
of England, Wales and
Ireland.
NW EUROPEAN STATUS
Widespread but local
and coastal, north to
S Scandinavia.

Sea Rocket *Cakile maritima*

HEIGHT To 25cm.
ECOLOGY & NATURAL HISTORY Straggling, fleshy and hairless annual that forms untidy-looking clumps.
HABITAT Found on sandy shores, at or above the highest strandline; occasionally also on gravel and shingle beaches.
FLOWERS 6–12mm across, pink or pale lilac and borne in terminal clusters, June to September.
FRUITS Green, fleshy pods that swell and bulge in middle and at base as they mature.
LEAVES Shiny and pinnately lobed.

B&I STATUS Widespread and locally common around coasts of Britain and Ireland.
NW EUROPEAN STATUS Widespread but local and coastal, north to N Norway and central Sweden.

Round-leaved Wintergreen *Pyrola rotundifolia* ssp. *maritima*

HEIGHT To 15cm.
ECOLOGY & NATURAL HISTORY
Low-growing perennial.
HABITAT Ssp. *maritima* grows in
damp, calcareous dune slacks,
often growing alongside Creeping
Willow *Salix repens* (see p. 43). Inland
counterpart ssp. *rotundifolia* favours
calcareous fens.
FLOWERS 8–12mm across, white
and bell-shaped; style is S-shaped
and protrudes beyond petals,
May to August.
FRUITS Capsules.
LEAVES Rounded, long-stalked
and form a basal rosette.

UK STATUS Local and habitat-
specific; populations fluctuate
but generally declining across
its range.
NW EUROPEAN STATUS Local
on coasts from NW France to
S Scandinavia.

PYROLACEAE – Wintergreens

Wild Mignonette *Reseda lutea*

HEIGHT To 70cm.
ECOLOGY & NATURAL HISTORY
Upright biennial or short-lived
perennial, often forming clumps.
HABITAT Sand dunes and
calcareous grassland; inland
on waste ground,
roadside verges and
disturbed grassland.
FLOWERS 6–8mm across and
yellowish green with 6 petals;
borne in compact spikes, June
to August.
FRUITS Upright and oblong pods.
LEAVES Pinnately divided with
wavy edges.

UK STATUS Widespread and
locally common in England,
scarce and very local elsewhere.
NW EUROPEAN STATUS
Widespread, north to S
Scandinavia, where it is
scattered and mainly coastal.

Heather *Calluna vulgaris*

HEIGHT To 50cm.

ECOLOGY & NATURAL HISTORY
Dense, evergreen undershrub that often carpets the ground where conditions suit it. Also sometimes known as Ling.

HABITAT Characteristic plant of acid soils on heaths and particularly evident, and often locally dominant, on maritime heaths.

FLOWERS 4–5mm, bell-shaped and usually pink but some-times white; borne in spikes, August to September.

FRUITS Capsules.

LEAVES Short, narrow and borne in 4 rows along the stem.

B&I STATUS Widespread and locally abundant throughout the region. On most maritime heaths it is the dominant plant.

NW EUROPEAN STATUS Widespread but local.

Bell Heather *Erica cinerea*

HEIGHT To 50cm.
ECOLOGY & NATURAL HISTORY Hairless, evergreen undershrub. Flowers are popular with pollinating insects.
HABITAT Grows on acid soils, typically favouring drier locations than Heather.
FLOWERS 5–6mm long, bell-shaped and purplish red; borne in groups along the stem that sometimes appear like elongated spikes, June to September.
FRUITS Capsules.
LEAVES Narrow, dark green and borne in whorls of 3 up the wiry stems.

Similar **Dorset Heath *Erica ciliaris*** has downy shoots, leaves in whorls of 3 and spikes of pinkish purple flowers; local on south Dorset heaths and coastal heaths in W Cornwall.

B&I STATUS Widespread and locally common especially in the west; it sometimes becomes the dominant plant on dry soils.
NW EUROPEAN STATUS NW France only.

Cornish Heath *Erica vagans*

HEIGHT To 90cm.
ECOLOGY & NATURAL HISTORY Forms low shrubs and, in suitable locations, covers extensive areas.
HABITAT Coastal heaths on base-rich soils.
FLOWERS Small and pale pink, borne in tall, dense spikes, August to September.
FRUITS Capsules.
LEAVES Produced in 4s or 5s.

B&I STATUS Native distribution confined mainly to the Lizard Peninsula and nearby sites in Cornwall; it puts on a particularly spectacular flowering display around Kynance Cove. Elsewhere its occurrence is widely scattered and in some locations it may have been introduced.
NW EUROPEAN STATUS NW France only.

Primrose *Primula vulgaris*

HEIGHT To 20cm.
ECOLOGY & NATURAL HISTORY Familiar herbaceous perennial.
HABITAT Grows in coastal grassland; widespread in meadows and woods inland.
FLOWERS 2–3cm across, 5-lobed and pale yellow, usually with deep yellow centres; solitary and borne on long hairy stalks that arise from the centre of the leaf rosette, February to May.
FRUITS Capsules.
LEAVES Oval, tapering, crinkly and up to 12cm long; they form a basal rosette.

B&I STATUS Widespread and locally common.
NW EUROPEAN STATUS Widespread and locally common.

Similar **Scottish Primrose** *Primula scotica* is low-growing (often just 5–6cm tall) with pinkish purple, yellow-centred flowers, May to June and again in August; it grows in coastal turf on clifftops and dunes in NE Scotland and West Mainland, Orkney.

Brookweed *Samolus valerandi*

HEIGHT To 12cm.
ECOLOGY & NATURAL HISTORY Hairless and pale green herbaceous perennial that grows in small colonies.
HABITAT Grows on damp ground, usually on saline or calcareous soil, often beside freshwater seepages on sea cliffs, in wet dune slacks and coastal lagoons.
FLOWERS 2–3mm across with 5 white petals, joined to halfway; in terminal clusters, June to August.
FRUITS Spherical capsules.
LEAVES Spoon-shaped; appear mainly as a basal rosette.

B&I STATUS Widespread but local and mainly coastal.
NW EUROPEAN STATUS Mainly coastal, NW France to S Sweden.

Sea-milkwort *Lysimachia maritima*

HEIGHT To 10cm.
ECOLOGY & NATURAL HISTORY Low-growing and generally creeping, hairless perennial. Previously known as *Glaux maritima*.
HABITAT Grows on the upper reaches of saltmarshes, wet shingle hollows and on sea walls.
FLOWERS 5–6mm across and comprise 5 pink, petal-like sepals; borne on upright shoots, May to September.
FRUITS Dark brown capsules.
LEAVES Ovate, succulent and arranged in opposite pairs along the trailing stems.

B&I STATUS Widespread and locally common on coasts throughout the region.
NW EUROPEAN STATUS Widespread on coasts throughout.

Bog Pimpernel *Lysimachia tenella*

HEIGHT Creeping.
ECOLOGY & NATURAL HISTORY Delicate and attractive hairless perennial with trailing stems; sometimes forms mats.
HABITAT Grows on damp ground, such as bogs and dune slacks, and mainly on acid soils.
FLOWERS Up to 1cm long, pink and funnel-shaped with 5 lobes; borne on slender, upright stalks, June to August.
FRUITS Capsules.
LEAVES Rounded, short-stalked and arranged in opposite pairs.

Similar **Chaffweed** *Lysimachia minima* is an insignificant (1–2cm tall) hairless annual that is easily overlooked in short grass on damp, sandy ground; its minute, pale pink flowers appear June to August, and its pinkish fruits are like miniature apples. Uniquely among British plants, its leaves have a black line around the margin of the under surface; it is widespread but very local.

B&I STATUS Widespread and locally common in the west but scarce in the east.
NW EUROPEAN STATUS Local, NW France to Netherlands.

Scarlet Pimpernel *Lysimachia arvensis*

HEIGHT Scrambling, up to 15cm.
ECOLOGY & NATURAL HISTORY Low-growing, hairless annual. Previously known as *Anagallis arvensis*.
HABITAT Grows on bare and disturbed ground on dunes, machair and cliffs, and also occurs in similar habitats and arable fields inland.
FLOWERS 5–7mm across with 5 scarlet or pinkish orange (sometimes blue) petals fringed with hairs; flowers open wide only in bright sunshine and are borne on slender stalks, June to August.
FRUITS Dry capsules.
LEAVES Oval and usually in pairs.

Similar **Yellow Loosestrife** *Lysimachia vulgaris* is up to 1.5m tall with a terminal array of yellow 5-lobed flowers to 10–15mm across. A wetland plant, it grows in damp dune slacks.

B&I STATUS Widespread and generally common. **NW EUROPEAN STATUS** Widespread and common, except in N.

PRIMULACEAE – Primroses and relatives

Rue-leaved Saxifrage *Saxifraga tridactylites*

HEIGHT To 15cm.
ECOLOGY & NATURAL HISTORY Stickily hairy annual with reddish, zigzag stems.
HABITAT Grows on cliffs, dry, bare ground and old walls, mainly on sandy or calcareous soils.
FLOWERS 4–6mm across with 5 white petals; borne in clusters, June to September.
FRUITS Dry capsules.
LEAVES Pinnately divided into up to 5 finger-like lobes.

B&I STATUS Widespread and very locally common.
NW EUROPEAN STATUS Very locally common in NW France; scarce and local north to S Scandinavia.

Wildflowers

Grass-of-Parnassus *Parnassia palustris*

HEIGHT To 25cm.
ECOLOGY & NATURAL HISTORY Distinctive, tufted and hairless perennial.
HABITAT Grows on damp, peaty grassland, in machair, dune slacks, marshes and moors.
FLOWERS 15–20mm across and superficially buttercup-like, with 5 white petals and greenish veins; on upright stalks with clasping leaves, June to September.
FRUITS Dry capsules.
LEAVES Deep green; basal leaves are heart-shaped and stalked.

B&I STATUS Locally common in N Britain and Ireland; scarce in, or absent from, the south.
NW EUROPEAN STATUS Local, north from Denmark and N Germany; scarce and very local elsewhere.

SAXIFRAGACEAE – Saxifrages and relatives

Navelwort *Umbilicus rupestris*

HEIGHT To 15cm.
ECOLOGY & NATURAL HISTORY Distinctive perennial.
HABITAT Grows on coastal walls, banks and cliffs, often in partial shade.
FLOWERS Whitish, tubular and drooping; borne in spikes, June to August.
FRUITS Dry, splitting capsules.
LEAVES Rounded and fleshy with a depressed centre above the leaf stalk.

B&I STATUS Widespread in W Britain and Ireland; scarce elsewhere.
NW EUROPEAN STATUS Widespread but local.

Roseroot *Rhodiola rosea*

HEIGHT To 30cm.
ECOLOGY & NATURAL HISTORY Distinctive, greyish perennial.
HABITAT Grows on sea cliffs; also found on mountain ledges.
FLOWERS Yellow and 4-petalled; borne in terminal, rounded clusters, May to July.
FRUITS Orange and superficially like the flowers.
LEAVES Succulent, oval and overlapping.

B&I STATUS Locally common in W Wales, N England, Scotland and Ireland.
NW EUROPEAN STATUS Widespread and locally common only in Norway.

Biting Stonecrop *Sedum acre*

HEIGHT To 10cm.
ECOLOGY & NATURAL HISTORY Distinctive mat-forming perennial.
HABITAT Grows on well-drained stable ground such as sand dunes, shingle, gravel tracks and old walls.
FLOWERS Star-shaped and 10–12mm across, with 5 bright yellow petals, May to July.
FRUITS Dry and splitting.
LEAVES Fleshy, crowded and pressed close to the stem; the English name reflects that fact that they taste hot.

B&I STATUS Widespread and locally common.
NW EUROPEAN STATUS Widespread but local, north to coastal N Norway and S Sweden.

White Stonecrop *Sedum album*

HEIGHT To 15cm.
ECOLOGY & NATURAL HISTORY Mat-forming, evergreen perennial.
HABITAT Grows on rocky ground, cliffs and shingle, usually near the sea.
FLOWERS Star-shaped, 6–9mm across, white above but often pinkish below; in terminal clusters, June to September.
FRUITS Dry and splitting.
LEAVES 6–12mm long, fleshy, shiny and green or reddish.

B&I STATUS Local, possibly native on coasts of SW England but widely naturalised elsewhere.
NW EUROPEAN STATUS Local, north to S Scandinavia; native in places, introduced elsewhere.

English Stonecrop *Sedum anglicum*

HEIGHT To 5cm.
ECOLOGY & NATURAL HISTORY Mat-forming perennial with wiry stems.
HABITAT Grows on rocky ground, sea cliff slopes, shingle and old walls.
FLOWERS Star-shaped and 12mm across with 5 white petals that are pink below, June to September.
FRUITS Dry and red.
LEAVES 3–5mm long, fleshy and often tinged red.

B&I STATUS Widespread and locally common, especially in W Britain and Ireland.
NW EUROPEAN STATUS Scattered range, mainly NW France and coastal S Norway.

Mossy Stonecrop *Crassula tillaea*

HEIGHT Prostrate.
ECOLOGY & NATURAL HISTORY Tiny, often reddish annual that is easily overlooked.
HABITAT Grows in dunes on bare and often seasonally damp sandy soil and gravel. Occurs inland on heaths.
FLOWERS Tiny, whitish and arising from leaf axils, June to September.
FRUITS Dry and splitting.
LEAVES 1–2mm long, oval and densely crowded on the slender stems.

B&I STATUS Extremely local, mainly in S and E England.
NW EUROPEAN STATUS Local, north to Low Countries.

CRASSULACEAE – Stonecrops and relatives

Bramble *Rubus fruticosus* agg.

HEIGHT To 3m.
ECOLOGY & NATURAL HISTORY Scrambling shrub that comprises hundreds of microspecies. Arching stems are armed with variably shaped prickles and root when they touch the ground.
HABITAT Grows in hedgerows and scrub.
FLOWERS 2–3cm across and white or pink, May to August.
FRUITS Familiar 'blackberries'.
LEAVES Have 3–5 toothed leaflets.

B&I STATUS Widespread and common.
NW EUROPEAN STATUS Widespread, north to S Scandinavia.

Wildflowers

Dewberry *Rubus caesius*

HEIGHT Scrambling.
ECOLOGY & NATURAL HISTORY Creeping perennial whose biennial stems bear weak prickles.
HABITAT Grows in dry, grassy and typically calcareous locations and does particularly well in stable dune slacks.
FLOWERS 2–2.5cm across with 5 white petals June to August.
FRUITS Bluish black, the large segments covered in a plum-like 'bloom'.
LEAVES Trifoliate and toothed.

B&I STATUS
Widespread and locally common.
NW EUROPEAN STATUS
Local, north to S Scandinavia.

Japanese Rose *Rosa rugosa*

HEIGHT To 1.5m.
ECOLOGY & NATURAL HISTORY Showy shrub with upright stems that bear rather straight thorns. If left unchecked, forms sizeable patches. Considered an invasive threat in some locations.
HABITAT Sand dunes, coastal scrub and grassland, and sea cliffs.
FLOWERS 6–9cm across with 5 pinkish purple or white petals, June to August.
FRUITS Spherical, red hips, 2–5cm across.
LEAVES Comprise 5–9 oval leaflets that are shiny above.

B&I STATUS Widely planted beside roads and grown in gardens, and often naturalised on the coast.
NW EUROPEAN STATUS
Scattered and introduced.

Burnet Rose *Rosa spinosissima*

HEIGHT To 50cm.
ECOLOGY & NATURAL HISTORY
Clump-forming shrub. Suckers and stems bear numerous straight thorns and stiff bristles. Previously known as *Rosa pimpinellifolia*.
HABITAT Grows on sand dunes, stabilised shingle beaches and coastal grassland favouring calcareous soils; favours similar soils inland.
FLOWERS 3–5cm across with 5 creamy white petals; usually solitary, May to July.
FRUITS Spherical, 5–6mm across and purplish black when ripe.
LEAVES Comprise 7–11 oval leaflets.

Similar **Pirri-pirri-bur** *Acaena novae-zelandiae* is an accidental introduction from New Zealand and Australia, best known for its spiny fruits that catch in clothing. It is an invasive problem species in several coastal areas.

B&I STATUS Widespread but only locally common.
NW EUROPEAN STATUS Local and coastal, north to Scandinavia.

Dog-rose *Rosa canina*

HEIGHT To 3m.
ECOLOGY & NATURAL HISTORY
Scrambling, variable shrub whose long, arching stems bear curved thorns. Several other dog-rose relatives occur in the region but *R. canina* is generally the commonest coastal 'wild rose'.
HABITAT Grows in coastal scrub, dunes and on cliffs. Widespread inland.
FLOWERS 3–5cm across, fragrant with 5 pale pink petals and yellow stamens; borne in clusters of up to 4 flowers, June to July.
FRUITS Red, egg-shaped hips that typically shed their sepals before they ripen.
LEAVES Comprise 5–7 hairless leaflets.

B&I STATUS Widespread and common throughout.
NW EUROPEAN STATUS Widespread and locally common.

Meadowsweet *Filipendula ulmaria*

HEIGHT To 1.25m.
ECOLOGY & NATURAL HISTORY
Striking perennial.
HABITAT Grows in wet dune slacks and coastal marshes. Widespread in marshes inland.
FLOWERS 4–6mm across, fragrant and creamy white; borne in sprays, June to September.
FRUITS Spirally twisted and one-seeded.
LEAVES Dark green and comprise 3–5 pairs of oval leaflets with smaller leaflets between.

B&I STATUS Widespread and locally common throughout.
NW EUROPEAN STATUS Widespread and locally common.

Silverweed *Potentilla anserina*

HEIGHT Creeping.
ECOLOGY & NATURAL HISTORY
Low-growing perennial with long, creeping stems. Tolerates trampling and light disturbance.
HABITAT Found in seasonally damp and drying, grassy places; does well on shores and dunes and above the strandline on saltmarshes, tolerating occasional inundation by brackish water.
FLOWERS 15–20mm across with 5 yellow petals, May to August.
FRUITS Dry and papery.
LEAVES Divided into up to 12 pairs of leaflets (with tiny ones between them) that are covered in silvery, silky hairs.

B&I STATUS Widespread and common.
NW EUROPEAN STATUS Widespread, north to coastal N Norway and S Sweden.

Creeping Cinquefoil *Potentilla reptans*

HEIGHT To 20cm.
ECOLOGY & NATURAL HISTORY
Creeping perennial whose trailing stems root at the nodes (unlike Tormentil).
HABITAT Grows in grassy places, including verges, dune slacks and coastal grassland.
FLOWERS 15–25mm across with 5 yellow petals, June to September.
FRUITS Dry and papery.
LEAVES Long-stalked, hairless and divided into 5–7 leaflets.

B&I STATUS Widespread and common throughout.
NW EUROPEAN STATUS Widespread, north to S Scandinavia.

Tormentil *Potentilla erecta*

HEIGHT To 30cm.
ECOLOGY & NATURAL HISTORY Creeping, downy perennial.
HABITAT Coastal grassy places and heaths, and similar habitats inland, on neutral to acid soils.
FLOWERS 7–11mm across with 4 yellow petals; borne on slender stalks, May to September.
FRUITS Dry and papery.
LEAVES Unstalked and trifoliate, but appear 5-lobed because of two large, leaflet-like stipules at the base.

B&I STATUS Widespread and often locally abundant.
NW EUROPEAN STATUS Widespread.

Parsley-piert *Aphanes arvensis*

HEIGHT To 10cm but often creeping and prostrate.
ECOLOGY & NATURAL HISTORY Spreading, fresh green downy annual.
HABITAT Forms carpets on dry, bare ground including stable sandy and shingle shores, and bare coastal grassland. Widespread inland.
FLOWERS Minute, petal-less and green; borne in dense clusters opposite leaf bases, April to October.
FRUITS Dry and papery.
LEAVES Fan-shaped, deeply divided into 3 lobes and superficially like culinary flat parsley in miniature.

Similar **Slender Parsley-piert *Aphanes australis*** shows subtle differences in stipules and fruits but is otherwise indistinguishable. Refer to Stace for further advice regarding identification.

B&I STATUS Widespread and generally common.
NW EUROPEAN STATUS Widespread and locally common.

Purple Oxytropis *Oxytropis halleri*

HEIGHT To 20cm.
ECOLOGY & NATURAL HISTORY Tufted perennial, covered in silky hairs.
HABITAT Grows in the far north on sea cliffs and coastal rocky outcrops, on calcareous soils; a mountain species further south.
FLOWERS 20mm long and deep purple, with a pointed tip to the keel; in stalked heads, May to June.
FRUITS Downy, 25mm-long pods.
LEAVES Up to 15cm long with 10–15 pairs of narrow leaflets.

B&I STATUS Extremely local. Easiest to see on N Scottish coast at Bettyhill Nature Reserve.
NW EUROPEAN STATUS Absent.

Purple Milk-vetch *Astragalus danicus*

HEIGHT To 30cm.
ECOLOGY & NATURAL HISTORY Attractive, downy and spreading perennial.
HABITAT Grows on dry, calcareous grassland; coastal habitats include sand dunes, machair and sea cliffs.
FLOWERS 15–18mm long and purple; borne in stalked clusters, May to July.
FRUITS Pods, covered in white hairs.
LEAVES Hairy and pinnate, comprising 6–12 pairs of oval leaflets.

B&I STATUS Local in eastern England and southern Scotland; scarce in Ireland.
NW EUROPEAN STATUS Very local, mainly Denmark and N Germany.

Wood Vetch *Ervilia sylvatica*

HEIGHT To 1.5m.
ECOLOGY & NATURAL HISTORY
Elegant, straggling perennial.
Previously known as *Vicia sylvatica*.
HABITAT Favours steep, coastal slopes and open woodland.
FLOWERS 12–20mm long, white and purple-veined; borne in spikes of up to 20 flowers, June to August.
FRUITS Black, hairless pods.
LEAVES Comprise 6–12 pairs of oblong leaflets and end in a branched tendril.

B&I STATUS Widespread but local; commonest in the west.
NW EUROPEAN STATUS Scattered range from Denmark and N Germany to coastal S Sweden and S Norway.

Yellow-vetch *Vicia lutea*

HEIGHT To 50cm.
ECOLOGY & NATURAL HISTORY
Straggling and hairless greyish green annual.
HABITAT Grows in a range of coastal habitats including rank cliff-side grassland and shingle.
FLOWERS 25–35mm long, and dull pale yellow; borne in groups of 1–3, June to September.
FRUITS Hairy, brown pods up to 4cm long.
LEAVES Comprise 3–10 pairs of bristle-tipped leaflets and branched tendrils.

B&I STATUS Very local and mainly coastal; casual colonist inland.
NW EUROPEAN STATUS Very local and mainly coastal.

Common Vetch *Vicia sativa*

HEIGHT To 75cm.
ECOLOGY & NATURAL HISTORY
Variable, downy annual. On
coastal shingle and sand, often
dwarfed and almost prostrate,
particularly subspecies *nigra*.
HABITAT Grows in grassy places
and hedgerows.
FLOWERS Pinkish purple and
2–3cm long; appear singly or in
pairs, April to September.
FRUITS Pods that ripen black.
LEAVES Comprise 3–8 pairs of
oval leaflets, ending in tendrils;
upper leaves of subspecies *nigra*
have narrow leaflets.

B&I STATUS
Widespread and
fairly common
throughout.
**NW EUROPEAN
STATUS** Widespread.

Spring Vetch *Vicia lathyroides*

HEIGHT To 20cm.
ECOLOGY & NATURAL HISTORY Rather delicate,
spreading and downy annual. Favours soils that
become desiccated in summer. Can be confused with
dwarf forms of *V. sativa* but note leaflet numbers and
relative sizes of flowers.
HABITAT Grows in short
grassland, mainly on
sandy soils near the sea.
FLOWERS 5–8mm long,
solitary and pinkish purple
(fade blue after flowering),
April to June.
FRUITS Black, hairless pods.
LEAVES Comprise 2–4 pairs of bristle-
tipped leaflets, some with unbranched tendrils.

B&I STATUS Local
throughout the region.
NW EUROPEAN STATUS
Local, NW France to
coastal S Scandinavia.

Tufted Vetch *Vicia cracca*

HEIGHT To 2m.
ECOLOGY & NATURAL HISTORY
Slightly downy, scrambling
perennial. Flowers are popular with
pollinating insects.
HABITAT Grows in grassy places,
hedgerows and scrub.
FLOWERS 8–12mm long and
bluish purple; borne in one-
sided spikes up to 8cm tall,
June to August.
FRUITS Hairless pods.
LEAVES Comprise up to
12 pairs of narrow leaflets
and end in a branched
tendril

B&I STATUS Widespread and
common throughout.
NW EUROPEAN STATUS
Widespread.

Bithynian Vetch *Vicia bithynica*

HEIGHT To 60cm.
ECOLOGY & NATURAL HISTORY
Scrambling perennial.
HABITAT Grows in rough coastal
grassland and undercliffs;
occasional inland.
FLOWERS 15–20mm long,
comprising creamy white
keel and wings and a purple
standard; singly or in pairs,
May to June.
FRUITS 3–5cm long, brown
and hairy pods.
LEAVES Comprise 2–3 pairs of
oval leaflets, branched tendrils
and large stipules.

B&I STATUS Very
local in the south.
**NW EUROPEAN
STATUS** Introduced
and also locally
native, NW France
only.

Sea Pea *Lathyrus japonicus*

HEIGHT To 12cm.

ECOLOGY & NATURAL HISTORY
Spreading, grey-green perennial with stems up to 1m long. The seeds remain viable even after floating for prolonged periods in seawater, which explains how colonisation of novel locations occurs.

HABITAT Entirely restricted to coastal shingle and, more rarely, sandy beaches.

FLOWERS 2cm long and purple, fading to blue; in heads of 2–15 flowers, June to August.

FRUITS Swollen pods, 5cm long.

LEAVES Comprise 2–5 pairs of oval leaflets and angular stipules.

Similar **Broad-leaved Everlasting-pea** *Lathyrus latifolius* is a scrambling perennial that is a garden escape. In places it causes conservation concern because of its invasive and smothering qualities.

B&I STATUS Mainly S and E England.

NW EUROPEAN STATUS Very local on coasts north from N France.

Yellow Vetchling *Lathyrus aphaca*

HEIGHT To 80cm.
ECOLOGY & NATURAL HISTORY Hairless,
scrambling annual with angled stems and
a waxy, grey-green appearance.
HABITAT Restricted to grassland on
calcareous soils, especially near the sea.
FLOWERS 12mm long and
yellow; solitary and borne
on long stalks, June to
August.
FRUITS Curved, brown
pods.
LEAVES True leaves
are reduced to tendrils
but note the leaf-like
stipules.

B&I STATUS Locally
common in southern
England only.
NW EUROPEAN STATUS
Local, mainly NW
France.

Meadow Vetchling *Lathyrus pratensis*

HEIGHT To 50cm.
**ECOLOGY &
NATURAL HISTORY**
Scrambling
perennial with long,
angled stems.
HABITAT Favours species-rich
and unimproved grassland.
FLOWERS 15–20mm long
and yellow; borne in open,
long-stalked terminal clusters of
4–12 flowers, May to August.
FRUITS 25–35mm long pods that
ripen black.
LEAVES Comprise 1 pair of narrow leaflets
with a tendril and large stipules.

B&I STATUS Widespread and
common.
NW EUROPEAN STATUS
Widespread.

Kidney Vetch *Anthyllis vulneraria*

HEIGHT To 30cm.
ECOLOGY & NATURAL HISTORY Perennial
covered in silky hairs.
HABITAT On the coast it favours calcareous
grassland, shingle, sand dunes and sea-cliffs.
FLOWERS Typically yellow or orange
but red in var. *coccinea*; borne in paired,
kidney-shaped heads, 3cm across, May to
September.
FRUITS Short pods.
LEAVES Comprise pairs of narrow leaflets,
the terminal leaflet being the largest.

B&I STATUS Widespread and
locally common.
NW EUROPEAN STATUS
Widespread but local; mainly
lowland.

Var. *coccinea*.

Ribbed Melilot *Melilotus officinalis*

HEIGHT To 1.5m.
ECOLOGY & NATURAL HISTORY Attractive, upright and hairless biennial.
HABITAT Grows in grassy places and on waste ground.
FLOWERS Bright yellow and borne in spikes up to 7cm long, June to September.
FRUITS Brown, wrinkled pods.
LEAVES Comprise 3 oblong leaflets.

B&I STATUS Locally common and possibly native in S England and S Wales; introduced elsewhere.
NW EUROPEAN STATUS Widespread, north to S Scandinavia.

Spiny Restharrow *Ononis spinosa*

HEIGHT To 70cm.
ECOLOGY & NATURAL HISTORY Similar to Common Restharrow but upright and bushy, with spiny stems.
HABITAT Favours grassland on clay and heavy soils; on coasts found on banked sea walls and grazing marshes.
FLOWERS 10–15mm long and deep pink, the wings shorter than the keel, July to September.
FRUITS Pods that are longer than the calyx.
LEAVES Trifoliate with narrow, oval leaflets.

B&I STATUS Local, mainly in England.
NW EUROPEAN STATUS Local, north to Denmark; scarce and very local in S Norway and S Sweden.

Common Restharrow *Ononis repens*

HEIGHT To 70cm.

ECOLOGY & NATURAL HISTORY Robust, creeping and woody perennial with hairy, spineless stems.

HABITAT Restricted to calcareous soils, favouring sand dunes and shingle on the coast.

FLOWERS 10–15mm long and pink, the wings and keel similar in length; in clusters, July to September.

FRUITS Pods that are shorter than the calyx.

LEAVES Stickily hairy and trifoliate with oval leaflets.

Similar **Small Restharrow *Ononis reclinata*** is a small, stickily hairy and spineless annual that grows on dunes and limestone cliffs in Devon (Berry Head), south Wales, southwest Scotland and the Channel Islands; its flowers are less than 10mm long and pink.

B&I STATUS Locally common.

NW EUROPEAN STATUS Local, north to S Scandinavia.

Greater Bird's-foot-trefoil *Lotus pedunculatus*

HEIGHT To 50cm.
ECOLOGY & NATURAL HISTORY
Hairy, hollow-stemmed perennial.
HABITAT Grows in damp grassy
places and fens.
FLOWERS 15mm long and yellow;
in heads on stalks up to 15cm long,
June to August.
FRUITS Slender pods; splayed like
a bird's foot when ripe.
LEAVES Comprise 5 dark green
leaflets but appear trifoliate,
because lower pair are sited at stalk
base.

B&I STATUS Locally common.
NW EUROPEAN STATUS Local,
north to Denmark; scarce and
very local in S Norway and
S Sweden.

Hairy Bird's-foot-trefoil *Lotus subbiflorus*

HEIGHT To 20cm, but typically
prostrate.
ECOLOGY & NATURAL HISTORY
Densely hairy prostrate annual.
HABITAT Grows in short cliff-
top grassland, and cultivated
field margins on Isles of Scilly.
FLOWERS Orange-yellow and
small, 5–9mm long; borne in
heads of 2–3 flowers, May to
August.
FRUITS Slender pods.
LEAVES Very hairy,
comprising 5 leaflets but
appearing trifoliate.

B&I STATUS Local in S and
SW England and Channel
Islands; scarce and very local
in S Ireland and SW Wales.
NW EUROPEAN STATUS Local,
mainly coastal NW France.

Common Bird's-foot-trefoil *Lotus corniculatus*

HEIGHT To 10cm.

ECOLOGY & NATURAL HISTORY
Sprawling, solid-stemmed and usually hairless perennial. The flowers are popular with pollinating insects and the foliage is the larval foodplant for the Common Blue butterfly *Polyommatus icarus*. The roots are food for larvae of the Six-belted Clearwing *Bembecia ichneumoniformis*, an unusual day-flying moth.

HABITAT Grows in grassy places.

FLOWERS Red in bud but yellow and 15mm long when open; in heads on stalks to 8cm long, May to September.

FRUITS Slender pods; splayed like a bird's foot when ripe.

LEAVES Comprise 5 leaflets but appear trifoliate (lower pair at stalk base).

Similar **Narrow-leaved Bird's-foot-trefoil** *Lotus glaber* has much narrower leaves and smaller flowers (6–12mm long); it is local in coastal grazing marshes, mainly in S and E England.

Above:
Six-belted
Clearwing
*Bembecia
ichneumoniformis*

Right:
Common Blue
*Polyommatus
icarus*

B&I STATUS Common and widespread.
NW EUROPEAN STATUS Widespread, north to coastal N Norway and S Sweden.

Black Medick *Medicago lupulina*

HEIGHT To 20cm.
ECOLOGY & NATURAL HISTORY
Downy annual.
HABITAT Grows in short grassland
and waste places.
FLOWERS Small and yellow;
borne in dense, spherical heads
(8–9mm across) of 10–50 flowers,
April to October.
FRUITS Spirally coiled pods,
spineless and black when ripe.
LEAVES Trifoliate, each
leaflet with an apical point.

B&I STATUS
Widespread and rather
common.
NW EUROPEAN STATUS
Widespread, north to
S Scandinavia.

Similar **Toothed
Medick** *Medicago
polymorpha*
grows in dry grass-
land and has spiny,
coiled pods.

Spotted Medick *Medicago arabica*

HEIGHT Prostrate.
ECOLOGY & NATURAL HISTORY Creeping
annual.
HABITAT Grows in dry, grassy
places, doing particularly
well near the sea.
FLOWERS Small and
yellow; borne in heads
(5–7mm across) of
1–6 flowers, April
to September.
FRUITS Spirally coiled
and spiny pods.
LEAVES Trifoliate,
the heart-shaped leaflets
bearing a dark central spot.

B&I STATUS Local in S and
E England, and mainly
coastal.
NW EUROPEAN STATUS
Mainly NW France to
Belgium.

Bird's-foot *Ornithopus perpusillus*

HEIGHT To 30cm.
ECOLOGY & NATURAL HISTORY
Low-growing, often trailing
downy annual.
HABITAT Grows on free-
draining acidic soils, including
sand dunes and cliff paths.
FLOWERS 3–5mm long,
creamy and red-veined; in
heads of 3–8 flowers,
May to August.
FRUITS Constricted pods,
splayed like a bird's foot
when ripe.
LEAVES Comprise 5–13 pairs
of leaflets.

B&I STATUS Locally common in
England and Wales but scarce
elsewhere.
NW EUROPEAN STATUS Local,
north to S Scandinavia.

Orange Bird's-foot *Ornithopus pinnatus*

HEIGHT To 20cm.
ECOLOGY & NATURAL HISTORY
Straggly annual, similar to
Bird's-foot but separated by
flower colour.
HABITAT Grows on wind-
pruned maritime heath and
stabilised hollows in sand dunes.
FLOWERS Orange-yellow
flowers, 5–7mm long, April
to September.
FRUITS Constricted pods,
splayed like a bird's foot when
ripe.
LEAVES Comprise 3–5 pairs
of leaflets.

B&I STATUS Grows on Isles of Scilly
(easiest to find on Bryher) and on the
Channel Islands. Bizarrely, this rarity
is widespread as an introduced alien in
Western Australia.
NW EUROPEAN STATUS Rare,
NW France only.

White Clover *Trifolium repens*

HEIGHT To 40cm.

ECOLOGY & NATURAL HISTORY
Creeping, hairless perennial that roots at the nodes.

HABITAT Grows in grassy places on a wide range of soil types.

FLOWERS Creamy white, becoming brown with age; borne in long-stalked rounded heads, 2cm across, May to September.

FRUITS Pods, concealed by the calyx.

LEAVES Trifoliate, the rounded leaflets often bearing a white mark and translucent lateral veins.

Similar **Alsike Clover** *Trifolium hybridum* has pink-flushed flowers and unmarked leaves. It is a relict of cultivation.

B&I STATUS Widespread and often extremely common throughout the region.

NW EUROPEAN STATUS Widespread.

Red Clover *Trifolium pratense*

HEIGHT To 40cm.
ECOLOGY & NATURAL HISTORY
Familiar downy perennial.
HABITAT Grows in grassy places
on a wide range of soil types.
FLOWERS Pinkish red and borne
in dense, unstalked heads
that are 2–3cm across,
May to October.
FRUITS Pods,
concealed by the calyx.
LEAVES Trifoliate, the oval leaflets
each bearing a white crescent-shaped
mark; stipules are triangular and
bristle-tipped.

Similar **Zigzag
Clover *Trifolium
medium*** has
deep pink flowers
and narrow,
unmarked leaflets;
it grows in grass-
land on heavy
soils.

B&I STATUS Widespread and
often extremely common
throughout the region.
NW EUROPEAN STATUS
Widespread.

Western Clover *Trifolium occidentale*

HEIGHT Prostrate.
ECOLOGY & NATURAL HISTORY Superficially
similar to White Clover but low-growing and
spreading, with differences in its leaves and
flowers.
HABITAT Dry ground, often beside coastal
paths and on compacted sand.
FLOWERS Borne in heads
2–3cm across that
are red-centred with
white flowers,
April to July.
FRUITS Pods,
concealed by the calyx.
LEAVES Trifoliate with
unmarked leaflets.

B&I STATUS Locally common
on Isles of Scilly; also found,
very locally, in Cornwall, N
Devon, SE Ireland and the
Channel Islands.
NW EUROPEAN STATUS Local,
NW France only.

Hare's-foot Clover *Trifolium arvense*

HEIGHT To 25cm.
ECOLOGY & NATURAL HISTORY Charming and distinctive annual that is covered in soft hairs.
HABITAT Grows in dry, grassy areas, on sandy or gravelly soils, including sand dunes and cliffs.
FLOWERS Pale pink and shorter than the filament-like calyx teeth; borne in dense egg-shaped to cylindrical heads, 2–3cm long, June to September.
FRUITS Pods, concealed by the calyx.
LEAVES Trifoliate and comprise narrow leaflets that are barely toothed.

B&I STATUS Widespread and locally common in England and Wales; absent from N Scotland and mainly coastal in Ireland.
NW EUROPEAN STATUS Widespread, north to S Scandinavia.

Rough Clover *Trifolium scabrum*

HEIGHT To 15cm.
ECOLOGY & NATURAL HISTORY Downy annual.
HABITAT Grows in short grassland; on coasts found on seasonally parched sea cliffs and slopes.
FLOWERS White and borne in unstalked heads that are 10mm long, May to July.
FRUITS Pods, concealed by the calyx.
LEAVES Trifoliate with oval leaflets that are hairy on both sides and have obvious lateral veins.

B&I STATUS Locally common in S England and S Wales but mainly coastal.
NW EUROPEAN STATUS Local, NW France and Belgium only.

Clustered Clover *Trifolium glomeratum*

HEIGHT To 20cm but often prostrate.
ECOLOGY & NATURAL HISTORY
Hairless annual.
HABITAT Short coastal grassland,
sand dunes and other bare ground.
FLOWERS Suffused deep pink and
4–5mm long, in globular heads with
reflexed or splayed sepals, June to
August.
FRUITS Pods, concealed by calyx.
LEAVES Trifoliate with sharp-
toothed margins, often tinged red.

B&I STATUS Locally
common on coasts of S
England; scarce elsewhere.
NW EUROPEAN STATUS
Local, NW France only.

Twin-headed Clover *Trifolium bocconei*

HEIGHT To 20cm.
ECOLOGY & NATURAL HISTORY Downy annual. In
Cornwall, its survival depends on a critical level of
grazing, typically by Rabbits, ensuring bare turf.
HABITAT Short, free-draining turf overlying
Serpentine rock near the sea.
FLOWERS White, tinged
with pink and 4–6mm
long, on compact
ovoid heads (typically
paired), May to June.
FRUITS Pods,
concealed by calyx.
LEAVES Trifoliate, the
leaflets hairless above
and downy below.

B&I STATUS Extremely rare and
found in a few sites on the Lizard
Peninsula, in Cornwall; also
occurs on Jersey.
NW EUROPEAN STATUS Rare,
NW France only.

Upright Clover *Trifolium strictum*

HEIGHT To 15cm.
ECOLOGY & NATURAL HISTORY Autumn-germinating downy annual that overwinters as a rosette and dies off by early summer.
HABITAT Short coastal grassland on free-draining soils, including Serpentine.
FLOWERS 5–7mm long and deep pink, in stalked, dense heads, May to June.
FRUITS Pods, concealed by calyx.
LEAVES Trifoliate, with narrow leaflets that have toothed margins.

B&I STATUS Very rare, known mainly from the Lizard Peninsula in Cornwall; very rare on Jersey.
NW EUROPEAN STATUS Rare, NW France only.

Knotted Clover *Trifolium striatum*

HEIGHT To 20cm.
ECOLOGY & NATURAL HISTORY Hairy annual.
HABITAT Grows in dry, grassy places, often on sand or gravel.
FLOWERS Pink and borne in unstalked, egg-shaped heads that are 15mm long, May to July.
FRUITS Pods, concealed by the calyx.
LEAVES Trifoliate with spoon-shaped leaflets that are hairy on both sides but lack obvious lateral veins.

B&I STATUS Locally common, mainly in the south.
NW EUROPEAN STATUS Local, NW France to S Scandinavia.

Wildflowers

Subterranean Clover *Trifolium subterraneum*

HEIGHT Prostrate.
ECOLOGY & NATURAL HISTORY Low-growing, hairy annual.
HABITAT Grows in short, coastal grassland on sand and gravel; occasional inland.
FLOWERS 8–12mm long and creamy white; in clusters of 2–6 in leaf axils, May to June.
FRUITS Pods that 'burrow' into the soil, pushed by elongating stalks.
LEAVES Trifoliate with broadly oval, notched leaflets.

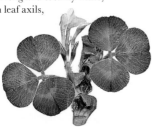

B&I STATUS Local, mainly in the south.
NW EUROPEAN STATUS Local, NW France to Netherlands.

Suffocated Clover *Trifolium suffocatum*

HEIGHT Prostrate.
ECOLOGY & NATURAL HISTORY Winter annual that is easily overlooked because it is low-growing and soon withers and dries.
HABITAT Bare, compacted and seasonally parched bare coastal ground and short turf.
FLOWERS Borne in dense, stalkless clusters, the whitish 3–4mm-long flowers shorter than the pointed bracts, April to May.
FRUITS Pods, concealed by calyx.
LEAVES Trifoliate, stalked leaves with triangular leaflets that radiate from the centre of the plant.

B&I STATUS Very local on coasts of S and E England, Isles of Scilly and Channel Islands.
NW EUROPEAN STATUS Local, NW France only.

Bird's-foot Clover *Trifolium ornithopodioides*

HEIGHT Prostrate.
ECOLOGY & NATURAL HISTORY Low-growing, hairless annual.
HABITAT Grows on bare, coastal grassland.
FLOWERS 5–8mm long, white or pale pink, in heads of 1–5 flowers, May to October.
FRUITS Small pods.
LEAVES Trifoliate with oval, toothed leaflets.

B&I STATUS Very local in S England, S Wales and S Ireland.
NW EUROPEAN STATUS Local, NW France only.

Strawberry Clover *Trifolium fragiferum*

HEIGHT To 15cm.
ECOLOGY & NATURAL HISTORY Perennial with creeping stems that root at the nodes.
HABITAT Grows in grassy places, mainly on clay and doing best near the sea.
FLOWERS Pink and borne in globular heads, 10–15mm across, July to September.
FRUITS Pods enclosed in inflated, pinkish heads; confusingly these resemble a pale raspberry rather than a strawberry.
LEAVES Trifoliate with oval, unmarked leaflets.

B&I STATUS Local in the south and mainly coastal.
NW EUROPEAN STATUS Local and often coastal, NW France to S Scandinavia.

Starry Clover *Trifolium stellatum*

HEIGHT To 20cm.
ECOLOGY & NATURAL HISTORY Upright hairy annual.
HABITAT Stable coastal shingle.
FLOWERS 13–17mm long surrounded by long, pointed calyx teeth; borne in ovoid to spherical heads, May to June.
FRUITS Small pods that are surrounded by calyx teeth that spread to create starry heads.
LEAVES Trifoliate, the leaflets toothed and notched at the tip.

B&I STATUS Introduced and established at a couple of spots on the English south coast.
NW EUROPEAN STATUS Local, NW France to S Scandinavia.

Long-headed Clover *Trifolium incarnatum* ssp. *molinerii*

HEIGHT To 30cm.
ECOLOGY & NATURAL HISTORY Robust, downy annual. Crimson Clover (ssp. *incarnatum*), with deep red flowers, is an occasional relict of cultivation.
HABITAT Grows in short grassland on coastal cliffs, restricted to schist rocks.
FLOWERS Pale pink (sometimes more intense, occasionally white), borne in cylindrical heads, 3–4cm long, May to June.
FRUITS Pods enclosed in inflated heads with spreading calyx teeth.
LEAVES Trifoliate with broad, oval leaflets.

Ssp. *incarnatum*

B&I STATUS Very local, found only on the Lizard Peninsula, S Devon and Jersey.
NW EUROPEAN STATUS Very local, NW France only.

Sea Clover *Trifolium squamosum*

HEIGHT To 30cm.
ECOLOGY & NATURAL HISTORY Downy annual.
HABITAT Grows in coastal grassland, typically on grassy sea walls built to protect low-lying land.
FLOWERS Pinkish flowers are borne in rounded to egg-shaped heads, 1cm long, June to July.
FRUITS Pods, produced in heads with spreading calyx teeth that resemble miniature Teasel heads.
LEAVES Trifoliate, with narrowly oval leaflets.

B&I STATUS Restricted and local in S England, with Thames and Severn estuaries as strongholds.
NW EUROPEAN STATUS Local, mainly NW France.

Hop Trefoil *Trifolium campestre*

HEIGHT To 25cm.
ECOLOGY & NATURAL HISTORY Low-growing, hairy annual.
HABITAT Grows in dry grassland.
FLOWERS 4–5mm long and yellow; borne in compact, rounded heads, 15mm across, May to October.
FRUITS Pods, cloaked by brown dead flowers in hop-like heads.
LEAVES Trifoliate; terminal leaflet has the longest stalk.

B&I STATUS Widespread and generally common; local in the north and in Ireland.
NW EUROPEAN STATUS Local, NW France only.

Wildflowers

Tree Lupin *Lupinus arboreus*

HEIGHT To 3m.
ECOLOGY & NATURAL HISTORY
Much-branched perennial shrub.
HABITAT Grows in sand dunes.
FLOWERS 14–16mm long and
yellow; borne in elongated spikes,
to 25cm tall, June to August.
FRUITS Pods.
LEAVES Palmate, with 5–12
narrow leaflets.

B&I STATUS Introduced from
California and colonising; its
invasive habits exclude native plants
and its arrival at a site is seldom
good for native biodiversity.
NW EUROPEAN STATUS Absent.

Dwarf Gorse *Ulex minor*

HEIGHT To 1m.
ECOLOGY & NATURAL HISTORY
Spreading, evergreen shrub with
spines that are soft, smooth and
10mm long. Often grows alongside
the other species of gorse, which can
lead to confusion.
HABITAT Grows on acid soils, mainly
on heaths.
FLOWERS 10–15mm-long, pale
yellow with 0.5mm long basal bracts,
July to September.
FRUITS Hairy pods.
LEAVES Mature plants lack leaves;
young plants have small trifoliate
ones.

B&I STATUS Local and
restricted mainly to
S and SE England.
NW EUROPEAN STATUS
Local, NW France
only.

Gorse *Ulex europaeus*

HEIGHT To 2m.
ECOLOGY & NATURAL HISTORY Evergreen shrub with straight, grooved spines, 15–25mm long.
HABITAT Grows on heaths and grassy places, mainly on acid soils.
FLOWERS 2cm long, bright yellow and coconut-scented with 4-5mm-long basal bracts, flowering year-round, but mainly February to May.
FRUITS Hairy pods.
LEAVES Mature plants lack leaves; young plants have small trifoliate ones.

Green Hairstreak *Callophrys rubi*, whose larval foodplants include the shoots and buds of Gorse.

B&I STATUS Widespread and common throughout.
NW EUROPEAN STATUS Locally common, mainly NW France to Denmark.

Wildflowers

Western Gorse *Ulex gallii*

HEIGHT To 1.5m.

ECOLOGY & NATURAL HISTORY
Dense, evergreen shrub with spines that are almost smooth and 25mm long. In suitable locations, forms dense swards and becomes an important component of maritime heath.

HABITAT Grows on acid soils, often near coasts.

FLOWERS 10–15mm long, bright yellow with 0.5mm-long basal bracts, July to September.

FRUITS Hairy pods.

LEAVES Mature plants lack leaves; young plants have small trifoliate ones.

Heather is the larval foodplant for the **Oak Eggar** *Lasiocampa quercus* moth. This huge moth (wingspan up to 7.5cm) often flies in the daytime over maritime heaths where Western Gorse predominates.

B&I STATUS Restricted mainly to W Britain and Ireland; common on coastal cliffs in the west.

NW EUROPEAN STATUS Local, NW France only.

Broom *Cytisus scoparius*

HEIGHT To 2m (ssp. *scoparius*), or prostrate (ssp. *maritimus*).

ECOLOGY & NATURAL HISTORY
Deciduous, branched and spineless shrub with ridged, 5-angled green twigs. Ssp. *scoparius* is widespread. Ssp. *maritimus* is a rare prostrate form with silky-hairy shoots, restricted to sea cliffs in southwest England, south Wales and the Channel Islands, growing flattened to rock faces.

HABITAT Ssp. *scoparius* favours acid, free-draining soils. Ssp. *maritimus* grows on rock faces, exposed to the sea and salt spray.

FLOWERS 2cm long, bright yellow and solitary, or in pairs, April to June.

FRUITS Oblong, blackening pods that explode on dry, sunny days.

LEAVES Trifoliate; those of ssp. *maritimus* are much hairier than ssp. *scoparius*.

Above and right:
Ssp. *maritimus*

Ssp. *scoparius*

B&I STATUS Ssp. *scoparius* is widespread and common. Ssp. *maritimus* is restricted to coasts of SW England, SW Wales, S Ireland and Channel Islands.

NW EUROPEAN STATUS Local, NW France to S Scandinavia.

Ssp. *maritimus*

Ssp. *scoparius*

Hairy Greenweed *Genista pilosa*

HEIGHT To 1m, but often almost prostrate.
ECOLOGY & NATURAL HISTORY Low-growing, spineless shrub.
HABITAT Maritime heaths and sea cliffs.
FLOWERS 7–10mm long, yellow and borne in terminal heads, May to June.
FRUITS Downy pods.
LEAVES Oval, smooth above and silvery-downy below.

B&I STATUS Rare, easiest to find on Lizard Peninsula, Cornwall but also occurs on N Cornish coast and W Wales.
NW EUROPEAN STATUS Local and scarce, mainly Belgium to S Scandinavia.

Dyer's Greenweed *Genista tinctoria*

HEIGHT To 1m but prostrate in ssp. *littoralis*.
ECOLOGY & NATURAL HISTORY Spineless, deciduous shrub.
HABITAT Ssp. *tinctoria* grows on clay or chalk soils while ssp. *littoralis* grows on cliffs and maritime heath on Cornwall's Lizard Peninsula.
FLOWERS 15mm long, bright yellow and Broom-like; borne in leafy, stalked spikes, June to August.
FRUITS Oblong, flat and hairless pods.
LEAVES Those of ssp. *tinctoria* are narrowly oval while in ssp. *littoralis* they are more broadly oval.

Ssp. *littoralis*

Ssp. *tinctoria*

B&I STATUS Ssp. *tinctoria* is locally common in England, Wales and S Scotland while ssp. *littoralis* is confined to N coasts of Cornwall and Lizard Peninsula.
NW EUROPEAN STATUS Local.

Ssp. *littoralis*

Common Evening-primrose *Oenothera biennis*

HEIGHT To 1.5m.
ECOLOGY & NATURAL HISTORY Downy biennial.
HABITAT Favours sandy soils, colonising waste land, disturbed ground and sand dunes.
FLOWERS 4–5cm across, yellow with green sepals; open only on dull days or evenings, June to September.
FRUITS Capsules.
LEAVES Lanceolate with red veins.

Similar **Fragrant Evening-primrose *Oenothera stricta*** is similar but has red-striped sepals. Grows on sandy soils, mainly near coasts in S England. Several other evening-primrose species and hybrids are found in the region.

B&I STATUS Introduced from N America and now widely naturalised.
NW EUROPEAN STATUS Widespread, NW France to S Scandinavia.

Rosebay Willowherb *Chamaenerion angustifolium*

HEIGHT To 1.5m.
ECOLOGY & NATURAL HISTORY Showy perennial.
HABITAT Grows in sand dunes; away from the coast favours disturbed ground, cleared woodland and recently burnt sites.
FLOWERS 2–3cm across with pinkish purple petals; borne in tall spikes, July to September.
FRUITS Pods that contain cottony seeds.
LEAVES Lanceolate and arranged spirally up the stems.

B&I STATUS Widespread and common throughout.
NW EUROPEAN STATUS Widespread.

Portland Spurge *Euphorbia portlandica*

HEIGHT To 40cm.
ECOLOGY & NATURAL HISTORY Hairless, greyish perennial with reddish stems that branch from the base.
HABITAT Grows in grassland and on cliffs near the sea.
FLOWERS Have lobes with long, crescent-shaped horns (petals and sepals are absent); borne in umbel-like clusters, April to September.
FRUITS Rough capsules.
LEAVES Spoon-shaped with a prominent midrib.

B&I STATUS Locally common on coasts of SW and W Britain.
NW EUROPEAN STATUS Local, NW France only.

Purple Spurge *Euphorbia peplis*

HEIGHT Prostrate.
ECOLOGY & NATURAL HISTORY Spreading annual with diagnostic forked reddish purple stems. Colonises by sea-borne seeds.
HABITAT Grows on sandy and gravel beaches.
FLOWERS Tiny and ovoid (petals and sepals are absent), July to September.
FRUITS Smooth capsules.
LEAVES Ovate and greyish green.

B&I STATUS Probably extinct but could reappear on suitable beaches in SW England.
NW EUROPEAN STATUS Rare, NW France only.

Sea Spurge *Euphorbia paralias*

HEIGHT To 60cm.
ECOLOGY & NATURAL HISTORY
Upright perennial.
HABITAT Grows on sandy beaches and dunes. It colonises and thrives in open, mobile dunes as a pioneer species. Naturalised elsewhere in the world and considered an invasive alien plant worthy of eradication in Western Australia.
FLOWERS Yellowish with petal-like bracts and horned lobes (petals and sepals are absent); in umbel-like heads, June to October.
FRUITS Capsule has wrinkly surface, recalling a miniature brain.
LEAVES Grey-green, fleshy and closely packed up stems.

B&I STATUS Widespread and locally common on coasts of S and W England, Wales and Ireland.
NW EUROPEAN STATUS Coastal and locally common, NW France to Netherlands.

Sea Spurge (continued)

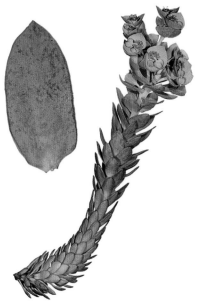

Pale Flax *Linum bienne*

HEIGHT To 60cm.
ECOLOGY & NATURAL HISTORY Slender annual or short-lived perennial. Easily overlooked when flowers not open.
HABITAT Grassy banks and grassland on free-draining soils near the sea.
FLOWERS Pale blue and 12–16mm across.
FRUITS Capsules.
LEAVES Narrow, up to 25cm long and alternate.

Similar **Fairy Flax *Linum cartharticum*** has white flowers 5–8mm across, which open only in sunshine. Grows in dune slacks and machair, and calcareous grassland inland.

B&I STATUS Local and mainly coastal in S England, Wales and SE Ireland.
NW EUROPEAN STATUS Locally common.

Bloody Crane's-bill *Geranium sanguineum*

HEIGHT To 25cm.
ECOLOGY & NATURAL HISTORY Clump-forming perennial.
HABITAT Grows in calcareous grassland; on coasts, favours sand dunes and cliffs.
FLOWERS 2–3cm across with 5 deep reddish purple petals; solitary on long stalks, June to August.
FRUITS End in a long 'beak'.
LEAVES Deeply divided, almost to the base, into 5–7 lobes.

B&I STATUS Locally common in Britain, except in SE; also occurs in W Ireland.
NW EUROPEAN STATUS Very local, NW France to S Scandinavia.

Herb-Robert *Geranium robertianum*

HEIGHT To 30cm.
ECOLOGY & NATURAL HISTORY Straggling, hairy annual; ssp. *maritimum* is prostrate.
HABITAT Grows in shady hedgerows, on rocky banks and in woodlands; ssp. *maritimum* grows on coastal shingle.
FLOWERS 12–15mm across with pink petals and orange pollen; borne in loose clusters, April to October.
FRUITS Hairy and form a long 'beak'.
LEAVES Hairy and deeply cut into 3 or 5 pinnately divided lobes; often tinged red.

B&I STATUS Common and widespread throughout; ssp. *maritimum* (mapped in red) is local and entirely coastal.
NW EUROPEAN STATUS Widespread, NW France to S Scandinavia.

Little-Robin *Geranium purpureum*

HEIGHT To 30cm.
ECOLOGY & NATURAL HISTORY Similar to Herb-Robert but overall more slender and straggly.
HABITAT Restricted to dry banks and coastal shingle.
FLOWERS 7–14mm across with pink petals and yellow pollen, April to September.
FRUITS Distinctly wrinkled.
LEAVES Hairy and deeply cut into 3 or 5 pinnately divided lobes.

B&I STATUS Local in SW England, S Wales and S Ireland.
NW EUROPEAN STATUS Local, NW France.

Musk Stork's-bill *Erodium moschatum*

HEIGHT To 25cm.
ECOLOGY & NATURAL HISTORY Stickily hairy annual that smells of musk.
HABITAT Grows on bare, disturbed sandy ground, and mainly coastal.
FLOWERS 25-30mm across with pink petals that are easily lost; borne in dense heads, May to July.
FRUITS Long and beak-like.
LEAVES Pinnate, the lobes oval and toothed, not feathery; stipules are broad.

B&I STATUS Local, mainly in SW.
NW EUROPEAN STATUS Scattered and local, mainly NW France to N Germany.

Sea Stork's-bill *Erodium maritimum*

HEIGHT Usually prostrate.
ECOLOGY & NATURAL HISTORY Stickily hairy annual.
HABITAT Grows on bare, coastal ground.
FLOWERS 3–5mm across; petals are tiny, whitish, often absent and usually fall by 9am, May to July.
FRUITS Long and beak-like.
LEAVES Oval, lobed and stalked.

B&I STATUS Local, commonest in SW Britain.
NW EUROPEAN STATUS Local and coastal, NW France to N Germany.

Common Stork's-bill *Erodium cicutarium*

HEIGHT To 30cm.
ECOLOGY & NATURAL HISTORY
Stickily hairy annual. Some coastal plants are extremely stickily hairy leading to confusion with Sticky Stork's-bill.
HABITAT Grows on bare, grassy places, doing especially well near the coast.
FLOWERS 8–14mm across with pink petals that are easily lost; borne in loose heads of 3–8 flowers, May to August. Pale-flowered (almost white) forms occur.
FRUITS 1.5–4mm long and beak-like.
LEAVES Finely divided and feathery; stipules are narrow.

B&I STATUS Widespread and locally common, especially SE England and near the sea.
NW EUROPEAN STATUS Widespread, NW France to S Scandinavia.

Sticky Stork's-bill *Erodium aethiopicum*

HEIGHT To 15cm.

ECOLOGY & NATURAL HISTORY Similar to Common Stork's-bill but leaves are even more stickily hairy and hairs are always glandular (with sticky blobs at the tip); beware, some forms of Common Stork's-bill also have this feature. Previously known as *Erodium lebelii*.

HABITAT Entirely coastal, restricted to sand dunes.

FLOWERS 6–7mm across with very pale petals, in heads of 2–3 flowers, May to August.

FRUITS Beak-like and less than 2.2cm long.

LEAVES Weakly divided and covered in sticky, glandular hairs, often with adhering sand grains.

B&I STATUS Very local and restricted to dunes in W and NW Britain.
NW EUROPEAN STATUS Local.

Certain identification of Sticky Stork's-bill requires microscopic examination of a tiny feature on the fruit. However, a combination of habitat, small stature, weakly divided leaves, small flowers, small fruits (if less than 1.5cm long) and copious sticky hairs when combined are good ID pointers.

GERANIACEAE – Geraniums and relatives

Common Ivy *Hedera helix*

HEIGHT To 20m.

ECOLOGY & NATURAL HISTORY Evergreen, self-clinging climber that also carpets the ground. The flowers are a source of nectar for butterflies, moths and hoverflies. The dense foliage is used by nesting and roosting birds.

HABITAT Wide range of habitats including coastal woodlands, hedgerows and scrub.

FLOWERS Yellowish green and 4-parted; borne in globular heads, September to November.

FRUITS Berries that ripen purplish black.

LEAVES Glossy, dark green and 3- or 5-lobed with paler veins.

B&I STATUS Widespread and common.

NW EUROPEAN STATUS Widespread, NW France to S Scandinavia.

So-called **Atlantic Ivy (*Hedera hibernica* aka *Hedera helix* ssp. *hibernica*)** is either a natural form or an escaped cultivar depending on which authority you follow. It has less angular leaves that can be almost heart-shaped.

Sea-holly *Eryngium maritimum*

HEIGHT To 60cm.
ECOLOGY & NATURAL HISTORY Distinctive, hairless perennial that forms tough clumps. Its flowers are extremely attractive to pollinating insects including bumblebees and hoverflies.
HABITAT Coastal shingle and sand.
FLOWERS Blue and borne in globular umbels, up to 4cm long, July to September.
FRUITS Bristly and spiky.
LEAVES Waxy, blue-green and holly-like with spiny, white margins and white veins.

Similar **Field Eryngo *Eryngium campestre*** is a much-branched, spindly version of Sea-holly (height to 50cm) yellowish green overall, with narrower, more deeply divided leaves and smaller flower umbels, June to July. It grows on dry ground in S Devon (e.g. Plymouth Hoe) and occasionally elsewhere.

On southern sand dunes, look out for a solitary wasp called the **Bee Wolf** *Philanthus triangulum*, which visits Sea-holly flowers for nectar. Its spread northwards over the last two decades from southern mainland Europe is best regarded not as a conservation good news story but rather a sign of the effects of global warming.

Rock Samphire *Crithmum maritimum*

HEIGHT To 40cm.

ECOLOGY & NATURAL HISTORY
Spreading, branched and hairless
perennial. Tolerates constant salt spray
and, in some locations, occasional
inundation during stormy weather
and particularly high tides. Formerly
collected, and the dangerous practice
of gathering on cliff faces is mentioned
by Shakespeare in King Lear as a
'...dreadful trade'.

HABITAT Characteristic of maritime
rocky habitats and stabilised coastal
shingle.

FLOWERS Greenish yellow and borne
in umbels, 3–6cm across, with 8–30
rays and numerous bracts, June to
September.

FRUITS Egg-shaped, ridged and corky,
green at first, ripening red.

LEAVES Divided into narrow, fleshy
lobes, triangular in cross-section.

B&I STATUS Widespread
and common around coasts
of S and W Britain and
Ireland.

NW EUROPEAN STATUS
Local and coastal, NW
France only.

Wildflowers

Hemlock *Conium maculatum*

HEIGHT To 2m.
ECOLOGY & NATURAL HISTORY Highly poisonous, hairless biennial with hollow, purple-blotched stems and an unpleasant smell when bruised.
HABITAT Grows on landward sides of beaches and cliffs and damp, wayside ground; inland, increasingly common on motorway verges and riversides.
FLOWERS White and borne in umbels that are 2–5cm across, June to July.
FRUITS Globular with wavy ridges.
LEAVES Up to 4 times pinnately divided into fine leaflets.

B&I STATUS Widespread and locally common except in far N.
NW EUROPEAN STATUS Widespread and locally common.

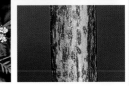

Fennel *Foeniculum vulgare*

HEIGHT To 2m.
ECOLOGY & NATURAL HISTORY Grey-green, strong-smelling and hairless perennial with solid young stems and hollow older ones.
HABITAT Grows on landward side of beaches and coastal grassland.
FLOWERS Yellow and borne in open umbels, 4–8cm across, July to September.
FRUITS Narrowly egg-shaped and ridged.
LEAVES Feathery, comprising thread-like leaflets.

B&I STATUS Locally common in S, scarcer and more local elsewhere.
NW EUROPEAN STATUS Local.

Alexanders *Smyrnium olusatrum*

HEIGHT To 1.25m.
ECOLOGY & NATURAL HISTORY Stout and sometimes clump-forming, hairless biennial.
HABITAT Grows on cliffs and other coastal sites including waste ground and roadside verges, doing particularly well with slight disturbance.
FLOWERS Yellowish and borne in umbels, 4–6cm across, with 7–15 rays, March to June.
FRUITS Globular, ridged and black when ripe.
LEAVES Dark green, shiny and 3 times trifoliate.

B&I STATUS Introduced but widely naturalised, mainly on S and SE coasts of England and Ireland.
NW EUROPEAN STATUS Local, NW France only.

Slender Hare's-ear *Bupleurum tenuissimum*

HEIGHT To 50cm.
ECOLOGY & NATURAL HISTORY Slender and easily overlooked annual.
HABITAT Entirely restricted to coastal grassland and upper reaches of saltmarshes.
FLOWERS Yellow and borne in tiny umbels, 3–4mm across, surrounded by bracts, and arising from leaf axils, July to September.
FRUITS Globular.
LEAVES Narrow and pointed.

B&I STATUS Local, confined to coasts in S and E England only.
NW EUROPEAN STATUS Very local and coastal, NW France to S Scandinavia.

Small Hare's-ear *Bupleurum baldense*

HEIGHT To 2cm.
ECOLOGY & NATURAL HISTORY Tiny, atypical umbellifer.
HABITAT Short turf on cliff-tops on calcareous soils.
FLOWERS Borne in umbels shrouded by pointed green bracts, June to July.
FRUITS Globular.
LEAVES Narrow and strap-like.

B&I STATUS Grows dangerously near the cliff edge at Beachy Head in Sussex, also in S Devon and on the Channel Islands. Such a small and insignificant plant may have been overlooked elsewhere.
NW EUROPEAN STATUS Rare, NW France only.

Marsh Pennywort *Hydrocotyle vulgaris*

HEIGHT Creeping.
ECOLOGY & NATURAL HISTORY
Low-growing perennial and an
atypical umbellifer.
HABITAT Grows in damp grassy
coastal habitats, including
dune-slacks and water-retaining
shingle hollows; inland, favours
fens, damp meadows and
marshes.
FLOWERS Tiny, pinkish and
hidden by the leaves; borne in
small umbels, June to August.
FRUITS Rounded and ridged.
LEAVES Round and dimpled
with broad, blunt teeth.

B&I STATUS Widespread
but commonest in the
west.
NW EUROPEAN STATUS
Local, NW France to
S Scandinavia.

Scots Lovage *Ligusticum scoticum*

HEIGHT To 80cm.
ECOLOGY & NATURAL HISTORY
Robust and hairless perennial;
often forms sizeable clumps.
Stems are ribbed and purplish
and hollow towards the base.
HABITAT Grows on cliffs,
and stabilised dunes and
grassland fringing rocky
and shingle shores.
FLOWERS White and borne in
flat-topped umbels, 4–6cm across,
on long, reddish stalks, June to August.
FRUITS Oval and flattened, with 4 wings.
LEAVES Bright green, shiny and 2 times trifoliate
with oval leaflets and inflated, sheathing stalks.

B&I STATUS Locally
common on Scottish
coasts and northern
coasts of Ireland.
NW EUROPEAN STATUS
Local, coastal Norway
and SW Sweden.

Parsley Water-dropwort *Oenanthe lachenalii*

HEIGHT To 1m.
ECOLOGY & NATURAL HISTORY
Upright, hairless perennial with
solid, ridged stems.
HABITAT Grows in damp meadows
and marshes; tolerates brackish
conditions.
FLOWERS White and borne in
open umbels, 2–6cm across, with
6–15 rays, June to September.
FRUITS Egg-shaped and ribbed.
LEAVES 2- or 3-pinnate, lower
leaves with narrow to oval, flat
leaflets, overall recalling young,
fresh Parsley leaves.

B&I STATUS Locally common
(mainly coastal) in England,
Wales and Ireland; scarce in
Scotland.
NW EUROPEAN STATUS
Local, coastal NW France to
Denmark and N Germany.

Corky-fruited Water-dropwort *Oenanthe pimpinelloides*

HEIGHT To 1m.
**ECOLOGY & NATURAL
HISTORY** Upright perennial
with solid stems.
HABITAT Grows in
unimproved, often grazed,
meadows.
FLOWERS White and borne
in crowded umbels, 2–5cm
across, with 6–15 rays, June
to August.
FRUITS Ribbed and parallel-
sided, styles as long as fruits.
LEAVES 2-pinnate, lower
leaves with wedge-shaped
leaflets.

B&I STATUS Locally
common only in central
S England.
NW EUROPEAN STATUS
Local, NW France only.

Wild and Sea Carrots *Daucus carota*

HEIGHT To 75cm.

ECOLOGY & NATURAL HISTORY Upright or spreading hairy perennial with solid, ridged stems.

HABITAT Grows in rough grassland, mostly on chalky soils or near the sea. Sea Carrot (ssp. *gummifer*) is restricted to coastal cliffs, rocky slopes and dunes.

FLOWERS White (pinkish in bud) and borne in long-stalked umbels, up to 7cm across, the central flower of which is red; note the divided bracts beneath, June to September. Umbel rays are typically smooth in ssp. *carota* (Wild Carrot) but hairy in ssp. *gummifer* (Sea Carrot)

FRUITS Egg-shaped with spiny ridges; fruiting umbels are concave when growing inland (ssp. *carota*) but flat or convex in Sea Carrot (ssp. *gummifer*).

LEAVES 2- or 3-pinnate with narrow leaflets; those of Sea Carrot ssp. *gummifer* are distinctly fleshy.

Sea Carrot

Wild Carrot

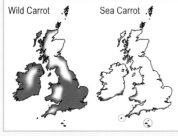

Wild Carrot

Wild Carrot   Sea Carrot

B&I STATUS Widespread and locally common, except in the north. Sea Carrot ssp. *gummifer* is entirely coastal and restricted mainly to SW and W Britain.

NW EUROPEAN STATUS Widespread.

Moon Carrot *Seseli libanotis*

HEIGHT To 70cm.
ECOLOGY & NATURAL HISTORY Downy biennial or perennial with ridged stems. Superficially similar to Wild Carrot beside which it sometimes grows. The plant base is often shrouded by old leaf remains; young compact plants recall small cauliflowers.
HABITAT Chalk grassland.
FLOWERS White and borne in domed umbels with narrow, unbranched bracts below, July to September.
FRUITS Ovoid, downy and ridged.
LEAVES Pinnate, the leaflet's plane angled relative to stalk in the manner of a stepladder.

B&I STATUS Grows on coastal downs near Seaford in Sussex (also inland, very locally, near Cambridge and Hitchin).
NW EUROPEAN STATUS Very local, NW France to S Scandinavia. Grows on the white chalk cliffs of N France on the opposite side of the English Channel from Seaford Head.

Wild Parsnip *Pastinaca sativa* ssp. *sylvestris*

HEIGHT To 1m.
ECOLOGY & NATURAL HISTORY Upright, downy perennial with ridged, hollow stems, that smell strongly when bruised. Ancestor of cultivated parsnip (ssp. *sativa*).
HABITAT Calcareous coastal grassland.
FLOWERS Yellowish and borne in open, bractless umbels, 3–9cm across, June to September.
FRUITS Oval, flattened and winged.
LEAVES Pinnate with oval, lobed and toothed leaflets.

B&I STATUS Widespread and locally common in lowland England; scarcer and more coastal elsewhere.
NW EUROPEAN STATUS Widespread, NW France to S Scandinavia.

Wild Celery *Apium graveolens*

HEIGHT To 1m.
ECOLOGY & NATURAL HISTORY
Upright, hairless biennial with a
characteristic strong smell of celery.
Stems are solid and grooved.
HABITAT Grows in rough, often
saline, grassland and its
distribution is mainly coastal.
FLOWERS White and borne in
short-stalked or unstalked umbels,
3–6cm across, June to August.
FRUITS Globular.
LEAVES Shiny and pinnate; basal
leaves are 1- or 2-pinnate with toothed
and lobed, diamond-shaped leaflets;
stem leaves appear trifoliate.

B&I STATUS Absent from
Scotland and commonest
in coastal S England.
NW EUROPEAN STATUS
Local and coastal, NW
France to Denmark and
N Germany.

Hogweed *Heracleum sphondylium*

HEIGHT To 2m.
ECOLOGY & NATURAL HISTORY
Robust, roughly hairy perennial with
hollow, ridged stems.
HABITAT Grows in meadows and
rough grassland, including
coastal cliffs and sand dunes.
FLOWERS Off-white, with
unequal petals; borne in umbels
with 40 or so rays, and up to
20cm across, May to August.
FRUITS Elliptical, hairless and
flattened.
LEAVES Up to 60cm long, broad,
hairy and pinnate, the lobes usually
rather oval.

B&I STATUS Widespread
and common through-
out the region.
NW EUROPEAN STATUS
Widespread, north to
S Scandinavia.

Honewort *Trinia glauca*

HEIGHT To 15cm.
ECOLOGY & NATURAL HISTORY
Compact, hairless, grey-green
and waxy perennial.
HABITAT Grows in short,
dry grassland on
limestone soils.
FLOWERS White,
with separate-sex
plants; male umbels are
1cm across, female 3cm
across, May to June.
FRUITS Egg-shaped and
ridged.
LEAVES 2- or 3-pinnate
with narrow lobes.

Top right: young male plant
Right and below: female plant

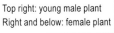

B&I STATUS Rare; found
only in S Devon and N
Somerset.
NW EUROPEAN STATUS
Rare and local, NW
France only.

Parsley *Petroselinum crispum*

HEIGHT To 40cm.
ECOLOGY & NATURAL HISTORY Hairless
biennial that is bright green at first but turns
yellow with age. Familiar as a kitchen herb.
HABITAT Grows in coastal grassy places
including cliffs, banks and stabilised shingle.
FLOWERS Greenish yellow; borne
in open umbels, 1–2cm across,
June to August.
FRUITS Globular.
LEAVES Shiny, roughly triangular
and 3-pinnate; cultivars have variably
crinkled leaflets.

Similar **Knotted
Hedge-parsley
*Torilis nodosa***
is spreading and
prostrate with small
bunches of flowers
at nodes, ripening
to spiny fruits.
Grows on banks and
free-draining soils.

B&I STATUS Exact status is hard
to determine: widely grown
in gardens and naturalised
occasionally as a presumed
archaeophyte.
NW EUROPEAN STATUS Locally
naturalised, NW France only.

Hog's Fennel *Peucedanum officinale*

HEIGHT To 1.5m.
ECOLOGY & NATURAL HISTORY
Hairless, dark green perennial
with solid stems. Sole foodplant for
larvae of Fisher's Estuarine Moth
Gortyna borelii, which feed inside
stems and roots.
HABITAT Restricted to coastal
grassland on clay soils.
FLOWERS Deep yellow and borne
in open umbels, 15–20cm across,
July to September.
FRUITS Narrow-ovate.
LEAVES 4- to 6-trifoliate with
flattened, narrow segments.

B&I STATUS Restricted to
a couple of locations on the
Thames Estuary.
NW EUROPEAN STATUS Rare
and very local in NW France.

Fisher's Estuarine Moth, *Gortyna borelii*.

Common Centaury *Centaurium erythraea*

HEIGHT To 25cm.

ECOLOGY & NATURAL HISTORY Variable, hairless and upright annual that usually branches from above the mid-point. Dwarf form var. *capitatum* (Dumpy Centaury) is short and densely-branched.

HABITAT Grows in dry, grassy places; coastal locations include chalk downland and sand dunes.

FLOWERS 10–15mm across, unstalked and pink (rarely white) with 5 petal-like lobes that open fully only in sunshine; borne in terminal clusters and on side shoots, June to September. Stigmas conical.

FRUITS Capsules.

LEAVES Grey-green and oval with a pointed tip; stem leaves narrower than the basal ones (10–20mm across), which form a rosette; all leaves have 3–7 veins.

var. *capitatum*

B&I STATUS Widespread and common, except Scotland; var. *capitatum* occurs very locally on coasts of England and Wales.
NW EUROPEAN STATUS Widespread, NW France to S Scandinavia.

Slender Centaury *Centaurium tenuiflorum*

HEIGHT To 35cm.

ECOLOGY & NATURAL HISTORY Much-branched, upright annual that lacks a basal rosette of leaves.

HABITAT Grows in damp fresh-water seepages on undercliffs.

FLOWERS 8–10mm across when open, and typically white and stalked; flowers have 5 petal-like lobes that open fully only in sunshine and mostly remain closed; borne in dense clusters, June to August.

FRUITS Capsules.

LEAVES Yellow-green and oval with a pointed tip; become narrower as they progress up the stem.

B&I STATUS Very rare and confined to a few landslips and undercliffs on Dorset's Jurassic Coast.
NW EUROPEAN STATUS Rare, NW France only.

Seaside Centaury *Centaurium littorale*

HEIGHT To 15cm.
ECOLOGY & NATURAL HISTORY
Similar to Common Centaury but more compact, with subtle differences in the leaves and flowers.
HABITAT Grows in sandy, coastal soils and mainly northern.
FLOWERS 12–16mm across, unstalked and pink (colour subtly more intense than Common Centaury) with 5 petal-like lobes; borne in dense, flat-topped clusters, June to August. Stigmas flat-topped.
FRUITS Capsules.
LEAVES Grey-green, parallel-sided and rounded at tip; basal leaves form a rosette and are 4–5mm wide while stem leaves are narrower.

B&I STATUS Locally common on coasts of N and NW Britain.
NW EUROPEAN STATUS Local and coastal, N France to S Scandinavia.

Lesser Centaury *Centaurium pulchellum*

HEIGHT To 15cm.
ECOLOGY & NATURAL HISTORY Slender annual that usually branches from near the base. Recalls a tiny Common Centaury but it lacks a basal rosette of leaves.
HABITAT Sand dunes, upper estuary margins, damp grassland; inland, found on open grassland and heaths.
FLOWERS 5–8mm across, short-stalked and dark pink; borne in open clusters, June to September.
FRUITS Capsules.
LEAVES Narrowly ovate, 3–7 veined and appear only on the stems.

B&I STATUS Widespread but local in England and Wales only; mainly coastal and most frequent in the south.
NW EUROPEAN STATUS Widespread but local, NW France to S Scandinavia.

Perennial Centaury *Centaurium portense*

HEIGHT To 25cm.
ECOLOGY & NATURAL HISTORY
Perennial with creeping stems and upright flowering stalks.
HABITAT Grows in short turf and restricted to few small areas of coastal cliffs. Common Centaury sometimes grows alongside, so beware the potential for misidentification.
FLOWERS 15–20mm across, stalked and pink; borne in few-flowered clusters, July to August.
FRUITS Capsules.
LEAVES Rounded and stalked on the creeping stems but narrower and unstalked on upright stems.

B&I STATUS Rare and restricted to cliffs in Pembrokeshire and SW Cornwall.
NW EUROPEAN STATUS Rare, NW France only.

Guernsey Centaury *Exaculum pusillum*

HEIGHT To 10cm.
ECOLOGY & NATURAL HISTORY Slender, branched annual, usually upright but sometimes prostrate.
HABITAT Short turf in dune slacks and threatened by inappropriate land management.
FLOWERS 4–6mm across with 4 pink petals, July to September.
FRUITS Capsules.
LEAVES Narrowly ovate.

B&I STATUS Very rare, restricted to Guernsey.
NW EUROPEAN STATUS Rare and coastal, NW France only.

Field Gentian *Gentianella campestris*

HEIGHT To 10cm.
ECOLOGY & NATURAL HISTORY Biennial, similar to Autumn Gentian but separable with care by studying the flowers.
HABITAT Grows in grassland on neutral or acid soils.
FLOWERS 10–12mm across and bluish purple,

sometimes creamy white; note the 4 corolla lobes and unequal calyx lobes, one pair much larger than the other, July to October.
FRUITS Capsules.
LEAVES Narrow ovate.

B&I STATUS Locally common in N England and Scotland; scarce or absent elsewhere.
NW EUROPEAN STATUS Scarce in NW France, widespread from N Germany to Norway and S Sweden.

Autumn Gentian *Gentianella amarella* ssp. *amarella*

HEIGHT To 25cm.
ECOLOGY & NATURAL HISTORY Variable and hairless biennial that is often tinged purple.
HABITAT Grows in grassy areas, mostly on calcareous soils and sand dunes.
FLOWERS 10–12mm across and purple, with 4 or 5 corolla lobes and equal calyx lobes; borne in upright spikes, July to October.
FRUITS Capsules.
LEAVES Form a basal rosette in the first year but wither before the flower stem appears in the second year.

B&I STATUS Widespread and locally common.
NW EUROPEAN STATUS Local and mainly coastal, N France to S Scandinavia.

Early Gentian *Gentianella amarella* ssp. *anglica*

HEIGHT To 5cm.

ECOLOGY & NATURAL HISTORY Superficially similar to Autumn Gentian but much shorter and flowering in the spring. Formerly assigned species status (*Gentianella anglica*) but now 'downgraded' to subspecies level.

HABITAT Short turf on calcareous grassland.

FLOWERS Reddish purple and 6–8mm across with 4 or 5 equal calyx lobes; borne in terminal and axillary clusters, April to June.

FRUITS Capsules.

LEAVES Ovate.

B&I STATUS Very local in S England, with strongholds on Isle of Wight and Dorset coast.
NW EUROPEAN STATUS Absent.

Dune Gentian *Gentianella amarella* ssp. *occidentalis*

HEIGHT To 15cm.

ECOLOGY & NATURAL HISTORY Upright annual or biennial that is sparsely branched (usually 1 or 2 internodes, top internode more than half the plant's height). Formerly assigned species status (*Gentianella uliginosa*) but now 'downgraded' to subspecies level.

HABITAT Dune slacks.

FLOWERS 10–12mm across and purple, with unequal, spreading calyx lobes; borne on long stalks, July to October.

FRUITS Capsules.

LEAVES Ovate.

B&I STATUS Local and rare, mainly S Wales but also isolated locations in N Devon (Braunton Burrows); plants on Colonsay (Scotland) are now known to be dwarf forms of ssp. *amarella*.
NW EUROPEAN STATUS Widespread but scarce.

Yellow-wort *Blackstonia perfoliata*

HEIGHT To 30cm.
ECOLOGY & NATURAL HISTORY
Upright and distinctive, grey-green annual.
HABITAT Grows in short, calcareous grassland and stable sand dunes.
FLOWERS 10–15mm across with 6–8 bright yellow petals that open only in sunshine, June to October.
FRUITS Capsules.
LEAVES Ovate and waxy, those on the stem are borne in opposite pairs that are fused at the base around the stem; basal leaves form a rosette.

B&I STATUS Locally common in England and Wales, mainly in the south.
NW EUROPEAN STATUS Local, NW France only.

GENTIANACEAE – Gentians and relatives

Bittersweet *Solanum dulcamara*

HEIGHT To 1.5m.
ECOLOGY & NATURAL HISTORY Downy and scrambling perennial that is woody at the base, hence the alternative name Woody Nightshade.
HABITAT Grows in hedgerows and scrub, and often on stabilised shingle beaches.
FLOWERS 10–15mm across with 5 purple, petal-like corolla lobes and projecting yellow anthers; borne in branched and hanging clusters, May to September.
FRUITS Poisonous, egg-shaped red berries, up to 1cm long.
LEAVES Oval and pointed.

B&I STATUS Widespread and common throughout, except in the north and in Ireland.
NW EUROPEAN STATUS Widespread, NW France to S Scandinavia.

Sea Bindweed *Calystegia soldanella*

HEIGHT Creeping.
ECOLOGY & NATURAL HISTORY Prostrate perennial, that trails and progresses through dune vegetation.
HABITAT Grows on sand dunes, and occasionally on stabilised shingle.
FLOWERS 3–5cm across, funnel-shaped and pink with 5 white stripes; on slender stalks, June to August.
FRUITS Capsules.
LEAVES Kidney-shaped, fleshy, up to 4cm long and long-stalked.

B&I STATUS Widespread on coasts but locally common only in the south.
NW EUROPEAN STATUS Local and coastal, NW France to Netherlands.

CONVOLVULACEAE – Bindweeds and relatives

Common Dodder *Cuscuta epithymum*

HEIGHT Climbing.
ECOLOGY & NATURAL HISTORY Bizarre, parasitic and leafless plant that lacks chlorophyll and gains its nutrition from host plants, which include Heather, Wild Thyme and Western Gorse.
HABITAT Grows in grassy places and on heaths, the slender, red stems twining through the vegetation and sometimes smothering it.
FLOWERS 3–4mm across, pink and borne in dense clusters, July to September.
FRUITS Capsules.
LEAVES Absent.

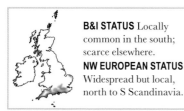

B&I STATUS Locally common in the south; scarce elsewhere.
NW EUROPEAN STATUS Widespread but local, north to S Scandinavia.

Oysterplant *Mertensia maritima*

HEIGHT Prostrate.
ECOLOGY & NATURAL HISTORY
Spreading plant that forms extensive
mats in sheltered locations.
HABITAT Grows on stony beaches,
around the high-tide mark.
FLOWERS Bell-shaped, pink in bud but
soon turning blue, June to August.
FRUITS Nutlets.
LEAVES Fleshy and blue-green.

B&I STATUS A northern
species; Shetland and
Orkney are the best British
locations for the species
where it is very locally
common.
NW EUROPEAN STATUS
Local and coastal, mainly
Norway.

Viper's-bugloss *Echium vulgare*

HEIGHT To 80cm.
ECOLOGY & NATURAL HISTORY
Upright biennial covered in reddish bristles.
HABITAT Grows in dry grassland, mainly on sandy and calcareous soils, often flourishing near the coast.
FLOWERS 15–20mm long, funnel-shaped and bright blue with protruding purplish stamens; borne in tall spikes, May to September.
FRUITS Rough nutlets.
LEAVES Narrow and pointed; basal leaves are stalked.

Similar **Purple Viper's-bugloss *Echium plantagineum*** is shorter with purplish blue flowers borne in curved clusters, June to September. A very rare archaeophyte, possibly native to W Cornwall, Isles of Scilly and the Channel Islands. Grows in dry, sandy ground and arable field margins.

B&I STATUS
Widespread and common in England and Wales; scarce elsewhere.
NW EUROPEAN STATUS Widespread but local, north to S Scandinavia.

Early Forget-me-not *Myosotis ramosissima*

HEIGHT To 10cm.
ECOLOGY & NATURAL HISTORY
Downy annual.
HABITAT Grows in bare grassy places including stabilised sand dunes.
FLOWERS Minute, 2–3mm across, 5-lobed and sky blue; borne in clusters, April to October.
FRUITS Nutlets.
LEAVES Ovate, basal ones forming a rosette.

B&I STATUS Widespread and common, except in the far north.
NW EUROPEAN STATUS Widespread and locally common.

Hound's-tongue *Cynoglossum officinale*

HEIGHT To 75cm.
ECOLOGY & NATURAL HISTORY
Upright, downy biennial whose crushed leaves smell strongly of mice.
HABITAT Grows in dry, grassy places, often on chalky soil and near the coast.
FLOWERS 5–7mm across, maroon and 5-lobed; borne in branched clusters, June to August.
FRUITS Comprise groups of 4 flattened, oval nutlets that are covered in hooked bristles.
LEAVES Narrow and hairy; lower ones are stalked.

B&I STATUS Widespread but commonest in S and E England.
NW EUROPEAN STATUS Local, north to S Scandinavia.

Betony *Betonica officinalis*

HEIGHT To 50cm.
ECOLOGY & NATURAL HISTORY Upright, unbranched and downy or hairless perennial. Previously known as *Stachys officinalis*.
HABITAT Grows on cliff tops and in dunes, typically on sandy or chalky soils; inland it is a plant of grassy waysides and hedgerows.
FLOWERS 12–18mm long and reddish purple; borne in showy, dense and terminal heads, reminiscent of marsh-orchid spikes, June to September.
FRUITS Nutlets.
LEAVES Stalked and oblong, typically heart-shaped at the base but narrower up the stem.

B&I STATUS Widespread and fairly common in England and Wales but scarce or absent elsewhere.
NW EUROPEAN STATUS Widespread from NW France to N Germany; mainly absent from Scandinavia and Low Countries.

Red Hemp-nettle *Galeopsis angustifolia*

HEIGHT To 30cm.
ECOLOGY & NATURAL HISTORY Branched and downy annual. Formerly an arable 'weed', now largely restricted to coastal habitats and nature reserves.
HABITAT Grows in disturbed ground and on shingle near the coast; more occasionally found in arable field margins.
FLOWERS 15–25mm long and reddish pink with a hooded upper lip and a 2-lobed lower lip, the corolla tube being twice as long as the calyx; borne in terminal heads, July to September.
FRUITS Nutlets.
LEAVES Narrow and very slightly toothed.

B&I STATUS Widespread but only locally common and encountered mainly in SE England.
NW EUROPEAN STATUS Very local in France; mainly absent elsewhere.

Red Dead-nettle *Lamium purpureum*

HEIGHT To 30cm.
ECOLOGY & NATURAL HISTORY Branched and spreading downy annual that is pungently aromatic when crushed. The whole plant sometimes acquires a purplish tinge when 'stressed' e.g. by drought.
HABITAT Grows on disturbed ground and cultivated soils.
FLOWERS 12–18mm long and purplish pink, with a hooded upper lip and the lower lip toothed at the base and twice the length of the calyx; borne in whorls on upright stems, March to October.
FRUITS Nutlets.
LEAVES Heart-shaped to oval, round-toothed and stalked.

B&I STATUS Widespread and common.
NW EUROPEAN STATUS Widespread and locally common.

Wild Thyme *Thymus drucei*

HEIGHT To 5cm.
ECOLOGY & NATURAL HISTORY Creeping and mat-forming perennial with slender, woody runners. The whole plant is faintly aromatic, smelling of culinary thyme.
HABITAT Grows in dry grassland and on coastal cliffs, dunes and heaths.
FLOWERS 3–4mm long and pinkish purple; borne in dense, terminal heads with dark, purplish calyx tubes, on 4-angled stems that are hairy on opposite sides, July to September.
FRUITS Nutlets.
LEAVES Ovate, short-stalked and borne in opposite pairs.

B&I STATUS Widespread and common throughout the region.
NW EUROPEAN STATUS Widespread but local, north to S Scandinavia.

White Horehound *Marrubium vulgare*

HEIGHT To 50cm.
ECOLOGY & NATURAL HISTORY
Robust, upright perennial that is coated with downy white hairs and is aromatic.
HABITAT Grows on dry, often disturbed, ground, mainly on chalky soil and near the coast.
FLOWERS 12–15mm long and white; borne in many-flowered whorls, only a few flowers appearing at any one time, June to October.
FRUITS Nutlets.
LEAVES Oval, toothed and wrinkled.

upper

under

B&I STATUS Local, mainly near the south coast of England; occasional elsewhere.
NW EUROPEAN STATUS Scarce and very local, NW France and Belgium; occasional in Denmark and S Sweden.

White Horehound is the sole larval food-plant of a moth called the **Horehound Plume Moth *Wheeleria spilodactylus***.

Wood Sage *Teucrium scorodonia*

HEIGHT To 40cm.
ECOLOGY & NATURAL HISTORY Downy perennial.
HABITAT Grows on coastal cliffs and heaths, and along woodland rides, mainly on acid soils.
FLOWERS 5–6mm long, yellowish and with the upper lip absent; borne in leafless spikes, June to September.
FRUITS Nutlets.
LEAVES Oval, heart-shaped at the base, and wrinkled.

B&I STATUS Widespread and locally common.
NW EUROPEAN STATUS Widespread but local from NW France to the Netherlands; occasional elsewhere.

Water Germander *Teucrium scordium*

HEIGHT To 35cm.
ECOLOGY & NATURAL HISTORY
Downy and spreading perennial
with creeping runners and
upright flowering stems.
HABITAT Grows in damp, grassy
places, typically on calcareous
soils and sometimes in dune
slacks.
FLOWERS 8–10mm long with
no upper lip but a pinkish purple
lower lip; in whorls up leafy
stems, July to September.
FRUITS Nutlets.
LEAVES Oblong, toothed and
unstalked.

B&I STATUS Rare, restricted
mainly to a few sites in S
England and W Ireland.
NW EUROPEAN STATUS
Rare and extremely
local, NW France to the
Netherlands.

Wild Clary *Salvia verbenaca*

HEIGHT To 80cm.
ECOLOGY & NATURAL HISTORY
Upright, downy and almost unbranched
perennial. Upper part of the flowering
stem, including the bracts and calyces,
are often tinged purple.
HABITAT Grows in dry grassland,
typically on calcareous soils and often
near the coast.
FLOWERS 8–15mm long and bluish
violet, the calyx being sticky and coated
with long, white hairs; borne in whorls in
rather compact spikes, May to August.
FRUITS Nutlets.
LEAVES Oval with jagged teeth, and
mainly basal.

B&I STATUS Widespread
but local in S and E
England only.
NW EUROPEAN STATUS
Local, mainly in NW
France.

Skullcap *Scutellaria galericulata*

HEIGHT To 40cm.
ECOLOGY & NATURAL HISTORY
Creeping, square-stemmed downy or hairless perennial with upright flowering stalks.
HABITAT Grows in damp ground, in dune slacks and coastal marshes; also on coastal boulder beaches in Scotland.
FLOWERS 10–15mm long and bluish violet; borne in pairs on upright, leafy stems, mainly towards the top, June to September.
FRUITS Nutlets.
LEAVES Oval, stalked and toothed.

B&I STATUS Widespread and very locally common throughout much of the region, except Ireland and N Scotland.
NW EUROPEAN STATUS Widespread but local, north to S Scandinavia.

LAMIACEAE – Mints, dead-nettles and relatives

Common Toadflax *Linaria vulgaris*

HEIGHT To 75cm.
ECOLOGY & NATURAL HISTORY Greyish green, hairless perennial that is upright and often much-branched.
HABITAT Grows in dry coastal grassland, on roadside verges and waste ground; inland, favours similar habitats.
FLOWERS 15–25mm long and yellow, with orange centres and long spurs; borne in tall, cylindrical spikes, June to October.
FRUITS Capsules.
LEAVES Narrow, linear and arranged up the length of the stem.

Similar **Sand Toadflax** *Linaria arenaria* is shorter (to 10cm tall) with small flowers (4–6mm long); grows in dunes, native to W France and introduced to Braunton Burrows in Devon.

B&I STATUS Widespread and locally common; scarce in Ireland.
NW EUROPEAN STATUS Widespread, north to coastal Scandinavia.

Foxglove *Digitalis purpurea*

HEIGHT To 1.5m.
ECOLOGY & NATURAL HISTORY Familiar, greyish and downy biennial or short-lived perennial.
HABITAT Grows on sea cliffs and heaths, and in woodland, thriving best on acid soils and appearing in good quantity on recently cleared ground.
FLOWERS 4–5cm long, the corolla pinkish purple (sometimes white forms are found) with darker spots in the throat; borne in tall and elegant, terminal spikes, June to September.
FRUITS Green capsules.
LEAVES 20–30cm long, downy, oval and wrinkled; form a rosette in the 1st year from which the flowering spike appears in the 2nd.

B&I STATUS Widespread and common throughout.
NW EUROPEAN STATUS Widespread but local, NW France, Belgium and SW Norway; introduced and occasional elsewhere.

Foxglove is the sole foodplant of a moth called the **Foxglove Pug** *Eupithecia pulchellata*, the larvae of which feed inside the flowers.

Wall Speedwell *Veronica arvensis*

HEIGHT To 20cm.
ECOLOGY & NATURAL HISTORY Softly hairy annual that forms low swards when Rabbit-grazed or lightly trampled.
HABITAT Grows in dry, bare locations including vegetated dunes, coastal tracks and banks; widespread inland too.
FLOWERS 2–4mm across, the corolla 4-lobed and blue; borne in dense, leafy spikes, the flowers often partly obscured by leaf-like bracts, March to October.
FRUITS Flattened, hairy and heart-shaped capsules with a projecting style.
LEAVES Oval and toothed; the lower ones are short-stalked while the upper ones are unstalked.

Similar **Germander Speedwell** *Veronica chamaedrys* grows in dune and machair grassland, and meadows elsewhere inland. Its blue flowers are 10–12mm across, are borne on slender stalks and appear from April to June.

B&I STATUS Widespread and locally common.
NW EUROPEAN STATUS Widespread and common.

Eyebright *Euphrasia officinalis* agg.

HEIGHT To 25cm.

ECOLOGY & NATURAL HISTORY
Branched or unbranched annuals, semi-parasitic on roots of other plants and sometimes tinged reddish. The plant's appearance is variable and 30 or so 'species' are recognised requiring expertise and experience to discern differences. Here, all Eyebrights (except *Euphrasia arctica*) are considered as a single aggregate species.

HABITAT Grows in undisturbed grassy places.

FLOWERS 5–10mm long (depending on the 'species' involved), the corolla 2-lipped (the lower lip 3-lobed) and whitish (sometimes tinged pink) with purple veins and a yellow throat; borne in leafy spikes, May to September.

FRUITS Capsules.

LEAVES Oval but sharply toothed, sometimes tinged bronze.

B&I STATUS Widespread and locally common.
NW EUROPEAN STATUS Widespread but local, north to S and coastal C Sweden.

Similar **Arctic Eyebright** *Euphrasia arctica* is relatively tall (to 35cm) with relatively long stalks between the nodes. Its flowers are 8–12mm long and it grows in meadows and machair. Subspecies *E. a. borealis* is widespread in N Britain, W Wales and Ireland; ssp. *E. a. arctica* is commonest on Orkney and Shetland.

Ivy-leaved Toadflax *Cymbalaria muralis*

HEIGHT Trailing
ECOLOGY & NATURAL HISTORY Hairless
perennial with trailing, purplish stems.
Sometimes forms extensive patches on
coastal shingle.
HABITAT Grows on rocks, walls and
stabilised shingle.
FLOWERS 10–12mm across and lilac
with yellow and white at the centre, and
a curved spur; borne on long stalks,
April to November.
FRUITS Capsules, borne on long stalks
that become recurved with maturity,
forcing the fruit into nooks and crannies.
LEAVES Long-stalked, ivy-shaped,
5-lobed and borne on long stalks.

B&I STATUS Originally a garden plant
but now widely naturalised throughout
much of the region, except in N
Scotland.
NW EUROPEAN STATUS Native in
NW France, also introduced there
and elsewhere.

Yellow Bartsia *Parentucellia viscosa*

HEIGHT To 40cm
ECOLOGY & NATURAL HISTORY
Stickily-hairy, unbranched annual
that is semi-parasitic on the roots
of other plants.
HABITAT Grow in damp, grassy
places, mostly near the sea and
often in dune slacks.
FLOWERS 15–35mm long, the
corolla bright yellow and
2-lipped, the lower lip
3-lobed; in leafy spikes,
June to September.
FRUITS Capsules.
LEAVES Lanceolate and
unstalked.

B&I STATUS Very locally common
near coasts of S and SW England
and W Ireland.
NW EUROPEAN STATUS Very
local, NW France and Denmark
only.

Yellow-rattle *Rhinanthus minor*

HEIGHT To 45cm.

ECOLOGY & NATURAL HISTORY Variable, upright and almost hairless annual that is semi-parasitic on the roots of other plants. The stems are stiff, 4-angled and often marked with dark spots and streaks.

HABITAT Grows in undisturbed meadows and stabilised dunes.

FLOWERS 10–20mm long, the corolla yellow, 2-lipped and somewhat tubular and straight, the 2 teeth on the upper lip are 1mm long; borne in spikes with triangular, toothed and leaf-like green bracts, May to September.

FRUITS Inflated capsules inside which the ripe seeds do indeed rattle.

LEAVES Oblong with rounded teeth.

B&I STATUS Widespread and common.

NW EUROPEAN STATUS Widespread but local.

Similar **Red Bartsia *Odontites vernus*** grows to 40cm tall on disturbed and trampled ground and tracks near the sea. Flowers are pink and borne in curved heads, June to September.

Similar **Greater Yellow-rattle *Rhinanthus angustifolius*** is branched and grows to 60cm tall. Its flowers are 15–20mm long, the corolla yellow, 2-lipped with a concave dorsal surface. In Britain and Ireland it is rare, restricted to a few scattered locations from S England to Scotland; it is widespread but local in mainland Europe.

Common Broomrape *Orobanche minor* ssp. *minor*

HEIGHT To 40cm.

ECOLOGY & NATURAL HISTORY Upright, unbranched annual that usually has a purplish-tinged stem. The whole plant lacks chlorophyll. Ssp. *minor* (the most widespread subspecies) is parasitic on a range of herbaceous plants including Pea family members, notably clovers.

HABITAT Grows in grassy places and sand dunes.

FLOWERS 10–18mm long with purple stigmas, the corolla pinkish yellow with purple veins, tubular with smoothly curved dorsal surface, and 2-lipped; in open, upright spikes, June to September.

FRUITS Egg-shaped capsules, concealed by the dead flowers.

LEAVES Scale-like.

B&I STATUS Locally common in C and S England, Wales and S Ireland.
NW EUROPEAN STATUS Widespread but local, mainly NW France and Low Countries.

Seaside specialists: Sea Carrot and Sea-holly Broomrapes

HEIGHT To 50cm.

ECOLOGY & NATURAL HISTORY Sometimes afforded subspecies status, these variations on the Common Broomrape theme show subtle differences in flower structure and have highly specific hosts: **var. *maritima*** parasitises almost exclusively Sea Carrot *Daucus carota* ssp. *gummifer* (see p. 188), sometimes Buck's-horn Plantain *Plantago coronopus* (see p. 218); while **var. *pseudoamethystea*** favours Sea-holly *Eryngium maritimum* (see p. 180).

HABITAT Coastal sand dunes and cliffs.

B&I STATUS Very local, on dunes on south coast and cliffs on the Isle of Wight.
NW EUROPEAN STATUS Scarce and local, mainly NW France.

Sea Carrot Broomrape, *Orobanche minor* var. *maritima*

FLOWERS 10–18mm long with purple stigmas, the corolla pinkish flushed yellow at base, with purple veins, tubular with a straight (not curved) dorsal surface; in open, upright spikes, June to July.
FRUITS Egg-shaped capsules, concealed by the dead flowers.
LEAVES Scale-like.

Sea-holly Broomrape, *Orobanche minor* var. *pseudoamethystea*

Thyme Broomrape *Orobanche alba*

HEIGHT To 25cm.
ECOLOGY & NATURAL HISTORY
Attractive, upright and rather stout plant that is tinged reddish. Parasitic on the roots of Wild Thyme *Thymus drucei* (see p. 204).
HABITAT Grows on base-rich coastal grassland.
FLOWERS 15–20mm long and fragrant with reddish stigmas, the corolla reddish; borne in comparatively short spikes, May to August.
FRUITS Egg-shaped capsules, concealed by the dead flowers.
LEAVES Scale-like.

B&I STATUS Scarce and local, restricted to suitable coastal grassland in SW England, W Scotland and Ireland.
NW EUROPEAN STATUS Local, NW France only.

Ivy Broomrape *Orobanche hederae*

HEIGHT To 60cm.
ECOLOGY & NATURAL HISTORY Upright plant with a downy, purple-tinged stem that is swollen at the base. Parasitic on Common Ivy *Hedera helix* (see p. 179). Also occurs as strikingly yellow var. *lutea*.
HABITAT Grows on coastal cliffs and in scrub, and does best on calcareous soils.
FLOWERS 12–20mm long with yellow stigmas, the corolla creamy white with purple veins, mainly straight but swollen at the base; borne in spikes, May to July.
FRUITS Egg-shaped capsules, concealed by the dead flowers.
LEAVES Scale-like.

Above: var. *lutea*

B&I STATUS Local, mainly in S and W Britain. Probably introduced elsewhere and inland.
NW EUROPEAN STATUS Local, mainly NW France.

Oxtongue Broomrape *Orobanche picridis*

HEIGHT To 55cm.
ECOLOGY & NATURAL HISTORY Tall broomrape that parasitises members of the daisy family (Asteraceae) especially Hawkweed Oxtongue *Picris hieracioides* (see p. 233). Previously known as *Orobanche artemisiae-campestris*.
HABITAT Chalk banks and undercliffs.
FLOWERS Yellowish white tinged purple with purple stigmas and hairy filaments; borne in spikes, June to July.
FRUITS Egg-shaped capsules, concealed by the dead flowers.
LEAVES Scale-like.

Similar **Bedstraw Broomrape** *Orobanche caryophyllacea* parasitises various species of bedstraws (see p. 217); it grows on sand dunes and cliffs mainly in Kent and is easiest to find at Sandwich Bay.

B&I STATUS Very rare and restricted to Isle of Wight, Sussex and Kent.
NW EUROPEAN STATUS Scarce and local, NW France and Low Countries.

Yarrow Broomrape *Phelipanche purpurea*

HEIGHT To 40cm.
ECOLOGY & NATURAL HISTORY
Upright plant with a downy,
bluish-tinged stem. Parasitic on
Yarrow *Achillea millefolium* (see
p. 247). Previously known as
Orobanche purpurea.
HABITAT Cliff-top grassland,
usually near the sea.
FLOWERS 8–30mm long with
white stigmas, the corolla tinged
bluish purple, June to July.
FRUITS Egg-shaped capsules,
concealed by the dead flowers.
LEAVES Scale-like.

B&I STATUS Rare and scattered
with records from Channel
Islands, Isle of Wight, coastal
W Wales and NE Norfolk.
NW EUROPEAN STATUS Scarce
and local, mainly NW France.

OROBANCHACEAE – Broomrapes

Harebell *Campanula rotundifolia*

HEIGHT To 40cm.
ECOLOGY & NATURAL HISTORY
Attractive and delicate, hairless
perennial with wiry stems.
HABITAT Grows in dry, grassy places,
both on calcareous and acid soils,
including sand dune grassland.
FLOWERS 15mm long, the corolla
blue and bell-shaped with sharp,
triangular teeth; nodding and borne
on slender stalks, July to October.
FRUITS Dry capsules.
LEAVES Comprise rounded ones
at the base of the plant, which soon
wither, and narrower stem leaves that
persist while the plant is in flower.

B&I STATUS Widespread and
common, except in southwest.
NW EUROPEAN STATUS
Widespread but mostly absent
from NW France.

Sheep's-bit *Jasione montana*

HEIGHT To 30cm.
ECOLOGY & NATURAL HISTORY
Attractive, spreading and downy biennial.
HABITAT Grows in dry grassland, and
on coastal cliffs, heaths and dunes,
favouring acid soils and absent from
calcareous locations.
FLOWERS Sky blue and borne in
rounded heads, 30–35mm across, on
slender stalks, May to September. Note
that the anthers do not project (cf. Devil's-
bit Scabious *Succisa pratensis* below).
FRUITS Dry capsules.
LEAVES Wavy-edged and hairy at the
base, forming a rosette, but narrow on
the stem.

B&I STATUS Widespread but
local, and commonest in the
west and near the sea.
NW EUROPEAN STATUS
Widespread but very local;
mainly NW France, N
Germany and S Scandinavia.

Similar **Devil's-bit Scabious**
Succisa pratensis (family
Dipsacaceae – Teasels)
grows to 70cm tall on heaths
and damp grassland. Lilac
or mauve flowers have
projecting anthers shaped
like the letter T, June to
September. Widespread
except in E England.

CAMPANULACEAE – Bellflowers and relatives

Red Valerian *Centranthus ruber*

HEIGHT To 75cm.
ECOLOGY & NATURAL HISTORY
Upright, branched, hairless and
greyish green perennial.
HABITAT Grows on broken, rocky
ground, chalk cliffs and old walls.
FLOWERS 8–10mm long,
the corolla reddish or pink
(sometimes white); borne
in dense terminal heads,
June to September.
FRUITS Have a
feathery pappus.
LEAVES Ovate,
untoothed and borne
in opposite pairs.

Similar **Common Valerian**
Valeriana officinalis
grows to 1.5m tall in wet
dune slacks, and grass-
land inland. The 5-lobed
very pale pink flowers are
borne in dense clusters
and appear from June to
August.

B&I STATUS Introduced
and widely naturalised
but most frequent in
coastal districts.
NW EUROPEAN STATUS
Locally common, NW
France only.

Wildflowers

Lady's Bedstraw *Galium verum*

HEIGHT To 30cm.
ECOLOGY & NATURAL HISTORY
Attractive, branched perennial
and the only true bedstraw with
yellow flowers. Stems are square
and the whole plant smells of hay.
HABITAT Grows in dry grassland.
FLOWERS 2–3mm across, yellow
and 4-petalled; in dense clusters,
June to September.
FRUITS Smooth nutlets that
ripen black.
LEAVES Narrow with down-
rolled margins; in whorls of
8–12; they blacken when dry.

Similar **Wild Madder *Rubia
peregrina*** is a straggling bed-
straw-relative with backward
pointing bristles on its stems
that aid its progress. The yellowish green, 5-lobed flowers
are 5–6mm across and borne
in clusters, and are followed
by black berries. It grows on
coastal cliffs and in maritime
scrub, mainly in the south.

B&I STATUS Widespread
and common.
NW EUROPEAN STATUS
Widespread but local,
north to lowland S
Scandinavia.

Heath Bedstraw *Galium saxatile*

HEIGHT To 50cm.
ECOLOGY & NATURAL HISTORY Spreading,
rather weak-stemmed perennial that is sometimes
almost prostrate and mat-forming. Whole plant
blackens when dry.
HABITAT Grows on heaths and grassland on acid
soils.
FLOWERS 3mm across, white and 4-petalled,
with a sickly smell; in clusters,
June to August.
FRUITS Hairless, warty
nutlets.
LEAVES Narrow-ovate
and bristle-tipped,
with forward-pointing
marginal bristles.

B&I STATUS Widespread and
locally common.
NW EUROPEAN STATUS
Widespread but local, north to
lowland S Scandinavia.

Greater Plantain *Plantago major*

HEIGHT To 20cm.
ECOLOGY & NATURAL HISTORY
Persistent and usually hairless
perennial.
HABITAT Disturbed and trampled
grassland and arable land.
FLOWERS 3mm across, pale
yellow with anthers that are
purple when young, turning
yellow later; borne on slender
spikes, 10–15mm long, June to
October.
FRUITS Capsules.
LEAVES Broad, oval, up to
25cm long, with 3–9 veins and a
distinct, narrow stalk; in
basal rosettes.

fruiting
spike

B&I STATUS Widespread
and common throughout.
NW EUROPEAN STATUS
Widespread.

Buck's-horn Plantain *Plantago coronopus*

HEIGHT To 15cm.
**ECOLOGY & NATURAL
HISTORY** Downy, greyish green
perennial.
HABITAT Grows in grassland,
and on disturbed ground and
rocky sites, mainly near the sea.
FLOWERS 2mm across with a
brownish corolla and yellow
stamens; borne in slender spikes,
2–4cm long, May to July.
FRUITS Capsules.
LEAVES 20cm long, 1-veined
and pinnately divided; in
dense basal rosettes.

B&I STATUS Widespread and
common around the coasts
of Britain and Ireland; also
occurs inland in SE England.
NW EUROPEAN STATUS
Coastal and local, NW France
to S Sweden.

Sea Plantain *Plantago maritima*

HEIGHT To 15cm.

ECOLOGY & NATURAL HISTORY
Characteristic coastal perennial, tolerant of salt spray and occasional immersion in seawater.

HABITAT Grows mainly in saltmarshes and on coastal cliffs.

FLOWERS 3mm across with a brownish corolla and yellow stamens; in slender spikes, 2–6cm long, June to August.

FRUITS Capsules.

LEAVES Narrow, strap-like and untoothed, with 3–5 faint veins; in dense basal rosettes.

B&I STATUS Widespread and common around coasts.

NW EUROPEAN STATUS Widespread but entirely coastal.

Ribwort Plantain *Plantago lanceolata*

HEIGHT To 15cm.
ECOLOGY & NATURAL HISTORY Persistent perennial.
HABITAT Grows in grassy places, including sand dunes and cliffs.
FLOWERS 4mm across with a brownish corolla and white stamens; borne in compact heads, 2cm long, on furrowed stalks up to 40cm long, April to October.
FRUITS Capsules.
LEAVES Lanceolate, up to 20cm long with 3–5 distinct veins; borne in spreading basal rosettes.

B&I STATUS Widespread and common throughout the region.
NW EUROPEAN STATUS Widespread, north to lowland S Scandinavia.

PLANTAGINACEAE – Plantains and relatives

Great Mullein *Verbascum thapsus*

HEIGHT To 2m.
ECOLOGY & NATURAL HISTORY Robust, upright biennial that is covered in a thick coating of white, woolly hairs.
HABITAT Grows in dry, grassy places, on roadside verges and waste ground.
FLOWERS 15–35mm across, 5-lobed and yellow, with whitish hairs on the upper 3 stamens only; borne in tall, dense spikes, sometimes with side branches, June to August.
FRUITS Egg-shaped capsules.
LEAVES Ovate and woolly; they form a basal rosette in the first year from which tall, leafy stalks arise in the second.

Similar **White Mullein** *Verbascum lychnitis* has white flowers and stems coated in white hairs. It favours calcareous soils and grows, locally, in dunes and on stabilised shingle.

B&I STATUS Widespread and locally common.
NW EUROPEAN STATUS Widespread, north to lowland S Scandinavia.

Hoary Mullein *Verbascum pulverulentum*

HEIGHT To 2m.
ECOLOGY & NATURAL HISTORY Upright biennial, covered in white, woolly hairs that easily rub off the leaves.
HABITAT Grows in dry calcareous grassland.
FLOWERS 15–35mm across, 5-lobed and yellow, with whitish hairs on all stamens; in branched spikes, July to September.
FRUITS Egg-shaped capsules.
LEAVES Ovate and woolly on both sides.

B&I STATUS Local and restricted mainly to East Anglia.
NW EUROPEAN STATUS Very local, NW France only.

Twiggy Mullein *Verbascum virgatum*

HEIGHT To 1.5m.
ECOLOGY & NATURAL HISTORY Upright, usually unbranched biennial that is covered in glandular hairs.
HABITAT Coastal shingle and cliffs, waste ground and tracks inland.
FLOWERS 3–4cm across, 5-lobed and yellow, with purple-haired stamens, lower 2 of which are much longer than upper 3; borne in spikes, June to August.
FRUITS Egg-shaped capsules.
LEAVES Stem leaves have clasping auricles; basal leaves taper gradually.

B&I STATUS Naturalised and established particularly in SW Britain; occasional elsewhere.
NW EUROPEAN STATUS Local, NW France only.

Balm-leaved Figwort *Scrophularia scorodonia*

HEIGHT To 70cm.
ECOLOGY & NATURAL HISTORY
Upright, branched and downy
grey perennial with stems that
are square and angled.
HABITAT Grows on rocky cliffs
and hedge banks.
FLOWERS 1cm long and
greenish with a maroon upper
lip; borne in open spikes,
June to September.
FRUITS Greenish capsules,
like miniature figs.
LEAVES Oval, toothed and
wrinkled, with downy hairs on
both surfaces.

B&I STATUS Locally
common in SW England
only.
NW EUROPEAN STATUS
Local, NW France only.

Common Figwort *Scrophularia nodosa*

HEIGHT To 70cm.
ECOLOGY & NATURAL HISTORY
Upright, hairless perennial with
stems that are solid and square
but not winged.
HABITAT Grows in damp
woodland and shady places.
FLOWERS 1cm long and
greenish with a maroon upper
lip, and narrow white borders
to the sepal lobes; borne in
open spikes, June to September.
FRUITS Greenish capsules,
recalling miniature figs.
LEAVES Oval and pointed,
with sharp teeth.

B&I STATUS Widespread
and common, except in
N Scotland.
NW EUROPEAN STATUS
Widespread, north to lowland
S Scandinavia.

Water Figwort *Scrophularia auriculata*

HEIGHT To 70cm.
ECOLOGY & NATURAL HISTORY
Upright, hairless perennial with
stems that are square with
prominent wings.
HABITAT Grows in damp ground, in
woodlands and beside fresh water.
FLOWERS 1cm long and greenish
with a maroon upper lip, and
broad white borders to the sepal
lobes; borne in open spikes, June to
September.
FRUITS Greenish capsules, like
miniature figs.
LEAVES Oval but blunt-tipped, with
rounded teeth; on winged stalks.

B&I STATUS Widespread and
common.
NW EUROPEAN STATUS
Widespread, NW France and
Low Countries only.

SCROPHULARIACEAE – Figworts and relatives

Sea Arrowgrass *Triglochin maritima*

HEIGHT To 50cm.
**ECOLOGY & NATURAL
HISTORY** Plantain-like tufted
perennial.
HABITAT Grows in saltmarshes.
FLOWERS 3-4mm across,
3-petalled and green, edged
with purple; borne in a
long, narrow spike, which
itself is long-stalked, May to
September.
FRUITS Egg-shaped with
6 segments.
LEAVES Long, narrow and
smooth.

B&I STATUS Widespread
and locally common
around all coasts.
NW EUROPEAN STATUS
Widespread but entirely
coastal.

Carline Thistle *Carlina vulgaris*

HEIGHT To 60cm.
ECOLOGY & NATURAL HISTORY
Upright, branched or unbranched
biennial, armed with stiff spines.
HABITAT Grows in dry
calcareous grassland.
FLOWERS Borne in golden
brown, rayless heads, 15–40mm
across, surrounded by spreading,
straw-coloured bracts; carried in
clusters, July to September; dead
flower heads persist.
FRUITS Have feathery pappus hairs.
LEAVES Oblong with wavy margins
and spiny lobes; lower leaves are
downy.

Similar **Dwarf Thistle *Cirsium
acaule*** has a characteristic
flattened rosette of spiny
leaves from which unstalked
flower heads, 3–5cm across,
arise, June to September;
widespread in the south, in
short turf on calcareous soil.

B&I STATUS
Locally common.
**NW EUROPEAN
STATUS**
Widespread,
north to lowland
S Scandinavia.

Milk Thistle *Silybum marianum*

HEIGHT To 1m.
**ECOLOGY & NATURAL
HISTORY** Upright annual or
biennial.
HABITAT Coastal waste
ground and similar disturbed
habitats inland.
FLOWERS Borne on spineless
stems in spherical heads,
4–5cm across, with reddish
purple florets and spine-like
bracts below.
FRUITS Have unbranched
hairs.
LEAVES Spiny and bright
green with pale veins.

B&I STATUS
Introduced
from S Europe,
occasional,
mainly coastal.
**NW EUROPEAN
STATUS** Local.

Slender Thistle *Carduus tenuiflorus*

HEIGHT To 1m.

ECOLOGY & NATURAL HISTORY
Upright, greyish biennial. Similar to Welted Thistle but stems are spiny-winged right up to the flower heads and extremely cottony.

HABITAT Grows in dry grassland, often near the sea.

FLOWERS Borne in egg-shaped heads, 5–10mm across, with pinkish red florets; in dense, terminal clusters, June to August.

FRUITS Have unbranched hairs.

LEAVES Pinnate, spiny and cottony below.

Similar **Plymouth Thistle *Carduus pycnocephalus*** has solitary flower heads borne on non-spiny stalks; naturalised on Plymouth Hoe in Devon, its appearance has been unpredictable in recent years but it was still present in 2021.

B&I STATUS Locally common around coasts, except the north.

NW EUROPEAN STATUS Local in NW France; occasional elsewhere

Welted Thistle *Carduus crispus*

HEIGHT To 1.3m.
ECOLOGY & NATURAL HISTORY Upright and much-branched biennial with cottony stems that have spiny wings along almost their entire length, except just below the flower heads.
HABITAT Grows in grassland, scrub, verges and open woodland.
FLOWERS Borne in cylindrical or egg-shaped heads, 2–3cm long, with reddish purple florets and woolly green bracts; heads are carried in clusters, June to August.
FRUITS Have unbranched hairs.
LEAVES Oblong, deeply pinnate, 3-lobed and spiny at base of plant; upper leaves are narrower and stalkless.

B&I STATUS Widespread and common throughout, except in Ireland and N Scotland.
NW EUROPEAN STATUS Widespread, north to lowland Scandinavia.

Spear Thistle *Cirsium vulgare*

HEIGHT To 1m.
ECOLOGY & NATURAL HISTORY Upright biennial with stems that are downy and spiny-winged between the leaves.
HABITAT Grows in grassland and on disturbed ground.
FLOWERS Borne in heads, 2–4cm across, that comprise purple florets topping a basal ball coated with spiny bracts; heads are solitary or in small clusters, July to September.
FRUITS Have feathery pappus hairs.
LEAVES Pinnately lobed and spiny.

B&I STATUS Widespread and common throughout the region.
NW EUROPEAN STATUS Widespread, north to lowland S Scandinavia.

Marsh Thistle *Cirsium palustre*

HEIGHT To 1.5cm.

ECOLOGY & NATURAL HISTORY Creeping perennial that produces upright long, slender flowering stems that are unwinged, downy and ridged.

HABITAT Grows in damp grassy places.

FLOWERS Borne in heads, 20–25mm across, with reddish purple florets and darker bracts; heads are solitary, June to July.

FRUITS Have feathery pappus hairs.

LEAVES Oval, toothed, green and hairy above and white cottony below.

B&I STATUS Locally common in S and central England, Wales and Ireland.

NW EUROPEAN STATUS Widespread, north to lowland Scandinavia.

Creeping Thistle *Cirsium arvense*

HEIGHT To 1m.

ECOLOGY & NATURAL HISTORY Creeping perennial with upright, unwinged and mostly spineless flowering stems.

HABITAT Grows in disturbed ground and grassy areas.

FLOWERS Borne in heads, 10–15mm across, with pinkish lilac florets and darker bracts; heads are carried in clusters, June to September.

FRUITS Have feathery pappus hairs.

LEAVES Pinnately lobed and spiny, the upper leaves clasping.

B&I STATUS Widespread and common throughout the region.

NW EUROPEAN STATUS Widespread, north to lowland Scandinavia.

Lesser Burdock *Arctium minus*

HEIGHT To 1m.
ECOLOGY & NATURAL HISTORY
Robust, downy biennial.
HABITAT Grows on waste
ground, verges and hedgerows.
FLOWERS Borne in egg-shaped
heads, 15–20mm across, with
purplish florets and greenish
yellow, hooked and spiny bracts;
carried in open spikes, July to
September.

FRUITS Globose and covered in hooked
spines (the burs) that cling to clothing
and animal fur and aid dispersal.
LEAVES Heart-shaped with hollow
stalks; basal leaves are wider than long.

Similar
**Greater
Burdock
*Arctium
lappa*** has
basal leaves
with solid
stalks.

B&I STATUS Widespread
and common.
NW EUROPEAN STATUS
Widespread, north to
lowland S Scandinavia.

Saw-wort *Serratula tinctoria*

HEIGHT To 75cm.
ECOLOGY & NATURAL HISTORY Slender,
hairless and spineless perennial with
grooved and rather stiff stems.
HABITAT Grows on cliff-tops and coastal
heaths; inland also in damp meadows
and along woodland rides.
FLOWERS Borne in heads, 15–20mm
long, that comprise pinkish purple florets
and close-pressed purplish bracts; heads
are carried in open, terminal clusters,
July to October.
FRUITS Have unbranched pappus hairs.
LEAVES Vary from undivided to deeply
lobed, but the edges are always saw-
toothed.

B&I STATUS Locally
common only in SW
England; scarce or absent
elsewhere.
NW EUROPEAN STATUS
Widespread but very local,
north to S Scandinavia.

Common Knapweed *Centaurea nigra*

HEIGHT To 1m.
ECOLOGY & NATURAL HISTORY Downy or hairy perennial that branches towards the top of the plant. The stems are stiff and grooved and are often swollen beneath the base of the flowers.
HABITAT Grassy places of all kinds, including coastal meadows and cliffs.
FLOWERS Borne in heads, 2–4cm across, with reddish purple florets atop a swollen, hard base covered in brown bracts; heads are usually solitary, June to September.
FRUITS Do not have pappus hairs.
LEAVES Narrow; basal leaves are slightly lobed.

B&I STATUS Widespread and common throughout.
NW EUROPEAN STATUS Widespread in NW France and Low Countries; local in coastal S Scandinavia.

Greater Knapweed *Centaurea scabiosa*

HEIGHT To 1m.
ECOLOGY & NATURAL HISTORY Upright perennial with tough, grooved and downy stems.
HABITAT Dry grassland, typically on calcareous soils and including cliffs and dunes.
FLOWERS Borne in solitary heads, 3–5cm across, with reddish purple disc florets, the outer ones of which are ray-like and radiating, the heads atop a swollen base coated with brown bracts, June to September.
FRUITS Hairless achenes.
LEAVES Oblong and usually deeply pinnate although some coastal plants in Scotland and Wales have undivided basal leaves.

B&I STATUS Locally common in lowland England; scarce and usually coastal, or absent, elsewhere.
NW EUROPEAN STATUS Patchy distribution, north to lowland S Scandinavia.

Red Star-thistle *Centaurea calcitrapa*

HEIGHT To 70cm.
ECOLOGY & NATURAL HISTORY
Branched and superficially thistle-like biennial.
HABITAT Dry, grassy slopes, usually on chalk.
FLOWERS Reddish purple and borne in heads, 8–10mm across, surrounded by much longer spiny bracts, July to September.
FRUITS Spiny achenes.
LEAVES Deeply pinnately divided, the lobes with spiny tips.

Similar **Rough Star-thistle *Centaurea aspera*** is much less spiny. A native of SW Europe, it is introduced on Jersey and Guernsey where it grows on dunes and is showing signs of having invasive qualities.

B&I STATUS Introduced to Britain but now established in a few sites, chiefly at Cuckmere Haven in Sussex.
NW EUROPEAN STATUS Local in NW France; very occasional elsewhere.

Cat's-ear *Hypochaeris radicata*

HEIGHT To 50cm.
ECOLOGY & NATURAL HISTORY
Tufted perennial with hairless stems.
HABITAT Grows in dry grassland.
FLOWERS Borne in heads, 25–40mm across, with yellow florets much longer than the bristly, purple-tipped bracts; the flower stalks branch 1–2 times and are swollen beneath the solitary heads, June to September. Scales are present between the florets.
FRUITS Beaked with some feathery hairs.
LEAVES Oblong, bristly, wavy-edged; they form a basal rosette.

B&I STATUS Widespread and common.
NW EUROPEAN STATUS Widespread, north to lowland S Scandinavia.

Similar **Smooth Cat's-ear *Hypochaeris glabra*** is a scarce hairless annual that grows in coastal dunes mainly in S and W Britain, and inland in East Anglia. The flower heads are 10–15mm across and open only in bright sunshine.

Spotted Cat's-ear *Hypochaeris maculata*

HEIGHT To 30cm.
ECOLOGY & NATURAL HISTORY
Distinctive, bristly perennial.
HABITAT Dry grassland and on
broken, rocky slopes, mainly on
calcareous soils.
FLOWERS Borne in heads 3–5cm
across, with lemon yellow florets,
blackish bracts and scales present
between the florets; the heads are
solitary and carried on bristly
stalks, June to August.
FRUITS With feathery hairs.
LEAVES Ovate, wavy-edged, bristly
and marked with reddish purple
spots.

B&I STATUS Rare and local. At its
most showy on the Lizard peninsula,
the N Cornish coast and on Jersey;
also rare on downland inland.
NW EUROPEAN STATUS Very local,
mainly N Germany and lowland
S Scandinavia.

Autumn Hawkbit *Scorzoneroides autumnalis*

HEIGHT To 25cm.
ECOLOGY & NATURAL HISTORY Variable
hairless or only slightly downy perennial.
Previously known as *Leontodon autumnalis*.
HABITAT Grows in stable dunes, dry
saltmarshes and dry, grassy places
everywhere.
FLOWERS Borne in heads, 15–35mm
across, with yellow florets; the involucre
tapers gradually to the stem that bears
numerous scale-like bracts below the
head, June to October. The flowering
stems branch 2–3 times.
FRUITS Form a white 'clock'.
LEAVES Oblong and deeply pinnately
lobed.

B&I STATUS
Widespread and
common.
NW EUROPEAN STATUS
Widespread.

Lesser Hawkbit *Leontodon saxatilis*

HEIGHT To 25cm.
ECOLOGY & NATURAL HISTORY
Perennial whose stems are hairless above but bristly below.
HABITAT Grows on dry ground, including dunes and bare coastal grassland, and grassy places generally inland.
FLOWERS Borne in heads, 20–25mm across, with yellow florets. The heads droop in bud and are solitary; scale-like bracts are absent from the flower stalk, June to October.
FRUITS Form a white 'clock'.
LEAVES Pinnately lobed and sparsely hairy.

B&I STATUS Common and widespread, except in the north.
NW EUROPEAN STATUS Widespread from NW France to N Germany; occasional elsewhere.

Bristly Oxtongue *Helminthotheca echioides*

HEIGHT To 80cm.
ECOLOGY & NATURAL HISTORY
Branched and upright annual or biennial whose stems are covered in stiff bristles. Previously known as *Picris echioides*.
HABITAT Grows in dry grassland, on cliffs, sea walls and disturbed ground.
FLOWERS Borne in heads, 20–25mm across, with pale yellow florets; carried in open clusters, June to October.
FRUITS Have feathery hairs.
LEAVES Oblong, the upper ones clasping the stem; leaf surface is covered in swollen-based bristles and pale spots.

B&I STATUS Locally common in S Britain but scarce elsewhere.
NW EUROPEAN STATUS Mainly NW France.

Hawkweed Oxtongue *Picris hieracioides*

HEIGHT To 70cm.
ECOLOGY & NATURAL HISTORY
Branched perennial with bristly stems
that are sometimes are tinged reddish
towards the base.
HABITAT Grows in dry grassland,
mainly on calcareous soils and near
the sea.
FLOWERS Borne in heads, 20–25mm
across, with yellow florets, July to
September.
FRUITS Have feathery hairs.
LEAVES Resemble those of Bristly
Oxtongue but are narrow-oblong,
toothed and covered in bristles that
are not swollen-based.

B&I STATUS Locally common
in S and SE England; scarce
and mainly coastal elsewhere.
NW EUROPEAN STATUS
Widespread but local.

Goat's-beard *Tragopogon pratensis*

HEIGHT To 60cm.
ECOLOGY & NATURAL HISTORY
Upright annual or perennial.
HABITAT Grows in sand dunes and
a wide range of grassy places.
FLOWERS Borne in heads, 3–4cm
across, with yellow florets and
long, narrow bracts; flowers close
by midday and remain closed on
dull mornings, May to August.
FRUITS Have pappus hairs,
produced in impressive white
'clocks', 8–10cm across.
LEAVES Narrow, grass-like and
clasping, or sheathing, at the
base.

B&I STATUS Locally
common only in England
and Wales; scarce or
absent elsewhere.
NW EUROPEAN STATUS
Widespread, north to
lowland S Scandinavia.

Similar **Salsify *Tragopogon
porrifolius*** has pinkish
purple florets. Grows in
rough grassy places,
mainly near the sea
and in S England.

Marsh Sowthistle *Sonchus palustris*

HEIGHT To 3m.
ECOLOGY & NATURAL HISTORY Tall and stately perennial.
HABITAT Waterlogged peaty marshland soil; tolerates brackish conditions.
FLOWERS Borne in heads, 3–4cm across, with pale yellow florets on branched inflorescence, July to September.
FRUITS Yellowish achenes.
LEAVES Pointed, pinnately divided or entire, with pointed basal auricles.

B&I STATUS Local and scarce; mainly coastal but reintroduced to E Anglian fens.
NW EUROPEAN STATUS Very local, mainly Low Countries, N Germany, Denmark and S Sweden.

Perennial Sowthistle *Sonchus arvensis*

HEIGHT To 2m.
ECOLOGY & NATURAL HISTORY Impressively
tall perennial whose broken stems exude a
milky sap.
HABITAT Grows above beach and saltmarsh
strandlines, on sea walls and in damp, grassy or
disturbed ground generally.
FLOWERS Borne in heads, 4–5cm across,
with yellow florets; the heads are carried in
branched, umbel-like clusters, July to September.
FRUITS Ribbed and flattened with feathery
pappus hairs that form a 'clock'.
LEAVES Narrow, shiny, dark green above and
greyish below, with pinnate lobes, soft marginal
spines and clasping, rounded
auricles at the base.

B&I STATUS Widespread
and common throughout.
NW EUROPEAN STATUS
Widespread, north to
lowland S Scandinavia.

Prickly Sowthistle *Sonchus asper*

HEIGHT To 1m.
ECOLOGY & NATURAL HISTORY
Upright, mainly hairless annual or
biennial whose broken stems exude a
milky sap.
HABITAT Grows on disturbed ground
and in rough grassland.
FLOWERS Borne in heads, 20–25mm
across, with rich yellow florets; the
heads are carried in umbel-like
clusters, July to October.
FRUITS Elliptical with pappus hairs
forming a 'clock'.
LEAVES Glossy green above with wavy,
crinkly and sharp-spined margins, and
rounded auricles clasping at the base.

B&I STATUS Widespread
and common throughout.
NW EUROPEAN STATUS
Widespread, north to
lowland S Scandinavia.

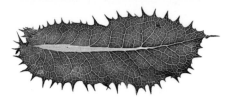

Stinking Hawk's-beard *Crepis foetida*

HEIGHT To 50cm.
ECOLOGY & NATURAL HISTORY Hairy annual or biennial that is superficially similar to other members of the genus but smells of bitter almonds when bruised. Flower heads droop in bud.
HABITAT Grows on stabilised shingle.
FLOWERS Borne in heads, which are 10–15mm across when open (only in morning sunshine), June to October.
FRUITS Curved, with pappus hairs.
LEAVES Deeply pinnately lobed and hairy; form a basal rosette that often withers before flowers and seed heads are mature. Stem leaves are similar but much smaller.

B&I STATUS Rare, and confined to coastal Sussex and Kent.
NW EUROPEAN STATUS Scarce and very local.

In terms of status, this plant has a chequered past but a promising future. Previously declared extinct, reintroductions have had varying degrees of success and managing Rabbit grazing appears important for its survival. It clings on at Dungeness, its original haunt, but has the best chance of success at Rye Harbour Nature Reserve thanks to the efforts of enthusiasts. See also page 39.

Beaked Hawk's-beard *Crepis vesicaria*

HEIGHT To 80cm.
ECOLOGY & NATURAL HISTORY Tough biennial with stiffly hairy stalks and stems.
HABITAT Rough grassland, sea walls and waste ground.
FLOWERS Borne in heads 25mm across, the yellow florets bearing an orange stripe beneath, May to July.
FRUITS Achenes with pappus hairs.
LEAVES Variably pinnately lobed, stem leaves clasping, basal leaves stalked.

B&I STATUS Widespread and locally common in lowland S Britain.
NW EUROPEAN STATUS Mainly NW France.

Mouse-ear-hawkweed *Pilosella officinarum*

HEIGHT To 25cm.

ECOLOGY & NATURAL HISTORY Variable, hairy and mat-forming perennial that has creeping runners (stolons) which seldom end in leaf rosettes. Stems produce a milky latex when broken.

HABITAT Grows in a wide range of dry, grassy places, including sand dunes, cliffs and meadows, on a range of soil types.

FLOWERS Borne in heads, 2–3cm across, with pale yellow florets that have a red stripe below; heads are solitary on leafless stems, May to October.

FRUITS Achenes with unbranched hairs.

LEAVES Spoon-shaped, green and hairy above and downy white below; arranged in a basal rosette.

B&I STATUS Widespread and common throughout.

NW EUROPEAN STATUS Widespread, north to lowland S Scandinavia.

Shaggy Mouse-ear-hawkweed *Pilosella peleteriana*

HEIGHT To 25cm.

ECOLOGY & NATURAL HISTORY Variable, extremely hairy perennial that spreads by creeping runners (stolons) which usually end with a leaf rosette, eventually forming congested mats.

HABITAT Grows in free-draining soils, including sand dunes and cliffs.

FLOWERS Borne in heads, 3–4.5cm across, with pale yellow florets that have a red stripe below, May to October; heads are solitary with densely-hairy bracts.

FRUITS Achenes with unbranched hairs.

LEAVES Spoon-shaped, green and hairy above and downy white below; arranged in a rosette.

B&I STATUS Very local, mainly on coasts of Channel Islands, SW Isle of Wight and Dorset; also occurs, extremely locally, inland.

NW EUROPEAN STATUS Very local, mainly NW France to S Scandinavia.

Dandelions *Taraxacum* spp.

HEIGHT To 30cm.

ECOLOGY & NATURAL HISTORY
Smooth perennials comprising 250 or so superficially similar 'species' that are a challenge for the beginner to separate with any degree of certainty. Identification is best attempted using the BSBI publication *Field Handbook to British and Irish Dandelions*.

HABITAT Grassy habitats including cliffs, sand dunes and coastal meadows; widespread inland in grassland and on roadside verges.

FLOWERS Borne in domed heads, 3–4cm across, on unbranched stalks, March to October.

FRUITS With pappus hairs, forming familiar white 'clocks'.

LEAVES Pinnately divided, arranged in a basal rosette.

B&I STATUS Widespread and common.

NW EUROPEAN STATUS Widespread and common.

Dandelions

Winter Heliotrope *Petasites pyrenaicus*

HEIGHT To 20cm
ECOLOGY & NATURAL HISTORY
Spreading perennial.
HABITAT Grows on damp
roadside verges, hedgerows and
coastal banks.
FLOWERS Pinkish lilac and
vanilla-scented heads, 10–12mm
across, and carried in open
spikes, December to March.
FRUITS Achenes.
LEAVES Up to 20cm across,
rounded and long-stalked with
toothed margins.

B&I STATUS Native of S
Europe, introduced and
spreading, especially near
coasts.
NW EUROPEAN STATUS
Introduced and occasional.

Golden Samphire *Limbarda crithmoides*

HEIGHT To 75cm.
ECOLOGY & NATURAL HISTORY
Attractive, tufted and upright
perennial. Previously known as
Inula crithmoides.
HABITAT Grows on saltmarshes,
coastal shingle, sea walls
and sea cliffs.
FLOWERS Borne in
heads, 15–30mm
across with
spreading, yellow
ray florets and
orange-yellow
central disc
florets; arranged
in terminal
clusters, July to
September.
FRUITS Achenes.
LEAVES Bright
green, narrow
and fleshy.

Similar **Plough-
man's-spikenard**
Inula conyzae
grows in calcareous
dune slacks (and
chalky ground
inland) and reaches
a height of 1m. Its
flowers are borne
in ovoid heads
8–10mm long
comprising yellow
florets and purplish
and green bracts.

B&I STATUS
Widespread and locally
common only around
the coasts of SW
Britain and Ireland.
NW EUROPEAN STATUS
Local and coastal, NW
France only.

Jersey Cudweed *Laphangium luteoalbum*

HEIGHT To 40cm.
ECOLOGY & NATURAL HISTORY Upright, mainly unbranched and extremely woolly greyish annual. Previously known as *Gnaphalium luteoalbum*.
HABITAT Grows in damp, sandy ground.
FLOWERS Yellowish brown, egg-shaped and borne in terminal clusters, June to August.
FRUITS Achenes with a pappus of hairs.
LEAVES Elongate with wavy margins.

B&I STATUS Local, mainly coastal and most reliable in N Norfolk, S Dorset and Isles of Scilly.
NW EUROPEAN STATUS Scarce, local and mainly coastal, north to N Germany.

Buttonweed *Cotula coronopifolia*

HEIGHT To 25cm
ECOLOGY & NATURAL HISTORY Creeping annual or perennial.
HABITAT Damp brackish soils and maritime grassy hollows; occasionally inland as well.

FLOWERS Borne in stalked, button-like heads 9–11mm across, comprising tightly packed yellow florets, July to August.
FRUITS Achenes.
LEAVES Narrow and variably pinnately lobed.

B&I STATUS Locally established introduction from the southern hemisphere.
NW EUROPEAN STATUS Introduced and very local, mainly NW France to N Germany.

Goldenrod *Solidago virgaurea*

HEIGHT To 75cm.
ECOLOGY & NATURAL HISTORY Variable, upright perennial that is sometimes slightly downy.
HABITAT Grows on clifftops and coastal heaths (plus woods, heaths and grassland inland); tolerates a range of soil types but favours acid conditions.
FLOWERS Yellow, the individual heads 5–10mm across and comprising ray and disc florets; borne in branched spikes, June to September.
FRUITS One-seeded with pappus hairs.
LEAVES Spoon-shaped and stalked at the base of the plant; stems leaves are narrow and unstalked.

B&I STATUS Widespread and locally common, especially in the west and north.
NW EUROPEAN STATUS Widespread but local, mainly NW France to N Germany.

Common Fleabane *Pulicaria dysenterica*

HEIGHT To 50cm.
ECOLOGY & NATURAL HISTORY
Creeping perennial with upright,
branched and woolly flowering stems.
HABITAT Grows in damp meadows
and ditches on heavy soils.
FLOWERS Borne in heads, 15–30mm
across, with spreading yellow ray
florets and deeper yellow, central disc
florets; arranged in open clusters, July
to September.
FRUITS Achenes with a hairy pappus.
LEAVES Downy, heart-shaped and
clasping; stem leaves persist, basal
ones soon wither.

B&I STATUS Common, except in
N Britain.
NW EUROPEAN STATUS
Widespread in NW France;
occasional and local north to
N Germany.

Blue Fleabane *Erigeron acer*

HEIGHT To 30cm.
ECOLOGY & NATURAL HISTORY Roughly hairy annual
or biennial; stems are stiff and tinged reddish.
HABITAT Grows on coastal shingle and dunes and dry,
grassy places elsewhere.
FLOWERS Borne in heads, 12–18mm across, with bluish
purple ray florets mainly concealing the yellow disc
florets; heads in clusters, June to August.
FRUITS Achenes.
LEAVES Basal leaves are spoon-shaped and stalked; stem
leaves are narrow and unstalked.

B&I STATUS Widespread
only in England and
Wales.
NW EUROPEAN STATUS
Widespread.

Sea Aster *Tripolium pannonicum*

HEIGHT To 75cm.
ECOLOGY & NATURAL HISTORY
Branched, hairless and salt-
tolerant perennial. Previously
known as *Aster tripolium*.
HABITAT Grows in saltmarshes,
saline grassland and on sea cliffs.
FLOWERS Umbel-like clusters of
flower heads, each 1–2cm across
and comprising yellow disc
florets and bluish lilac ray florets,
July to September. In var.
flosculosus only yellow florets
are present.
FRUITS Achenes.
LEAVES Fleshy and
narrow, with a
prominent midrib.

The flowers of Sea Aster are food for the larvae of an
interesting moth called the **Star-wort *Cucullia asteris***.

B&I STATUS Locally common
around the coasts of Britain
and Ireland.
NW EUROPEAN STATUS
Widespread but entirely
coastal, north to S
Scandinavia.

Var. *flosculosus*

Sea Aster (continued)

Sea Aster

Seaside Daisy *Erigeron glaucus*

HEIGHT To 30cm.
ECOLOGY & NATURAL HISTORY
Spreading, evergreen perennial.
Native of coastal Oregon and
California.
HABITAT Planted in a wide
range of coastal habitats and
often becomes naturalised on
cliffs and banks.
FLOWERS Borne in heads, to
3cm across, comprising pinkish
lilac ray florets and yellow disc
florets, May to October.
FRUITS Achenes.
LEAVES Fleshy and spoon-
shaped.

B&I STATUS Widely
planted in Britain
and Ireland and often
naturalised on coasts.
NW EUROPEAN STATUS
Occasional.

Clouded Yellow *Colias croceus*

Corn Marigold *Glebionis segetum*

HEIGHT To 50cm.
ECOLOGY & NATURAL HISTORY
Attractive, hairless and upright
annual. Previously known as
Chrysanthemum segetum.
HABITAT Grows in arable fields
and cultivated ground, usually
on acid, sandy soils.
FLOWERS Comprise heads,
3–6cm across, with orange-
yellow disc florets and yellow
ray florets, June to October.
FRUITS Achenes.
LEAVES Narrow, deeply lobed
or toothed, and slightly fleshy;
upper leaves clasp the stem.

B&I STATUS Naturalised
archaeophyte whose range and
abundance are decreasing.
Occasional nowadays, often
near the sea or where planted.
NW EUROPEAN STATUS
Occasional.

Goldilocks Aster *Galatella linosyris*

HEIGHT To 60cm.
**ECOLOGY & NATURAL
HISTORY** Upright
perennial. Previously
known as *Aster linosyris*.
HABITAT Coastal grassland and rocky cliffs on
limestone.
FLOWERS Inflorescence
comprises numerous heads
of yellow flowers, 13–17mm
across, July to September.
FRUITS Achenes.
LEAVES Numerous, long
and slender, arranged up
stem.

B&I STATUS Rare and
restricted mainly to a few
limestone outcrops on coasts
of SW Britain.
NW EUROPEAN STATUS
Local and rare, NW France
only.

Daisy *Bellis perennis*

HEIGHT To 10cm.
ECOLOGY & NATURAL HISTORY Familiar, downy and rosette-forming perennial.
HABITAT Grows in lawns but also occurs in short, trampled and grazed coastal grassland, in dune slacks and on clifftop paths.
FLOWERS Borne in solitary heads, 15–25mm across, on slender stems; they comprise yellow disc florets and white (often faintly crimson-tipped) ray florets, March to October.
FRUITS Achenes.
LEAVES Spoon-shaped and form prostrate rosettes from which flower stalks arise.

B&I STATUS Widespread and common throughout.
NW EUROPEAN STATUS Widespread, north to lowland S Scandinavia.

Yarrow *Achillea millefolium*

HEIGHT To 50cm.
ECOLOGY & NATURAL HISTORY Strongly aromatic, upright and downy perennial with creeping stems and upright, furrowed flowering stalks.
HABITAT Grows in sand dunes and on coastal shingle, and a wide range of grassy habitats and waste ground inland.
FLOWERS Borne in heads, 4–6mm across, comprising yellowish disc florets and pinkish white ray florets; the heads are arranged in flat-topped clusters, June to November.
FRUITS Achenes.
LEAVES Finely divided, feathery and dark green.

B&I STATUS Widespread and common throughout.
NW EUROPEAN STATUS Widespread.

Sea Mayweed *Tripleurospermum maritimum*

HEIGHT To 60cm.
ECOLOGY & NATURAL HISTORY Branched, spreading and mat-forming perennial.
HABITAT Grows mainly on coastal shingle and sand.
FLOWERS Borne in clusters of solitary, long-stalked heads, 20–40mm across, with yellow disc florets and white ray florets, April to October. There are no scales between the disc florets. Receptacle is domed and solid.
FRUITS Achenes.
LEAVES Much divided into cylindrical and fleshy segments.

B&I STATUS Widespread around coasts.
NW EUROPEAN STATUS Widespread but coastal.

      Wildflowers

Scentless Mayweed *Tripleurospermum inodorum*

HEIGHT To 75cm.
ECOLOGY & NATURAL HISTORY Scentless, hairless and rather straggly annual. Formerly considered to be conspecific with Sea Mayweed, which is now assigned species status.
HABITAT Disturbed and cultivated ground, seldom in similar habitats to Sea Mayweed.
FLOWERS Borne in clusters of solitary, long-stalked heads, 20–40mm across, comprising yellow disc florets and white ray florets, April to October. There are no scales between the disc florets. The receptacle is domed and solid.
FRUITS Achenes tipped with black oil glands.
LEAVES Feathery and much divided.

B&I STATUS Widespread and common.
NW EUROPEAN STATUS Widespread.

Oxeye Daisy *Leucanthemum vulgare*

HEIGHT To 60cm.
ECOLOGY & NATURAL HISTORY Downy or hairless perennial.
HABITAT Grows in stable sand dunes and on cliffs, and widespread inland in dry grassland; usually absent from acid soils.
FLOWERS Borne in solitary heads, 30–50mm across, with yellow disc florets and white ray florets, May to September. There are no scales between the disc florets.
FRUITS Achenes.
LEAVES Dark green and toothed; lower leaves are spoon-shaped, stalked and form a rosette, stem leaves are pinnately lobed.

B&I STATUS Widespread and common throughout.
NW EUROPEAN STATUS Widespread, north to lowland Scandinavia.

Chamomile *Chamaemelum nobile*

HEIGHT To 25cm.
ECOLOGY & NATURAL HISTORY Creeping, downy and greyish perennial that is pleasantly aromatic.
HABITAT Grows in short grassland on sandy soils where trampling or exposure to wind and salt spray maintain a short sward.
FLOWERS Borne in solitary heads, 18–24mm across, with yellow disc florets and white ray florets, June to September. Scales are present between the disc florets.
FRUITS Achenes.
LEAVES Feathery and pinnately divided into fine, bristle-tipped lobes that are hairless below.

Similar **Pineappleweed** *Matricaria discoidea* grows to 12cm tall, on trampled ground, track ruts and field margins. Flowers comprise domed heads of yellowish green disc florets, June to October. Whole plant smells of pineapple when crushed.

B&I STATUS Locally common only in S Britain and Ireland.
NW EUROPEAN STATUS Local, NW France only.

Cottonweed *Achillea maritima*

HEIGHT To 50cm.
ECOLOGY & NATURAL HISTORY Distinctive and grey-looking perennial whose stems and leaves are coated in thick, white woolly hairs. Previously known as *Otanthus maritimus*.
HABITAT Grows on stabilised shingle beaches.
FLOWERS Borne in heads that are yellow and terminal, August to October.
FRUITS Achenes.
LEAVES Oval, cloaked with cottony hairs, margins either entire or smoothly-toothed.

B&I STATUS Formerly rare but scattered around English and Irish coasts, it has declined due to human disturbance; now restricted to one location (and perhaps just 12 plants) in Co. Wexford, Ireland. It is being grown in Ireland's National Botanic Gardens.
NW EUROPEAN STATUS A plant of Atlantic and Mediterranean shores, with its northern outpost in Brittany, France.

Sea Wormwood *Artemisia maritima*

HEIGHT To 65cm.

ECOLOGY & NATURAL HISTORY Highly aromatic, much branched perennial with both upright and spreading stems that are woody at the base.

HABITAT Grows in saltmarshes and on sea walls, and tolerates salt spray and occasional inundation.

FLOWERS Borne in tiny egg-shaped, slightly nodding and yellow heads, 1–2mm across; these are carried in branched and leafy spikes, August to October.

FRUITS Achenes.

LEAVES Pinnately divided and downy on both sides.

B&I STATUS Locally common on suitable coasts of England and Wales; scarce elsewhere.

NW EUROPEAN STATUS Widespread but local and entirely coastal.

Dune Wormwood *Artemisia crithmifolia*

HEIGHT To 1m.

ECOLOGY & NATURAL HISTORY Perennial low shrub. Formerly treated as a subspecies of Field Wormwood (*Artemisia campestris* ssp. *maritima*) but Stace now suggests that British plants should be regarded as *A. crithmifolia*, a coastal European species.

HABITAT Grows in sand dunes.

FLOWERS Borne in tiny yellow heads, 3–4mm across in leafy spikes, August to October.

FRUITS Achenes.

LEAVES Pinnately divided and felty.

B&I STATUS Known only from Lancashire (discovered in 2004) and Glamorgan (known since 1956); possibly native.

NW EUROPEAN STATUS Widespread but local on coasts of W France.

Wormwood *Artemisia absinthium*

HEIGHT To 80cm.
ECOLOGY & NATURAL HISTORY
Highly aromatic, upright
perennial that has silkily
hairy stems.
HABITAT Grows in disturbed
coastal grassland and inland
on roadside verges and
disturbed ground.
FLOWERS Borne in yellowish heads
that are 3–5mm across, bell-shaped
and nodding; these are carried in tall,
branched spikes, July to September.
FRUITS Achenes.
LEAVES Pinnately divided into deeply cut
lobes that are silvery-hairy on both sides.

B&I STATUS Locally common in
England and Wales but scarce
or absent elsewhere.
NW EUROPEAN STATUS Local
and entirely coastal, north to
S Scandinavia.

Mugwort *Artemisia vulgaris*

HEIGHT To 1.25m.
ECOLOGY & NATURAL HISTORY Aromatic,
upright and branched perennial with ribbed,
reddish and downy stems.
HABITAT Grows on disturbed ground near
the sea, and inland on roadside
verges and waste ground.
FLOWERS Borne in reddish
heads, 2–3mm across,
arranged in tall, branched
spikes, July to September.
FRUITS Achenes.
LEAVES Pinnate and dark
green, hairless above but silvery
downy below; lower leaves are
stalked, upper ones are unstalked.

B&I STATUS
Widespread and
common throughout.
**NW EUROPEAN
STATUS** Widespread,
north to lowland
Scandinavia.

Least Lettuce *Lactuca saligna*

HEIGHT To 1m.
ECOLOGY & NATURAL HISTORY
Slender annual that is easy to overlook when its flower heads are not open: frustratingly, flowers only open on sunny days, between around 9–11am.
HABITAT Stabilised shingle and dry coastal ground.
FLOWERS Borne in yellow heads, around 1cm across when fully open, appearing at intervals up the stem, July to August.
FRUITS Achenes.
LEAVES Range from narrow and linear to pinnate, all clasping the stem at the base.

B&I STATUS Rare and restricted to a few sites around the Thames Estuary (mainly N Kent) and Rye Harbour in Sussex.
NW EUROPEAN STATUS Rare and very local, N France and Low Countries.

Prickly Lettuce *Lactuca serriola*

HEIGHT To 2m.
ECOLOGY & NATURAL HISTORY
Upright annual or biennial.
HABITAT Sea walls, stabilised shingle and disturbed ground near the sea; verges and wayside ground inland.
FLOWERS Borne in yellow heads, 8–10mm across when open, July to September. Usually only open in full sun.
FRUITS Dark grey-green achenes.
LEAVES Pinnate, with spiny margins, a spiny, grey-green midrib and clasping base. Often held upright and arranged in a north-south orientation up stem.

Similar **Great Lettuce** *Lactuca virosa* is similar in appearance and range but its leaves have a purplish midrib and are not arranged in a geometric manner; its fruits are blackish achenes.

B&I STATUS Locally common in lowland S Britain.
NW EUROPEAN STATUS Widespread but local, north to coastal S Scandinavia.

Groundsel *Senecio vulgaris*

HEIGHT To 40cm.
ECOLOGY & NATURAL HISTORY
Branched annual plant that is
either upright or spreading.
HABITAT Grows in sand dunes and
on coastal cliffs, and cultivated
and disturbed ground inland.
FLOWERS Borne in cylindrical
heads, 10mm long, of yellow disc
florets, with black-tipped greenish
bracts; carried in clusters, all year
but mainly April to August.
FRUITS Hairy achenes.
LEAVES Pinnately lobed; lower
leaves are stalked while upper ones
clasp the stem.

B&I STATUS Widespread and
common throughout.
NW EUROPEAN STATUS
Widespread.

Sticky Groundsel *Senecio viscosus*

HEIGHT To 60cm.
ECOLOGY & NATURAL HISTORY
Annual that recalls Groundsel and
Heath Groundsel but whole plant is
stickily hairy and pungent.
HABITAT Grows in free-draining
coastal shingle and sand dunes,
and dry disturbed ground inland.
FLOWERS Comprise conical heads,
12mm long, of yellow disc florets,
recurved ray florets and bracts that
are not black-tipped; borne in open
clusters, July to September.
FRUITS Hairless achenes.
LEAVES Pinnately divided.

B&I STATUS Locally common.
NW EUROPEAN STATUS
Widespread, north to lowland
Scandinavia.

Heath Groundsel *Senecio sylvaticus*

HEIGHT To 70cm.
ECOLOGY & NATURAL HISTORY
Similar to Sticky Groundsel but
taller and more robust.
HABITAT Favours acid soils and
grows on sea cliffs and coastal
sand, and inland on heaths and in
woodlands.
FLOWERS Comprise stickily
hairy, conical heads, 10mm long,
of yellow disc florets, recurved
ray florets and bracts that are not
black-tipped; heads are carried in
open clusters, June to September.
FRUITS Hairy achenes.
LEAVES Deeply pinnately divided.

B&I STATUS Locally
common throughout.
NW EUROPEAN STATUS
Widespread but local, north
to lowland S Scandinavia.

Common Ragwort *Jacobaea vulgaris*

HEIGHT To 1m.
ECOLOGY & NATURAL HISTORY Upright,
hairless biennial or short-lived perennial.
Foodplant of larvae of the Cinnabar
Moth *Tyria jacobaeae* (below).
Previously known as *Senecio jacobaea*.
HABITAT Grows in grassland; thrives
in grazed areas (animals avoid eating
the plant).
FLOWERS Yellow and borne in heads,
15–25mm across; these are carried in
dense, flat-topped clusters, June to October.
FRUITS Those of disc florets are downy
achenes; ray floret fruits hairless.
LEAVES Pinnate with a blunt end lobe, and
essentially hairless.

B&I STATUS Common
and widespread.
NW EUROPEAN STATUS
Widespread, north to
lowland S Scandinavia.

Cinnabar
Moth larva

Hoary Ragwort *Jacobaea erucifolia*

HEIGHT To 1.2m.
ECOLOGY & NATURAL HISTORY Upright
perennial. Previously known as *Senecio
erucifolius*.
HABITAT Grows on coastal shingle
and sand dunes, inland in rough
grassland and on verges.
FLOWERS Yellow and borne
in heads, 15–20mm across;
these are carried in flat-topped
clusters, June to October.
Inflorescence is more open than
that of Common Ragwort.
FRUITS Achenes.
LEAVES Pinnate with a small pointed tip;
undersides of leaves are coated in soft grey hairs.

B&I STATUS Common and
widespread.
NW EUROPEAN STATUS
Widespread, north to N Germany.

Silver Ragwort *Jacobaea maritima*

HEIGHT To 80cm.
ECOLOGY & NATURAL HISTORY
Clump-forming, silvery grey and woody
perennial. Previously known as *Senecio
cineraria*.
HABITAT Grows on coastal cliffs and walls.
FLOWERS Yellow and borne in heads,
15–25mm across, with silvery woolly
stalks and bracts; heads appear in scruffy-
looking clusters (with only a few flowers
looking pristine at any given time), June
to August.
FRUITS Downy achenes.
LEAVES Pinnate and green but fresh leaves
have a coating of white woolly hairs, which
rub off with time on the upper surface.

upper

under

B&I STATUS Introduced and
naturalised on the coasts of SW
England; planted elsewhere.
NW EUROPEAN STATUS Introduced
and very occasional in N France.

South Stack Fleawort *Tephroseris integrifolia* ssp. *maritima*

HEIGHT To 65cm.
ECOLOGY & NATURAL HISTORY Showy, downy perennial.
HABITAT Grows on sea cliffs.
FLOWERS Borne in heads, 15–25mm across, with orange-yellow disc florets and yellow ray florets, May to July.
FRUITS Hairy achenes.
LEAVES Oval, toothed and sparsely coated in silky hairs; basal ones form a rosette while stem leaves are few, narrow and clasping.

B&I STATUS Rare and confined to cliffs on Anglesey, notably near South Stack. Ssp. *integrifolia* is smaller and grows very locally inland on calcareous grassland.
NW EUROPEAN STATUS Ssp. *maritima* is endemic to Wales and found nowhere else.

Bluebell *Hycanithoides non-scripta*

HEIGHT To 50cm.
ECOLOGY & NATURAL HISTORY
Familiar bulbous perennial.
HABITAT Despite being
associated primarily with
woodland, it also grows
extensively on coastal cliffs,
particularly those exposed to
battering winds and salt spray.
FLOWERS Bell-shaped with 6
recurved lobes at the mouth;
mainly bluish purple (very
occasionally pink or white) and
borne in 1-sided drooping-
tipped spikes, April to June.
FRUITS Capsules.
LEAVES Long, 15mm wide,
glossy green and arising
from the base.

Hyacinthoides x massartiana
is a hybrid between Bluebell
and introduced, garden escape
Spanish Bluebell *Hycanithoides.
hispanica*. It is widespread but
still relatively scarce, thankfully
so since it poses a competitive
threat to our native species. Its
flower spikes are not one-sided
but otherwise its characters are
variably intermediate between
its parents.

B&I STATUS
Widespread
throughout the region
and sometimes locally
abundant.
**NW EUROPEAN
STATUS** Widespread
but local, mainly
NW France.

Spring Squill *Scilla verna*

HEIGHT To 5cm.
ECOLOGY & NATURAL HISTORY Compact, hairless perennial.
HABITAT Grows in dry, short coastal grassland, typically in sight of the sea.
FLOWERS Bell-shaped, 10–15mm across and lilac-blue; borne in upright, terminal clusters, each flower on a short stalk with a bluish purple bract, April to June. Flowers open in succession.
FRUITS Capsules.
LEAVES Wiry, curly, basal and 4–6 in number; they appear in early spring, before the flowers.

B&I STATUS Very locally common on the coasts of W Britain and E Ireland; scarce or absent elsewhere.
NW EUROPEAN STATUS Scarce and local, NW France only.

Autumn Squill *Scilla autumnalis*

HEIGHT To 7cm.
ECOLOGY & NATURAL HISTORY Similar to Spring Squill but separable by flowering time and subtle difference in appearance of the flowers.
HABITAT Grows only in coastal grassland.
FLOWERS 10–15mm across, bell-shaped and bluish purple; borne in compact, terminal clusters on a slender stalk, the flowers lacking an accompanying bract, July to September. Flowers open in succession, typically only two or three flowers at a time.
FRUITS Capsules.
LEAVES Wiry, basal and appear in autumn.

Similar **Tassel Hyacinth** *Muscari comosum* appears in spring and has a tassel of sterile flowers topping an array of bell-like fertile ones. Widespread in dunes in W Europe and naturalised near coasts in a few spots in SW England and Jersey.

B&I STATUS Restricted to coasts of SW England.
NW EUROPEAN STATUS Local, NW France only.

Wild Asparagus *Asparagus prostratus*

HEIGHT To 1.5m.

ECOLOGY & NATURAL HISTORY
Branched, hairless and prostrate perennial. Related Garden Asparagus *Asparagus officinalis* is upright with longer internodes; its young shoots are the familiar vegetable.

HABITAT Grows in free-draining grassy places.

FLOWERS 4–6mm long, greenish and bell-shaped; borne in leaf axils, with separate-sex plants, June to September.

FRUITS Red berries.

LEAVES Reduced to tiny bracts; what appear to be leaves are in fact slender, branched stems (cladodes); these are stiff in Wild Asparagus, flexible in Garden Asparagus.

Wild Asparagus

Wild Asparagus

Garden Asparagus

Garden Asparagus

B&I STATUS Wild Asparagus is native on sea cliffs in SW Britain and SE Ireland. Garden Asparagus is locally naturalised on coasts, especially on dunes.

NW EUROPEAN STATUS Scarce, local and coastal, NW France to S Scandinavia.

Wild Onion *Allium vineale*

HEIGHT To 60cm.
ECOLOGY & NATURAL HISTORY Bulbous perennial.
HABITAT Sea walls, cliffs and dry coastal grassland; roadside verges and grassland inland.
FLOWERS Borne in heads (sometimes multiple heads) each 2–5cm across, June to July. Typical variety has just greenish red bulbils (which sometimes 'sprout') and a papery bract, but occasionally seen as a mix of bulbils and pale pink long-stalked flowers, or rarely flowers only.
FRUITS Capsules like miniature bulbs; the straw-coloured heads are a familiar sight in coastal grassland in summer.
LEAVES Grey-green, hollow and semi-circular in cross-section.

B&I STATUS Common in the south; scarce or absent elsewhere.
NW EUROPEAN STATUS Widespread but local, north to coastal S Scandinavia.

Chives *Allium schoenoprasum*

HEIGHT To 40cm.
ECOLOGY & NATURAL HISTORY Tufted, bulbous perennial.
HABITAT Grows in damp, grassy places on limestone rocks.
FLOWERS Purplish and borne in heads, 2–4cm across, comprising 10–30 flowers and 2 papery bracts, June to July.
FRUITS Capsules.
LEAVES Grey-green, hollow and cylindrical.

Similar **Rosy Garlic *Allium roseum*** is up to 60cm tall, and a naturalised escape from cultivation; it is widespread but local in grassland, especially near coasts in S England. Flowers are pink and borne in umbels, with or without deep red bulbils.

B&I STATUS Rare native of limestone cliffs and grassland, mainly in W Britain; also widely cultivated and occasionally naturalised.
NW EUROPEAN STATUS Scarce and local, mainly coastal S Scandinavia.

Sand Leek *Allium scorodoprasum*

HEIGHT To 1m.
ECOLOGY & NATURAL HISTORY Upright, bulbous perennial; prior to flowering, it resembles a slender leek.
HABITAT Grows in dry grassland on sandy soils.
FLOWERS Ovoid, stalked and purplish, borne in rounded umbels, 3–4cm across, with purple bulbils and 2 papery bracts, on long, slender stems, July to August.
FRUITS Capsules.
LEAVES Keeled, rough-edged and 1–2cm wide.

B&I STATUS Local, mainly N England and S Scotland; naturalised elsewhere.
NW EUROPEAN STATUS Scarce and local, mainly coastal Scandinavia.

Three-cornered Leek *Allium triquetrum*

HEIGHT To 45cm.
ECOLOGY & NATURAL HISTORY Bulbous perennial that smells strongly of garlic when bruised.
HABITAT Grows in hedges and disturbed ground, and locally on sea cliffs.
FLOWERS Bell-shaped, 2cm long and white with narrow green stripes; borne in drooping umbels on 3-sided stems, March to June.
FRUITS Capsules.
LEAVES Narrow, keeled and three per plant.

Three-cornered Leeks and Bluebells

B&I STATUS Introduced and naturalised locally, mainly in SW Britain and S Ireland.
NW EUROPEAN STATUS Local, mainly NW France.

stem cross-section

Wild Leek *Allium ampeloprasum*

HEIGHT To 2m.
ECOLOGY & NATURAL HISTORY Robust and upright bulbous perennial with a rounded stem. Three varieties are recognised: var. *ampeloprasum* has umbels with just flowers; both var. *bulbiferum* and var. *babingtonii* (aka Babington's Leek) have umbels with flowers and bulbils.
HABITAT Grows in grassy places near the sea.
FLOWERS 6–8mm long and purplish, with yellow anthers; borne in spherical heads, up to 9cm across, June to August. Numerous bulbils may be present.
FRUITS Capsules.
LEAVES Flat, narrow, up to 50cm long, and waxy with finely toothed margins.

Above:
Var. *ampeloprasum*

Right:
Var. *babingtonii*

B&I STATUS Rare and coastal: var. *ampeloprasum* is found in SW England and Wales; var. *bulbiferum* is confined to the Channel Islands; and var. *babingtonii* occurs in SW England, Wales and W Ireland.
NW EUROPEAN STATUS Absent.

Sea Daffodil *Pancratium maritimum*

HEIGHT Flower stems to 60cm.
ECOLOGY & NATURAL HISTORY Grows from a bulb buried deep in sandy soil.
HABITAT Coastal sand dunes.
FLOWERS White, daffodil-like and 2–3cm across; borne in umbels, July to September.
FRUITS Capsules.
LEAVES Green, strap-like and up to 20cm long; often withering before flowers appear.

B&I STATUS Introduced or possibly native to dunes on S coasts of Devon and Cornwall.
NW EUROPEAN STATUS Local and scarce, NW France only.

Montbretia *Crocosmia x crocosmiflora*

HEIGHT To 80cm.
ECOLOGY & NATURAL HISTORY Clump-forming perennial.
HABITAT Grows in coastal scrub and on cliffs; also widespread inland.
FLOWERS 3–5cm across and orange; borne in flattened spikes of 10–15, September to October.
FRUITS Brown.
LEAVES Sword-shaped, 5–15mm wide.

B&I STATUS A naturalised garden escape, often thriving on western coasts.
NW EUROPEAN STATUS Locally naturalised.

Stinking Iris *Iris foetidissima*

HEIGHT To 60cm.
ECOLOGY & NATURAL HISTORY Tufted perennial.
HABITAT Grows in coastal scrub and woodland, mostly on calcareous soils.
FLOWERS 7–8cm across, purplish and veined, May to July.
FRUITS Green, oblong and 3-sided, drying and splitting to reveal orange seeds.
LEAVES Dark green and sword-shaped, with an unpleasant smell.

B&I STATUS Locally common only in S England and S Wales.
NW EUROPEAN STATUS Local, NW France only.

Similar **Yellow Iris *Iris pseudacorus*** has large yellow flowers and grows in wet dune slacks and coastal freshwater marshes; widespread inland as well.

Sand Crocus *Romulea columnae*

HEIGHT To 1cm.
ECOLOGY & NATURAL HISTORY Low-growing perennial.
HABITAT Grows in sandy turf and on cliff slopes.
FLOWERS Star-shaped, bluish lilac, 1cm across, and opening only in sunshine, March to May.
FRUITS Capsules.
LEAVES Wiry and curled, up to 10cm long and basal.

B&I STATUS Rare and restricted to Dawlish Warren in Devon, one spot on the S Cornish coast, and the Channel Islands.
NW EUROPEAN STATUS Scarce and local, NW France only.

IRIDACEAE – Irises and relatives

Bee Orchid *Ophrys apifera*

HEIGHT To 30cm.
ECOLOGY & NATURAL HISTORY Attractive and distinctive perennial.
HABITAT Grows in sand dunes and coastal grassland; widespread in grassland inland, mainly on calcareous soils.
FLOWERS Have pink sepals and green upper petals; lower petal is 12mm across, expanded, furry and maroon with variable, pale yellow markings (vaguely bumblebee-like). Flowers carried in spikes, June to July.
FRUITS Egg-shaped.
LEAVES Green and oval, forming a basal rosette, with 2 sheathing leaves on stem.

B&I STATUS Locally common only in England, Wales and S Ireland.
NW EUROPEAN STATUS Very local, mainly NW France.

Early Spider-orchid *Ophrys sphegodes*

HEIGHT To 35cm (often much shorter).

ECOLOGY & NATURAL HISTORY Distinctive perennial.

HABITAT Grows in free-draining coastal grassland on calcareous soils; also, more locally in similar habitats inland.

FLOWERS Comprise green sepals and yellowish green upper petals; the lower lip is 12mm across, expanded, furry and maroon-brown, variably marked with a metallic blue H-shaped mark. Flowers carried in spikes, April to May.

FRUITS Egg-shaped.

LEAVES Green and seen mainly as a basal rosette.

B&I STATUS Local, in S England only; Dorset (Purbeck) and Kent (e.g. Samphire Hoe) coasts are strongholds.

NW EUROPEAN STATUS Scarce and very local, mainly NW France.

Similar **Late Spider-orchid** *Ophrys fuciflora* has pink sepals and upper petals, and a well-marked maroon-brown lower petal. Very rare on chalk downs in Kent; formerly on chalk cliffs on Kent coast and could conceivably be overlooked. This mainly Mediterranean species occurs sparingly in NW France.

Marsh Helleborine *Epipactis palustris*

HEIGHT To 50cm.

ECOLOGY & NATURAL HISTORY Upright and elegant perennial; as *Epipactis* helleborines go, this is a distinctive species.

HABITAT Grows in wet dune-slacks, and in marshes and fens inland.

FLOWERS Comprise reddish green or brownish green sepals, narrow, whitish upper petals that are marked with red, and a frilly, whitish lip marked with red streaks towards the base; borne in open spikes of 15 or more flowers, July to August.

FRUITS Pear-shaped.

LEAVES Broad and oval towards the base of the plant but narrower up the stem.

B&I STATUS Very locally common in S England, S Wales and S Ireland; scarce or absent elsewhere.

NW EUROPEAN STATUS Widespread but local, north to lowland S Scandinavia.

Dune Helleborine *Epipactis dunensis*

HEIGHT To 65cm.
ECOLOGY & NATURAL HISTORY Upright perennial.
HABITAT Grows in dune slacks and under colonising pines; recently recognised/discovered inland (where rare) in riverside woodland and other damp habitats.
FLOWERS Comprise rather narrow, greenish white sepals and upper petals, and a broadly heart-shaped lip that is greenish white, sometimes pink-tinged towards the centre, and curved under at the tip; flowers only occasionally open fully and are carried in open spikes, June to July.
FRUITS Pear-shaped.
LEAVES Oval.

So-called **Lindisfarne Helleborine** is treated here as a subspecies (**ssp. *sancta***) although some authorities continue to assign it species status (*Epipactis sancta*). It is confined to Lindisfarne National Nature Reserve in Northumberland where 'classic' Dune Helleborine does not occur. Differences are subtle, including slightly smaller flowers and colour of the base of the flower stalk – pink in Dune but green in Lindisfarne. So-called **Tyne Helleborine** (var. *tynensis*) grows beside the River Tyne and has a narrow, pointed lip; superficially it has most in common with Lindisfarne Helleborine.

B&I STATUS Rare, restricted to N Wales and N England.
NW EUROPEAN STATUS Absent.

Broad-leaved Helleborine *Epipactis helleborine*

HEIGHT To 75cm.

ECOLOGY & NATURAL HISTORY Upright and clump-forming perennial with rather downy stems.

HABITAT Grows in dune slacks and coastal woodland; inland, widespread in shady woodland and scrub.

FLOWERS Comprise broad, greenish sepals that are tinged purple around the margins, broad upper petals that are strongly purple-tinged, and purplish, heart-shaped lip, the tip of which is usually curved under; borne in dense spikes of up to 100 flowers, July to September.

FRUITS Pear-shaped.

LEAVES Broadly oval and strongly veined.

B&I STATUS
Locally common in most parts, except N Scotland.
NW EUROPEAN STATUS
Widespread and locally common.

ssp. *neerlandica*

typical form

Similar **Dark Red Helleborine** *Epipactis atrorubens* has deep pinkish magenta flowers and is a rare plant of coastal limestone cliff ledges in NW Britain; it also occurs, very locally, inland in N Britain.

So-called **Dutch Helleborine** (**ssp.** *neerlandica*) (**above left**) is restricted to dunes in S Wales (Oxwich and Kenfig are important locations) and the Low Countries; it is compact, with rather congested, mainly basal leaves and a dense inflorescence. **Young's Helleborine** (*Epipactis helleborine* **var.** *youngiana*) was formerly assigned species status but is now regarded as merely a variety; it has an open inflorescence and grows in Northumberland.

Wildflowers

Green-flowered Helleborine *Epipactis phyllanthes*

HEIGHT To 50cm.
ECOLOGY & NATURAL HISTORY Slender, upright perennial with rather insignificant-looking flowers.
HABITAT Grows locally in coastal sand dunes; more widespread but still local inland, in shady woods on calcareous soils.
FLOWERS Comprise yellowish green sepals and petals; flowers are pendent, invariably do not open fully and are borne in open spikes, July to September.
FRUITS Pear-shaped.
LEAVES Narrow-ovate and strongly veined.

B&I STATUS Local in S England and Wales; very local and scarce in N Britain and Ireland.
NW EUROPEAN STATUS Local, NW France to Denmark.

Common Twayblade *Neottia ovata*

HEIGHT To 50cm.
ECOLOGY & NATURAL HISTORY A distinctive orchid, presumably named for its diagnostic paired leaves (tway is said to be derived from the word twain, an archaic term for two).
HABITAT Grows in dune slacks and sand dunes, and inland in woodland and grassland on a wide range of soil types.
FLOWERS Yellowish green, with a distinct hood and a deeply forked lower lip that is 10–15mm long; borne in a loose spike of 20 or more flowers, May to July.
FRUITS Ovoid, they form and swell at the base of the flowers as they wither.
LEAVES Comprise a pair of broad, oval basal leaves, up to 16cm long, that appear well before the flowering stem.

B&I STATUS Widespread and locally common where conditions suit it.
NW EUROPEAN STATUS Widespread but local, north to lowland S Scandinavia.

Fen Orchid *Liparis loeselii*

HEIGHT To 20cm.

ECOLOGY & NATURAL HISTORY In normal circumstances this species grows in newly-stablished young dune slacks with short vegetation. These days, active management (to remove encroachment by vigorous plants and scrub) is required to provide the right conditions for its survival.

HABITAT Grows in lightly vegetated dune slacks, and inland in East Anglian fens.

FLOWERS Yellow with narrow, spreading perianth segments; the flowers are borne in spikes, June to July.

FRUITS Ovoid and swollen, the result being that fruiting plants are conspicuous.

LEAVES Paired and basal, forming a cup-like arrangement from which the flower stem arises.

In fruit

B&I STATUS Rare and restricted to S Wales dunes (mainly Kenfig) and formerly in N Devon; fen populations are found in Norfolk.

NW EUROPEAN STATUS Rare and extremely local, mainly Low Countries, Denmark and N Germany.

Coralroot Orchid *Corallorhiza trifida*

HEIGHT To 25cm (usually much shorter).

ECOLOGY & NATURAL HISTORY Intriguing, yellowish green saprophytic perennial that lacks leaves and feeds on decaying plant matter. Easily overlooked and often easiest to spot when scanned for at ground level. Tread carefully when you do, to avoid damage.

HABITAT Grows in dune slacks, with inland populations in damp, shady northern woodland.

FLOWERS Greenish white, the lip often tinged and streaked with red; borne in open spikes, June to July.

FRUITS Ovoid.

LEAVES Absent.

B&I STATUS Widespread and very locally common only in N England and Scotland.

NW EUROPEAN STATUS Local, mainly N Germany and Scandinavia.

Autumn Lady's-tresses *Spiranthes spiralis*

HEIGHT To 15cm.

ECOLOGY & NATURAL HISTORY Delicate and distinctive little orchid that is easy to overlook. An autumn-flowerer and typically the last orchid species to be seen each year.

HABITAT Grows in short, dry grassland, both inland and on coastal turf and dunes.

FLOWERS Pure white and both the petals and sepals are downy; borne in a spiral up the grey-green stem, August to September.

FRUITS Egg-shaped and downy.

LEAVES Appear as a basal rosette of oval leaves that wither long before the flower stem appears.

B&I STATUS Locally common in S England, Wales and SW Ireland.

NW EUROPEAN STATUS Widespread but local in NW France; occasional and scarce in Low Countries and N Germany

Irish Lady's-tresses *Spiranthes romanzoffiana*

HEIGHT To 25cm.

ECOLOGY & NATURAL HISTORY
Distinctive, upright perennial.
Widespread across northern North
America, the species' presence here is
perhaps evidence of ancient pre-glacial
links between land masses now separated
by the Atlantic.

HABITAT Grows in waterlogged grassland
and marshes.

FLOWERS Greenish white and borne in a
triple spiral up the stem, creating a rather
conical spike, July to August.

FRUITS Egg-shaped.

LEAVES Appear as a basal rosette of
narrowly oval leaves, and narrower ones
up the stem.

B&I STATUS Rare and
restricted to S and N
Ireland, NW Scotland and
Wales: formerly occurred
on Dartmoor but presumed
extinct there.

NW EUROPEAN STATUS
Widespread in North America
but in Europe confined to
Britain and Ireland.

Frog Orchid *Coeloglossum viride*

HEIGHT To 20cm.

ECOLOGY & NATURAL HISTORY
Compact orchid that often blends in well with its surroundings. In the recent past it was classified as *Dactylorhiza viridis* but Stace currently regards its identity as being that by which it was known historically.

HABITAT Grows in dunes and short base-rich coastal grassland; favours calcareous grassland inland.

FLOWERS Fancifully frog-like; the sepals and upper petals form a greenish hood and the lip is 6–8mm long and yellowish brown; the flowers are borne in an open spike, June to August.

FRUITS Ovoid, forming at the base of the withered flowers.

LEAVES Broad, oval and form a basal rosette, with narrower leaves partially sheathing the lower part of the stem.

B&I STATUS Widespread and locally common.
NW EUROPEAN STATUS Widespread but local; absent from or patchily distributed in Low Countries and S Sweden.

SPOTTED-ORCHIDS AND MARSH-ORCHIDS
Genus *Dactylorhiza*

Leaf through books written on the subject of British orchids over the last 20 years, and floras that include the group, and you will discover almost as many ways of classifying this iconic group of plants as there are titles. In the past, morphology and pollination strategies were among the tools used to inform opinion. However, today DNA analysis is a more reliable (although perhaps not infallible) way of making determinations about the ancestry, lineage and relationships between species and genera.

Among orchids, few groups have been subjected to more revisions than the genus *Dactylorhiza*. Although the group is widespread inland in Britain and Ireland, its members are very much a feature of coastal habitats and always arouse disproportionate interest among botanists, hence their relatively thorough coverage in this book. Their treatment notwithstanding, this book is not the vehicle to explore radical options and, therefore, we have by and large adopted the conventions of the latest edition of Stace (to many, the botanical bible).

The current consensus appears to be that, apart from Early Marsh-orchid *D. incarnata* all other genus members have hybrid origins, albeit ancient ones; this challenges the notion of how we define the term 'species'. Anyway, as a result of recent reclassification, some former species have 'vanished' while new ones have made an appearance. A species formerly known as Western Marsh-orchid *D. majalis* is now represented by Irish Marsh-orchid *D. kerryensis* in Ireland and a subspecies of Northern Marsh-orchid *D. purpurella* in Wales. The species known formerly as Lapland Marsh-orchid *D. lapponica* and Hebridean Marsh-orchid *D. ebudensis* have 'disappeared' and are treated today as subspecies of Narrow-leaved Marsh-orchid *D. traunsteineriodes*, however unlikely this relationship might seem based on outward appearances.

Stylised flowers of spotted-orchids and marsh-orchids, members of the genus *Dactylorhiza*

Common Spotted-orchid
Dactylorhiza fuchsii
flowers have a distinctly 3-lobed lip, and are pink or whitish overall with bold, darker markings including 'loops'.
p. 278

Heath Spotted-orchid
Dactylorhiza maculata
flowers have a broad lip that is less obviously 3-lobed; overall they are usually very pale, with subtle purplish dots and 'loops'.
p. 279

Early Marsh-orchid
Dacytlorhiza incarnata flowers have a lip that is folded back along the mid-line; the colour is variable but typically either flesh-pink (var. *incarnata*) or magenta (var. *coccinea*).
p. 280

Southern Marsh-orchid
Dacytlorhiza praetermissa
flowers usually have a broadly rounded lip with a smallish, rounded central projecting lobe.
p. 281

Northern Marsh-orchid
Dactylorhiza purpurella
flowers usually have a broadly diamond-shaped lip with a smallish central projecting lobe.
p. 282

Narrow-leaved Marsh-orchid
Dactylorhiza traunsteinerioides
flowers have a rather elongate and distinctly 3-lobed lip that broadens towards its lower margin.
p. 283

Irish Marsh-orchid
Dactylorhiza kerryensis
flowers often have a rather undulating-margined 3-lobed lip.
p. 282

Common Spotted-orchid *Dactylorhiza fuchsii*

HEIGHT To 60cm.
ECOLOGY & NATURAL HISTORY
Robust, widespread and familiar
orchid.
HABITAT Grows in dune-slacks
and calcareous coastal grassland;
inland it favours open woods,
meadows and verges, on base-
rich or neutral soils.
FLOWERS Vary in colour from
plant to plant, ranging from pink
to white; darker streaks and hoops
adorn the lower lip, which has 3
lobes, the central one narrow,
the others broad and sometimes
square-shaped. Flowers are borne
in open spikes, May to August.
FRUITS Egg-shaped.
LEAVES Green, glossy and
dark-spotted; borne in a basal
rosette before flower stalk appears;
narrower leaves sheath the lower
flower stalk.

B&I STATUS
Locally common.
**NW EUROPEAN
STATUS**
Widespread.

A distinctive form
(called **Hebridean
Spotted-orchid**
*Dactylorhiza
fuchsii* var.
hebridensis) has
flowers that are
pinkish magenta
with a broad, frilly
lip and leaves
that are often un-
marked; grows in
coastal grassland
in Cornwall, and
machair in Scot-
land and N Ireland.

Heath Spotted-orchid *Dactylorhiza maculata*

HEIGHT To 50cm.

ECOLOGY & NATURAL HISTORY
Superficially similar to Common Spotted-orchid but separable on flower shape and habitat preference.

HABITAT Damp, acid and peaty soils of heaths, bogs and acid grassland, including coastal sites in the north and west.

FLOWERS Vary from pale pink to white, depending on the plant. The lip is broad and comprises a relatively small central lobe framed by much larger, broader side lobes; usually less well-marked than Common Spotted-orchid, dark markings on the lip comprising dots and streaks, sometimes aligning as interrupted loops. Borne in compact spikes, May to July.

FRUITS Egg-shaped.

LEAVES Green and variably spotted, typically much less so than Common Spotted-orchid.

B&I STATUS Locally common on suitable soils.
NW EUROPEAN STATUS Widespread.

Early Marsh-orchid *Dactylorhiza incarnata*

HEIGHT To 60cm.

ECOLOGY & NATURAL HISTORY Compact-flowered and medium-sized marsh-orchid.

HABITAT Grows in dune slacks, and inland in damp meadows, typically on calcareous soils, but occasionally on acid ground.

FLOWERS Usually flesh pink, but sometimes reddish purple or very occasionally pure white; the sides of the 3-lobed lip are strongly reflexed along the mid-line hence the flower is narrow when viewed front-on. Flowers are borne in spikes, May to June.

FRUITS Egg-shaped.

LEAVES Yellowish green, usually unmarked, narrow-lanceolate, keeled and often hooded at the tip.

var. *incarnata*

var. *coccinea*

var. *incarnata*

B&I STATUS Locally common throughout.

NW EUROPEAN STATUS Widespread.

Five varieties (sometimes referred to as subspecies) are recognised in Britain and Ireland, two of which are locally common in coastal habitats: nominate **var. *incarnata*** typically has salmon pink flowers and is widespread in suitable habitats; **var. *coccinea*** has deep red flowers and is confined mainly to dune slacks and machair.

Southern Marsh-orchid *Dactylorhiza praetermissa*

HEIGHT To 70cm.

ECOLOGY & NATURAL HISTORY Robust orchid and a commonly encountered and striking species in damp coastal grassland, mainly south of a line between the rivers Humber and Mersey.

HABITAT Grows in wet dune slacks, and inland in water meadows and fens, mostly on calcareous soils.

FLOWERS Range from pink to pinkish purple depending on plant and location, with a broad 3-lobed lip, the central lobe bluntly pointed, the side lobes rounded; dark spots and streaks are confined to the lip centre. Flowers are borne in tall, dense spikes, May to June.

FRUITS Egg-shaped.

LEAVES Glossy dark green, unmarked (very rarely ring-spotted) and broadly lanceolate, largest at the base and becoming narrower and sheathing up the stem.

B&I STATUS Locally common in the southern half of Britain. **NW EUROPEAN STATUS** Widespread, commonest in the south.

Northern Marsh-orchid *Dactylorhiza purpurella*

HEIGHT To 60cm.

ECOLOGY & NATURAL HISTORY Northern counterpart of Southern Marsh-orchid.

HABITAT Grows in dune slacks and coastal grassland, and inland in damp meadows.

FLOWERS Deep reddish purple, the lip broadly diamond-shaped with indistinct lobes and dark streaks; borne in dense spikes, June to July.

FRUITS Egg-shaped.

LEAVES Green and narrow, including those at the base, and mostly unmarked.

Similar **Irish Marsh-orchid** *Dactylorhiza kerryensis* has in the past been known by a number of other names, notably Western Marsh-orchid *D. occidentalis* or *D. majalis* ssp. *occidentalis*. Endemic to Ireland, it grows in dune slacks and damp coastal grassland; its magenta or purple flowers have a lip with variable markings and three broad, rounded lobes.

B&I STATUS Locally common in N and W Britain and Ireland.

NW EUROPEAN STATUS Widespread, commonest in the south.

Narrow-leaved Marsh-orchid *Dactylorhiza traunsteinerioides*

HEIGHT To 40cm.

ECOLOGY & NATURAL HISTORY
Delicate, rather open-flowered orchid whose flower stem is usually flushed red towards the top. Previously known, and sometimes still referred to, as Pugsley's Marsh-orchid.

HABITAT Grows in machair, dunes and coastal grassland on calcareous soils; inland, found in fens and marshes on base-rich soils.

FLOWERS Pinkish purple with darker markings, a noticeably long spur, a pronounced hood and a 3-lobed lip, the central lobe of which projects while the side ones are sometimes folded back down from the midline. Borne in relatively few-flowered spikes, May to June.

FRUITS Egg-shaped.

LEAVES Usually 3–4, narrow, lanceolate, keeled and variably spotted.

B&I STATUS Very local, mainly in N Britain and Ireland. East Anglian plants are the subject of debate as to their true identity.
NW EUROPEAN STATUS Absent.

Hebridean *Dactylorhiza* orchids with intensely purple-spotted leaves were formerly called Hebridean Marsh-orchid *D. ebudensis*; and plants with similarly dark-blotched leaves from NW Scotland were previously treated as Lapland Marsh-orchid *D. lapponica*. Both are now regarded as ecologically distinct variations on the *traunsteinerioides* theme belonging to **ssp. *francis-drucei***.

Lesser Butterfly-orchid *Platanthera bifolia*

HEIGHT To 40cm.
ECOLOGY & NATURAL HISTORY Distinctive perennial.
HABITAT Undisturbed grassland including dune slacks; widespread but patchy across much of Britain, favouring a range of soil types.
FLOWERS Greenish white with a long, narrow lip, a long spur (25–30mm) and pollen sacs that are parallel; borne in open spikes, May to July.
FRUITS Egg-shaped.
LEAVES Pair of large oval leaves at the base and much smaller scale-like leaves up the stem.

B&I STATUS Widespread but local.
NW EUROPEAN STATUS Widespread but local.

Marsh Fragrant-orchid *Gymnadenia densiflora*

HEIGHT To 40cm.
ECOLOGY & NATURAL HISTORY Distinctive perennial.
HABITAT Grows in calcareous dune slacks, and similarly damp calcareous habitats inland.
FLOWERS Borne in dense cylindrical spikes of fragrant flowers, May to June; typical forms are pink but white-flowered plants do occur.
FRUITS Egg-shaped.
LEAVES Narrow and unspotted.

B&I STATUS Widespread but local.
NW EUROPEAN STATUS Widespread but local.

Early-purple Orchid *Orchis mascula*

HEIGHT To 40cm.
ECOLOGY & NATURAL HISTORY
Attractive, spring-flowering
perennial.
HABITAT Grows in coastal grassland,
and inland in woodland, scrub and
meadows, doing especially well on
neutral or calcareous grassland.
FLOWERS Pinkish purple, with a long
spur and 3-lobed lower lip, unmarked
except for a scattering of dark spots on
an otherwise pale 'throat'; compared
to superficially similar Green-winged
Orchid, hood is unmarked. Borne in
tall, open spikes, April to June.
FRUITS Egg-shaped.
LEAVES Glossy and dark green with
dark spots; leaves appear first as a
rosette, from January onwards, from
which the flower stalk arises later in
spring.

B&I STATUS Widespread
and locally common.
NW EUROPEAN STATUS
Widespread, north to
lowland Scandinavia.

Pyramidal Orchid *Anacamptis pyramidalis*

HEIGHT To 30cm.

ECOLOGY & NATURAL HISTORY
Distinctive and easily recognised orchid. Where conditions suit it, the species can be very locally abundant.

HABITAT Grows in stabilised sand dunes and grassland; usually associated with calcareous soils.

FLOWERS Deep pink, with a 3-lobed lip and a long spur; borne in dense, conical or domed flower heads, June to August.

FRUITS Egg-shaped.

LEAVES Grey-green, lanceolate and usually carried upright, partially sheathing the flower stem.

B&I STATUS Locally common in parts of England, Wales and Ireland.

NW EUROPEAN STATUS Local and patchily distributed, mainly NW France to N Germany.

Loose-flowered Orchid *Anacamptis laxiflora*

HEIGHT To 1m.
ECOLOGY & NATURAL HISTORY Tall, elegant perennial.
HABITAT Grows in damp grassland.
FLOWERS Pinkish purple, the lip with a pale, dark spotted centre and reflexed sides; borne on long stalks in open spikes, May to July.
FRUITS Egg-shaped.
LEAVES Narrow, grey-green and unmarked.

B&I STATUS Confined to Jersey and Guernsey.
NW EUROPEAN STATUS Very local and scarce, mainly NW France.

Green-winged Orchid *Anacamptis morio*

HEIGHT To 40cm.
ECOLOGY & NATURAL HISTORY Distinctive orchid.
HABITAT Grows in dune slacks and coastal grassland; inland favours undisturbed grassland on neutral to base-rich soils.
FLOWERS Colour varies from plant to plant, ranging from pinkish purple to almost white; note the dark veins on the hood (cf. Early-purple Orchid); lip sides are often reflexed and centre is usually pale and well-marked with spots. Borne in rather open spikes, May to June.
FRUITS Egg-shaped.
LEAVES Glossy green, unmarked and appear as a basal rosette, and sheathing the stem.

B&I STATUS Locally common in central and S England, S Wales and central Ireland.
NW EUROPEAN STATUS Local, north to S Scandinavia but absent from much of Low Countries and Denmark.

Dense-flowered Orchid *Neotinea maculata*

HEIGHT To 20cm.
ECOLOGY & NATURAL HISTORY Short, compact orchid that is easily overlooked.
HABITAT Grows in dunes and short grassland on limestone soils.
FLOWERS Tiny and white or pinkish, depending on the plant; borne in congested heads, April to June.
FRUITS Egg-shaped.
LEAVES Broad at the base, narrowing up the stem, often withering and yellowing by the time the flower spike appears.

Similar **Small-flowered Tongue-orchid** *Serapias parviflora* has flowers with a narrow maroon lip (the 'tongue') and grows in bare grassy places. Possibly native to S Cornwall where it has not been seen recently. Very occasional elsewhere in England but widespread on the Atlantic coast of France.

B&I STATUS Rare and restricted to W Ireland, notably The Burren in Co. Clare.
NW EUROPEAN STATUS Absent.

Lizard Orchid *Himantoglossum hircinum*

HEIGHT To 1m.

ECOLOGY & NATURAL HISTORY Impressive and extraordinary orchid. Bizarrely, the flowers smell of goats.

HABITAT Grows in stabilised dunes and calcareous grassland.

FLOWERS Comprise a greenish grey hood, adorned on the inside with reddish streaks, and an extremely long and twisted lip (up to 5cm); borne in tall spikes, May to July.

FRUITS Egg-shaped.

LEAVES Comprise oval basal leaves that soon wither, and smaller stem leaves that persist.

B&I STATUS Regularly seen only in E Kent (Sandwich Bay) and Cambridgeshire; very occasionally turns up elsewhere.

NW EUROPEAN STATUS Scarce and local, mainly NW France.

Beaked Tasselweed *Ruppia maritima*
Spiral Tasselweed *Ruppia spiralis*

HEIGHT To 60cm (aquatic and trailing).
ECOLOGY & NATURAL HISTORY Superficially very
similar to one another (except for their flowers), these
are submerged aquatic perennials with slender stems.
Both Beaked and Spiral Tasselweeds have been known
as *Ruppia cirrhosa* in the past, the name's association
with the latter species lingering until relatively recently.
HABITAT Grow in brackish coastal pools and ditches.
FLOWERS Submerged, minute, easily overlooked and
borne in stalked umbels comprising greenish stamens
and no petals, July to September; stalks elongate and
rise to the surface in fruit.
FRUITS Swollen, egg-shaped and borne in umbels.
Beaked Tasselweed stalks are 2–3cm long and wavy;
those of Spiral Tasselweed are obviously spiralled and
4–6cm long.
LEAVES Narrow (1mm wide) and linear; those of
Spiral Tasselweed are rounded at the tip, while
Beaked Tasselweed's leaf tips are pointed.

Sharing the same brackish habitats and overall
appearance are **Fennel Pondweed** *Potamoge-
ton pectinatus*, which has terminal spikes
of flower and fruits; and **Horned Pondweed**
Zannichellia palustris, which has unstalked
clusters of flowers and fruits.

Beaked Tasselweed   Spiral Tasselweed

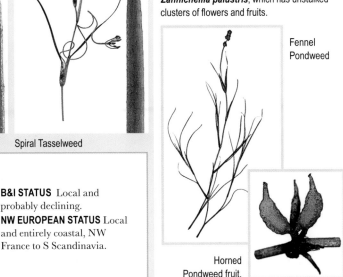

Fennel
Pondweed

Horned
Pondweed fruit.

B&I STATUS Local and
probably declining.
NW EUROPEAN STATUS Local
and entirely coastal, NW
France to S Scandinavia.

EELGRASS

Eelgrasses belong to the genus *Zostera* and, as their name implies, they are flowering plants rather than seaweeds, despite the fact that they live exclusively in the marine environment. Our two species are important ecologically, binding sediment with their roots and consequently reducing erosion and creating stability in the sheltered waters of bays and estuaries. They also provide a safe haven for marine creatures and serve as food for wildfowl.

Eelgrass *Zostera marina*

HEIGHT To 60cm, submerged and trailing.
ECOLOGY & NATURAL HISTORY Grass-like marine perennial that forms extensive beds when undisturbed. The underwater 'meadow' habitat this species creates provides shelter to and home for a range of marine creatures, from the Long-snouted (Spiny) Seahorse *Hippocampus guttulatus* and species of pipefish (*Entelurus* spp. and *Syngnathus* spp.) to stalked jellyfish such as *Haliclystus salpinx* and the sea-slug *Elysia viridis*.
HABITAT Grows in sand and silt substrates, typically below the low-water mark, hence rarely exposed to air and only by extreme tides.
FLOWERS Small, greenish and borne in branched clusters, enclosed by sheaths, June to September.
FRUITS Spongy.
LEAVES Linear, up to 1cm wide and 5cm long.

In the past, a third species was recognised: *Zostera angustifolia*. It is now considered to be a growth-form variety of *Z. marina*, one that has smaller, narrower leaves that are uncovered by all but the weakest of low tides.

B&I STATUS Widespread but local.
NW EUROPEAN STATUS Widespread, local and entirely coastal, NW France to N Norway and S Sweden.

Above: sea-slug *Elysia viridis*
Right: stalked jellyfish

Dwarf Eelgrass *Zostera noltei*

HEIGHT To 20cm, submerged and trailing.
ECOLOGY & NATURAL HISTORY Similar to Eelgrass
but smaller. Provides food in autumn and early winter
for wildfowl, including Brent Geese *Branta bernicla* and
Wigeon *Mareca penelope*.
HABITAT Typically associated with estuaries where it
grows between mid-water and low-water marks.
FLOWERS Small, greenish and borne in branched
clusters, enclosed by sheaths, June to September.
FRUITS Spongy.
LEAVES Linear, up to 1.5mm wide and 12cm long.

B&I STATUS
Widespread but local.
NW EUROPEAN
STATUS Widespread,
local and entirely
coastal, NW France
to S Sweden.

Brent Goose

Sea Rush
Juncus maritimus

HEIGHT To 1m.
ECOLOGY & NATURAL HISTORY Upright, stiff and clump-forming perennial.
HABITAT Grows in the drier upper reaches of saltmarshes, and among coastal rocks.
FLOWERS Straw-coloured and borne in loose clusters below a sharp-pointed bract, June to July.
FRUITS Brown, ovoid and bluntly pointed; similar length to the perianth.
LEAVES Sharply pointed.

B&I STATUS Locally common on coasts.
NW EUROPEAN STATUS Scarce, local and entirely coastal, NW France to S Sweden.

Sharp Rush
Juncus acutus

HEIGHT To 1.5m.
ECOLOGY & NATURAL HISTORY Clump-forming perennial that lives up to its name with its fearsomely-sharp leaves. In a few locations, it does so well that control measures are considered necessary by some.
HABITAT Stabilised dunes and dry coastal grassland.
FLOWERS Brown and borne in rounded clusters that are shorter than the spine-tipped bract, June to July.
FRUITS Ovoid, brown and twice the length of the perianth.
LEAVES Stiff, with an extremely sharp point.

B&I STATUS Local, and confined mainly to SW Britain and Channel Islands.
NW EUROPEAN STATUS Scarce and local, NW France only.

Jointed Rush
Juncus articulatus

HEIGHT To 80cm.
ECOLOGY & NATURAL HISTORY Prostrate perennial with upward-arching flowering stems.
HABITAT Margins of pools in dune slacks and coastal grassland.
FLOWERS Brown and borne in much-branched sprays.
FRUITS Ovoid and black.
LEAVES Curved and flattened laterally.

Similar **Blunt-flowered Rush *Juncus subnodulosus*** is an upright perennial (to 120cm tall) of damp, base-rich dune slacks and brackish marshes, and calcareous marshes and fens inland; its flowers are straw-coloured, borne in open, widely-spreading heads with blunt tepals, and it is widespread but local.

Similar **Bulbous Rush *Juncus bulbosus*** is a small perennial (often 10–15cm tall) with a bulbous base and branching sprays of blunt flowers and fruits; it favours damp, acid soils.

B&I STATUS Widespread and common.
NW EUROPEAN STATUS Widespread, north to lowland S Scandinavia.

Compact Rush
Juncus conglomeratus

HEIGHT To 1m.
ECOLOGY & NATURAL HISTORY Upright perennial. Similar to compact-flowered form of Soft Rush but stems are darker green, ridged, rough and not glossy.
HABITAT Damp, grazed grassland, mainly on acid soils.
FLOWERS Brown and borne in compact clusters, May to July.
FRUITS Dark brown, ovoid and as long as perianth.
LEAVES Absent.

B&I STATUS Locally common.
NW EUROPEAN STATUS Widespread, north to lowland S Scandinavia.

Hard Rush
Juncus inflexus

HEIGHT To 1.2m.
ECOLOGY & NATURAL HISTORY Tufted perennial with stiff, ridged and bluish or greyish green stems.
HABITAT Grows in damp, grassy places but avoids acid soils.
FLOWERS Brown and borne in loose clusters below a long bract, June to August.
FRUITS Brown and ovoid with a tiny point.
LEAVES Absent.

B&I STATUS Widespread and common except in the north.
NW EUROPEAN STATUS Widespread from NW France to Low Countries and N Germany; scarce or absent elsewhere.

Soft Rush
Juncus effusus

HEIGHT To 1.5m.
ECOLOGY & NATURAL HISTORY Clump-forming perennial with yellowish green, glossy and smooth stems.
HABITAT Grows on overgrazed grassland, mostly on acid soils.
FLOWERS Pale brown and borne in loose or open clusters near the stem tops, June to August.
FRUITS Yellow-brown, ovoid, indented at the tip and shorter than perianth.
LEAVES Absent.

B&I STATUS Widespread and common.
NW EUROPEAN STATUS Widespread, north to lowland S Scandinavia.

Saltmarsh Rush
Juncus gerardii

HEIGHT To 50cm.
ECOLOGY & NATURAL HISTORY Characteristic rush of saltmarshes, often covering extensive areas.
HABITAT Upper reaches of saltmarshes, saline grassland and margins of brackish pools behind seawalls.
FLOWERS Dark brown and borne in loose clusters, flanked by leaf-like bracts, June to July.
FRUITS Brown, ovoid, glossy and equal in length to the perianth.
LEAVES Dark green and arise at the base of the plant, and on stems.

B&I STATUS Locally common around coasts.
NW EUROPEAN STATUS Widespread but entirely coastal, north to S Norway and Baltic coasts.

Baltic Rush
Juncus balticus

HEIGHT To 70cm.
ECOLOGY & NATURAL HISTORY Creeping perennial, superficially similar to feeble-flowering specimens of both Hard and Soft rushes.
HABITAT Dune slacks.
FLOWERS Brown and borne in rather one-planed clusters, June to August.
FRUITS Brown and ovoid.
LEAVES Absent.

B&I STATUS Widespread in N Scotland, absent elsewhere.
NW EUROPEAN STATUS Northern species, found mainly in Scandinavia and around the Baltic.

Dwarf Rush
Juncus capitatus

HEIGHT To 5cm.
ECOLOGY & NATURAL HISTORY Tiny, tufted annual that often turns reddish in maturity.
HABITAT Grows in damp, seasonally-parched bare coastal ground.
FLOWERS Borne in a terminal cluster with 2 leaf-like bracts, May to June.
FRUITS Brown, ovoid and shorter than perianth.
LEAVES Wiry, entirely basal and soon withering.

B&I STATUS Rare and restricted to S Cornwall, Anglesey and the Channel Islands.
NW EUROPEAN STATUS Rare and local, NW France to S Baltic coasts.

Toad Rush
Juncus bufonius

HEIGHT To 40cm.
ECOLOGY & NATURAL HISTORY
Tufted annual that often turns red when stressed by drought.
HABITAT Grows in damp ground in dune slacks and coastal marshes, often in damp hollows; also found inland in a wide range of seasonally-drying bare ground.
FLOWERS Greenish white with pointed inner tepals; borne in branched clusters along the stems, topped by a sharp spine, May to September.
FRUITS Brown, ovoid and shorter than perianth.
LEAVES Narrow and grooved.

B&I STATUS Widespread and common.
NW EUROPEAN STATUS Widespread, north to lowland Scandinavia.

Similar **Frog Rush *Juncus ranarius* (ambiguus)** is the saltmarsh/saline soil counterpart of Toad Rush and is widespread on coasts. Certain identification requires hand lens examination of minute flower structure and reference to Stace. Pointers in the field (apart from habitat) include its generally prostrate habit and the fact that inflorescences are mainly borne in terminal clusters and not along the length of the stem.

Curved Sedge
Carex maritima

HEIGHT To 12cm.
ECOLOGY & NATURAL HISTORY Creeping perennial that is distinctive by sedge standards.
HABITAT Coastal sand and fine gravel, just above tide line and alongside other colonising plants.
FLOWERS Brown and arranged in dense, egg-shaped terminal heads without bracts; borne on curved stalks, June to July.
FRUITS Beaked and blackish brown.
LEAVES Curved and stiff, with inrolled margins.

B&I STATUS Local, restricted to Scotland and NE England.
NW EUROPEAN STATUS Scarce and local, mainly coast of Norway.

Divided Sedge
Carex divisa

HEIGHT To 75cm.
ECOLOGY & NATURAL HISTORY Creeping perennial.
HABITAT Dune slacks and brackish grassland.
FLOWERS Brown and borne in 3–7 dense clusters, the bottom 2 often slightly separate, May to June.
FRUITS Pale brown and flask-shaped.
LEAVES Narrow and inrolled.

B&I STATUS Local, restricted mainly to S and E coasts of England.
NW EUROPEAN STATUS Scarce and local, mainly NW France and Low Countries.

Sand Sedge
Carex arenaria

HEIGHT To 35cm.
ECOLOGY & NATURAL HISTORY
Creeping perennial. The
progress of its underground
stems can be detected by
aerial shoots, which run
in straight lines.
HABITAT Grows in sand dunes.
FLOWERS Comprise pale
brown spikes, in a terminal
head, male flowers above
females, May to July.
FRUITS Yellowish brown and
beaked.
LEAVES Slender, flat and as
long as flowering stem.

B&I STATUS Locally
common on most suitable
coasts.
NW EUROPEAN STATUS
Widespread but local,
mainly NW France to
Denmark.

Long-bracted Sedge
Carex extensa

HEIGHT To 40cm but sometimes prostrate.
ECOLOGY & NATURAL HISTORY Tufted
perennial.
HABITAT Upper saltmarsh zone, margins of
coastal pools and brackish grassland.
FLOWERS Spike of tawny brown, male flowers
topping widely separated spikes of greenish
brown female flowers, May to June. Note the
extremely long, leaf-like bracts (longer than
inflorescence).
FRUITS Greenish brown.
LEAVES Green, 2–3mm wide and often
inrolled.

B&I STATUS Locally
common in N and
exclusively coastal;
virtually absent from SE.
NW EUROPEAN STATUS
Local.

Distant Sedge
Carex distans

HEIGHT To 1m.
ECOLOGY & NATURAL HISTORY
Tufted perennial.
HABITAT Upper saltmarsh, margins of
coastal pools and brackish grassland.
FLOWERS Spike of tawny brown, male
flowers topping widely separated spikes
of greenish brown female
flowers, May to June.
FRUITS Greenish brown
and flask-shaped, flattened
on one side.
LEAVES Grey-green and
3–5mm wide.

B&I STATUS
Widespread but local.
**NW EUROPEAN
STATUS** Scarce and
local, mainly NW
France to Baltic
coasts.

Dotted Sedge
Carex punctata

HEIGHT To 70cm.
**ECOLOGY & NATURAL
HISTORY** Tufted perennial.
HABITAT Brackish
grassland and freshwater
seepages on sea cliffs.
FLOWERS Spike of brown
male flowers tops spikes of
yellowish green female
flowers, June to July.
FRUITS Yellowish green,
held at right-angles to stalk.
LEAVES Yellow-green and
5–7mm wide.

B&I STATUS
Extremely local
and exclusively
coastal.
**NW EUROPEAN
STATUS** Scarce
and local.

Sea Club-rush
Bolboschoenus maritimus

HEIGHT To 1.25m.
ECOLOGY & NATURAL HISTORY
Creeping, robust perennial whose stems
are rough and triangular in cross-
section.
HABITAT Grows on the margins of
brackish water near the sea.
FLOWERS Comprise a tight, terminal
cluster of egg-shaped spikelets, flanked
by a long, leafy bract, July to August.
FRUITS Dark brown.
LEAVES Rough and keeled.

B&I STATUS Locally
common.
NW EUROPEAN STATUS
Widespread but local
and coastal, north to S
Scandinavia and S Baltic.

Grey Club-rush
Schoenoplectus tabernaemontani

HEIGHT To 1.5m.
ECOLOGY & NATURAL HISTORY Grey-green, creeping perennial. Where conditions are suitable it can form extensive stands.
HABITAT Brackish water, in coastal grassland, lagoons, saltmarshes and dune slacks.
FLOWERS Reddish brown spikelets, borne on stalks and over-topped by a bract.
FRUITS Dark brown nut.
LEAVES Absent.

B&I STATUS Widespread and locally common in the south.
NW EUROPEAN STATUS Local and coastal, mainly Low Countries and S Baltic shores.

Black Bog-rush
Schoenus nigricans

HEIGHT To 80cm.
ECOLOGY & NATURAL HISTORY Tussock-forming perennial.
HABITAT Dune slacks, wet base-rich flushes on sea cliffs and drier reaches of saltmarshes; fens and bogs inland.
FLOWERS Blackish spikelets, borne in dense heads overtopped by long bract, May to June.
FRUITS Blackish nuts.
LEAVES Slender and all arising from the base.

B&I STATUS Widespread and locally common, although declining due to habitat loss.
NW EUROPEAN STATUS Widespread but local.

Round-headed Club-rush
Scirpoides holoschoenus

HEIGHT To 1.4m.
ECOLOGY & NATURAL HISTORY Tufted perennial.
HABITAT Dune slacks.
FLOWERS Borne in spherical heads, 6–10mm in diameter, July to August.
FRUITS Brown nuts.
LEAVES Slender and rush-like.

B&I STATUS Rare and local, restricted to N Devon and Somerset, and S Wales.
NW EUROPEAN STATUS Local from W France southwards.

Saltmarsh Flat-sedge
Blysmus rufus

HEIGHT To 40cm.
ECOLOGY & NATURAL HISTORY Slender, creeping perennial. Where conditions suit it, Saltmarsh Flat-sedge can form sizeable patches; when you have your eye in, the deep brown heads of flowers and fruits are striking.
HABITAT Damp, brackish ground in saltmarshes, dune slacks and beside coastal ditches.
FLOWERS Terminal cluster of brown spikelets, often overtopped by a bract.
FRUITS Brown nut.
LEAVES Narrow, inrolled and rush-like.

B&I STATUS Locally common in NW Britain and Ireland.
NW EUROPEAN STATUS Local on suitable coasts in N Europe.

Spike-rushes
Eleocharis spp.

HEIGHT To 50cm.
Spike-rushes are a group of superficially rush-like plants that like to grow in damp, sometimes waterlogged ground. A number of rather similar species occur in our region, including on the coast, requiring close scrutiny of their flower structure (and reference to Stace) to determine their identity with certainty. The most widespread is **Common Spike-rush *Eleocharis palustris***, which is found in damp dune slacks and coastal marshes with stems that are usually 2–4mm in diameter. More exclusively coastal, and with a northern bias to its distribution, is **Slender Spike-rush *E. uniglumis***, which favours dune slacks, saltmarshes and damp saline grassland; it is called 'Slender' for a good reason, the stems being no more than 1.5mm in diameter. All spike-rushes have terminal heads of brown spikelets; those of *E. palustris* are usually 10–25mm long; those of *E. uniglumis* are usually 5–10mm long and often set at a jaunty angle with the lowest glume embracing the base of the spikelet (a feature requiring hand lens scrutiny for certainty).

Common Spike-rush

Slender Spike-rush

Slender Spike-rush
B&I STATUS Local.
NW EUROPEAN STATUS Local and coastal, mainly Low Countries to Scandinavia.

Wildflowers

Lyme-grass
Leymus arenarius

HEIGHT To 1.5m.
ECOLOGY & NATURAL HISTORY
Blue-grey perennial.
HABITAT Grows in sand dunes and
on sandy beaches.
FLOWERS Borne in tall heads of
paired, grey-green spikelets, June
to August.
FRUITS Small, dry nutlets.
LEAVES Up to 15mm wide, with
inrolled margins.

B&I STATUS Widespread,
mainly in E Britain.
NW EUROPEAN STATUS
Locally common and
coastal, mainly Low
Countries to Scandinavia
and Baltic shores.

This grass is the sole foodplant for caterpillars of the
plant's namesake moth,
the **Lyme Grass Lon-
galatedes elymi**, whose
range matches that of the
plant; its stronghold is on
the east coast of Britain.

Bermuda-grass
Cynodon dactylon

HEIGHT To 30cm.
ECOLOGY & NATURAL HISTORY Spreading,
mat-forming perennial.
HABITAT Dunes and short grassland on sandy
soils.
FLOWERS Spreading, hand-like umbel of 3–6
spikes, each bearing rows of paired, purplish
spikelets, August to September.
FRUITS Tiny nutlets.
LEAVES Green, flat and 2–4mm wide.

B&I STATUS Mostly
introduced and
naturalised, but possibly
native in Cornwall.
NW EUROPEAN STATUS
Local, mainly NW France.

Sea Barley
Hordeum marinum

HEIGHT To 35cm (often much less).
ECOLOGY & NATURAL HISTORY Tufted annual. Green at first, yellowish brown when dry.
HABITAT Grows on bare ground and dry, grassy places near the sea.
FLOWERS Borne in long, unbranched spikes, 3–6cm long, the spikelets in 3s, each with stiff, spreading awns 1–2.5cm long, June to July; middle spikelet glumes are smooth (hand lens needed).
FRUITS Small, dry nutlets.
LEAVES 1–4mm wide.

B&I STATUS Local and exclusively coastal.
NW EUROPEAN STATUS Scarce and local, mainly NW France to Low Countries.

Wall Barley
Hordeum murinum

HEIGHT To 30cm.
ECOLOGY & NATURAL HISTORY Tufted annual of bare ground.
HABITAT Waste places, often near the sea.
FLOWERS Borne in long, unbranched spikes, 9–10cm long, with spikelets in 3s, each with stiff awns 1–3cm long, May to July; middle spikelet glumes have marginal hairs (hand lens needed).
FRUITS Small, dry nutlets.
LEAVES 3–8mm wide with short, blunt ligules.

B&I STATUS Widespread and locally common.
NW EUROPEAN STATUS Widespread and locally common.

Soft-brome
Bromus hordaceus

HEIGHT To 50cm, often much shorter on cliffs.
ECOLOGY & NATURAL HISTORY Variable annual. Represented by several subspecies including widespread ssp. *hordaceus* (sometimes dwarfed near coast) and ssp. *ferronii* which is exclusively coastal.
HABITAT Grows beside tracks and open grassland; ssp. *ferronii* is restricted to coastal cliffs and banks, and stabilised shingle.
FLOWERS Borne in spikes of greenish, ovate and downy spikelets, May to June; spikes are stiff and upright in ssp. *ferronii* but often droop in other subspecies.
FRUITS Nutlets.
LEAVES 3–7mm wide and softly hairy.

Ssp. *ferronii*
B&I STATUS Ssp. *hordaceus* is widespread and common; ssp. *ferronii* is restricted to SW Britain.
NW EUROPEAN STATUS Widespread but local.

BENT-GRASSES

Agrostis grasses are important grassland components. When in full flower they have small florets borne on slender, branches in a whorled, open panicle; in some species the panicle branches contract when flowering has finished. Identification is a challenge but to follow are a couple of species commonly encountered in coastal grassland.

Common and Creeping Bents
B&I STATUS Widespread and common.
NW EUROPEAN STATUS Widespread and common.

Common Bent
Agrostis capillaris

HEIGHT To 40cm.
ECOLOGY & NATURAL HISTORY Tufted perennial with creeping rhizomes.
HABITAT Widespread in grassland, including sand dunes, favouring neutral to slightly acid soils.
FLOWERS Small, one-flowered purplish brown spikelets borne in whorled panicles up to 20cm tall, June to August.
FRUITS Nutlets.
LEAVES Flat and 2–5mm wide.

Creeping Bent
Agrostis stolonifera

HEIGHT To 40cm.
ECOLOGY & NATURAL HISTORY Perennial with leafy, creeping runners that root at the joints.
HABITAT Brackish grassland, dune slacks and upper saltmarshes; also widespread inland.
FLOWERS Small, one-flowered purplish brown spikelets borne in whorled panicles up to 12cm tall, June to August.
FRUITS Nutlets.
LEAVES Flat and 1–5mm wide.

Common Reed *Phragmites australis*

HEIGHT To 2m.

ECOLOGY & NATURAL HISTORY
Familiar, robust perennial that often forms extensive stands. Plant turns brown and persists through winter.

HABITAT Grows around margins of coastal pools (brackish and freshwater), and on damp ground and in marshes.

FLOWERS Spikelets start purplish brown then fade to straw-coloured; borne in branched, 1-sided terminal clusters, August to September.

FRUITS Brown.

LEAVES Broad and long.

B&I STATUS
Widespread and common.

NW EUROPEAN STATUS
Widespread, north to lowland Scandinavia.

Common Reed is a colonising grass of water margins and the reedbeds that result from its vigorous growth are significant enough ecologically to warrant special mention. Numerous animals call this habitat home, some almost exclusively so. Although reedbeds are found inland as well as on the coast, it is near the sea where they come into their own, both in terms of extent and accessibility to naturalists.

A reedbed is a transition habitat, spanning the divide between open water and dry land; this range of habitats within a habitat is reflected in the species distribution of its invertebrate communities and notably its moths, many species of which have larvae that live and feed inside reed stems. Some favour reeds growing in water and pupate inside the stems of the plant; **Brown-veined Wainscot *Archanara dissoluta*, Twin-spotted Wainscot *Lenisa geminipuncta*** and **Silky Wainscot *Chilodes maritima*** are examples, the latter species having carnivorous tendencies and occasionally turning its attention to the larvae and pupae of fellow stem-dwelling moths. Others live in reeds growing in drier zones, the larvae feeding inside the stems but pupating in leaf litter; the **Reed Leopard *Phragmataecia castaneae*** is an example of this strategy.

A number of bird species are associated exclusively, or nearly so, with reedbeds including the **Reed Warbler *Acrocephalus scirpaceus*,** a summer visitor that nests among reeds and feeds on insects. Most endearing of all is the **Bearded Tit *Panurus biarmicus*** whose diet ranges from invertebrates to seeds depending on season and availability.

Above:
Reed Leopard

Left:
Silky Wainscot

Below:
Twin-spotted
Wainscot

Left: Bearded Tit
Below: Reed Warbler

Yorkshire Fog
Holcus lanatus

HEIGHT To 1m.
ECOLOGY & NATURAL HISTORY Variable, tufted perennial with grey-green, downy stems.
HABITAT Grows in meadows, and a wide range of grassland habitats.
FLOWERS Borne in heads that are tightly packed at first but then spread; comprise reddish-tipped, grey-green, 2-flowered spikelets, May to August.
FRUITS Small, dry nutlets.
LEAVES Grey-green and downy.

Similar **Creeping Soft-grass** *Holcus mollis* is soft to the touch and has a greyish look about it; it favours acid soils.

Bulbous Meadow-grass
Poa bulbosa

HEIGHT To 40cm.
ECOLOGY & NATURAL HISTORY Tufted perennial with a bulbous base.
HABITAT Stabilised shingle and sand dunes.
FLOWERS Borne in a compact inflorescence of reddish green spikelets.
FRUITS Nutlets, but leafy, proliferous plantlets appear in var. *vivipara*.
LEAVES 1–2mm wide, with purplish sheaths.

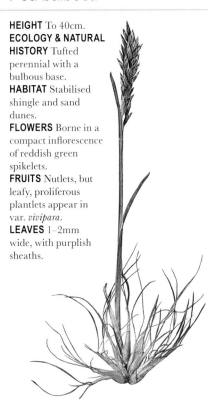

Early Meadow-grass
Poa infirma

HEIGHT To 10cm.
ECOLOGY & NATURAL HISTORY Tufted and often prostrate annual.
HABITAT Grows on bare ground near the sea.
FLOWERS Inflorescence has spikelets along the length of its branches, March to May.
FRUITS Nutlets.
LEAVES Yellowish green, narrow and flat.

B&I STATUS Local, in S England.
NW EUROPEAN STATUS Local, NW France only.

Similar **Annual Meadow-grass *Poa annua*** is taller (to 25cm) with green leaves and spikelets at the ends of inflorescence branches.

Yellow Oat-grass
Trisetum flavescens

HEIGHT To 50cm.
ECOLOGY & NATURAL HISTORY Slender, softly hairy perennial.
HABITAT Grows in dry grassland on calcareous soils in mature sand dunes; widespread inland.
FLOWERS Borne in an open inflorescence of yellowish, 2–4-flowered spikelets, each with a bent awn, June to July.
FRUITS Small dry nutlets.
LEAVES Narrow and flat with a blunt ligule.

B&I STATUS Widespread and locally common, except in the north.
NW EUROPEAN STATUS Widespread and locally common.

TRUE FESCUES

Members of the genus *Festuca*, fescues are important grassland components. Their spikelets comprise three or more florets and the panicles comprise branches that arise singly or in pairs, never in whorls. Red and Sheep's Fescues are common but extremely, and often confusingly, variable with an array of subspecies and forms adding to the identification challenges.

Red Fescue
Festuca rubra

HEIGHT To 60cm.
ECOLOGY & NATURAL HISTORY Clump-forming perennial.
HABITAT Wide range of grassy habitats, including upper reaches of saltmarshes, sea cliffs and sand dunes.
FLOWERS Borne in an inflorescence, the spikelets 7–10mm long and usually reddish, May to July.
FRUITS Small, dry nutlets.
LEAVES Either inrolled, wiry and stiff (on non-flowering stems) or flat (on flowering stems).

Red Fescue is an extremely variable plant represented by a bewildering array of subspecies and appearances; confusingly only certain coastal forms are red. What they have in common, however, is that the leaf sheath is fused almost to its tip, not just inrolled. Superficially similar **Rush-leaved Fescue** *Festuca arenaria* has all its leaves inrolled; it grows on sand dunes and shingle.

B&I STATUS Widespread and common.
NW EUROPEAN STATUS Widespread.

Sheep's Fescue
Festuca ovina

HEIGHT To 30cm.
ECOLOGY & NATURAL HISTORY Variable, tufted and hairless perennial.
HABITAT Grows in calcareous grassland including cliffs and dunes.
FLOWERS Borne in branched but compact heads of grey-green spikelets, each with a short awn, May to July.
FRUITS Small, dry nutlets.
LEAVES Short, narrow, inrolled, hair-like and waxy.

B&I STATUS Widespread and locally common.
NW EUROPEAN STATUS Widespread and locally common.

Dune Fescue
Vulpia fasciculata

HEIGHT To 20cm.
ECOLOGY & NATURAL HISTORY Tufted annual.
HABITAT Sand dunes and sandy shingle.
FLOWERS A curved, 1-sided inflorescence (to 10cm long) of long-awned spikelets, May to June.
FRUITS Nutlets.
LEAVES Narrow and becoming inrolled when dry, the sheaths of upper leaves inflated.

B&I STATUS Local, on coasts of S Britain and Ireland.
NW EUROPEAN STATUS Scarce and local, NW France only.

Bearded Fescue
Vulpia ciliata

HEIGHT To 30cm.
ECOLOGY & NATURAL HISTORY Tufted annual.
HABITAT Sand dunes and other areas of bare ground on sandy soils.
FLOWERS A 1-sided inflorescence (to 12cm long) of long-awned spikelets, May to June.
FRUITS Nutlets.
LEAVES Narrow, with inflated sheaths.

Similar **Squirrel-tail Fescue *Vulpia bromoides*** has long-awned, one-sided inflorescences like its relatives. It reaches 50cm in height but is usually shorter in coastal settings such as dunes.

B&I STATUS Local, confined mainly to S and E England.
NW EUROPEAN STATUS Scarce and local, NW France only.

THE *SPARTINA* STORY

Cord-grasses *Spartina* spp. are present in many estuaries, and their root systems and stems help bind substrates and consolidate vegetation. At a glance, they seem integral to saltmarsh communities. However, appearances can be deceptive and, in some situations, one species in particular has a worryingly negative environmental impact. Unsurprisingly, this downside has a human dimension, one whose origins can be traced back to Victorian times.

Once upon a time, British saltmarshes hosted just one species of *Spartina*, namely Small Cord-grass *S. maritima*. All was well until early in the 19th Century when an event occurred that would profoundly impact saltmarsh and mudflat communities in the centuries that followed, not just in Britain and Ireland but worldwide. The story begins in the 1820s when Smooth Cord-grass *S. alterniflora* appeared on the shores of Southampton Water, in Hampshire; the arrival of this North American species is assumed to have been accidental and ship-assisted.

Cord-grass flowers have characteristic bottle-brush-like stigmas whose feathery structure is designed to maximise the chances of 'catching' airborne pollen.

A novelty at first, it soon hybridised with *S. maritima* to produce a sterile hybrid, known today as Townsend's Cord-grass *S. x townsendii*. So far, not so bad. However, before long natural chromosome doubling created a fertile new 'species' that today is called Common Cord-grass *S. anglica*. As far back as the late Victorian era it was promoted and planted to turn tidal saltmarsh into dry land, a role that it plays here and abroad to this day. The plant doesn't need much human assistance and under its own steam it now dominates many British and Irish saltmarsh communities, to the point where its relatively feeble native parent *S. maritima* has been all-but excluded by its vigorous offspring.

So what, you might ask? Surely one *Spartina* species is much the same as another? Sadly, the answer is no and *S. anglica*'s spread has led to a wide range of environmental problems, the result of the plant's aggressive ability to accelerate the process of transition from daily inundated mudflats to dry land. It is not just estuarine flora that suffers. Invertebrate communities too are affected, particularly relevant being those that depend

Small Cord-grass

Common Cord-grass

Common Cord-grass

Smooth Cord-grass

Townsend's Cord-grass

on mudflats themselves. The vast numbers of burrowing annelid worms, crustaceans and molluscs that live unseen in the mud are important in their own right. But more profoundly they are part of a largely overlooked ecosystem, and serve as food for countless wintering birds. With rising sea levels and global warming realities, the effects of *Spartina anglica* seem set to be felt more widely here and abroad.

Cord-grasses (*Spartina* spp.) are represented in our region by three species, only one of which is common and widespread, plus one hybrid. They are plants of saltmarshes and estuaries, and flower from July to September.

Small Cord-grass *Spartina maritima* grows to 0.5m tall, has leaves that are 3.5–4.5mm wide, ligules that are 0.2–0.6mm long, downy glumes and flower spikes up to 8cm long. Restricted mainly to the Solent and East Anglian coast but declining, much-diminished and hard to discover these days. In NW Europe, restricted to NW France where it is scarce and local.

Common Cord-grass *Spartina anglica* (right) grows to 1.3m tall, has leaves that are 6–15mm wide, ligules that are 2–3mm long, downy glumes and flower spikes up to 24cm long. The only widespread and common cord-grass, locally common on most suitable coasts although absent from the far north. Widespread but local on Atlantic coasts of NW Europe.

Smooth Cord-grass *Spartina alterniflora* grows to 1.2m tall, has leaves that are 6–15mm wide, ligules that are 1–1.8mm long, smooth glumes and flower spikes up to 15cm long. Its occurrence is much-reduced nowadays and it is probably confined to just one extensive patch beside Southampton Water. Absent from elsewhere in NW Europe.

Townsend's Cord-grass *Spartina* x *townsendii* grows to 1.3m tall, has leaves that are 6–15mm wide, ligules that are 1–1.8mm long, downy glumes and flower spikes up to 22cm long. Sterile, it arises spontaneously and spreads vegetatively. Local and declining with a similar overall range to *S. anglica*. Scarce and declining on Atlantic coasts of NW Europe.

Common Saltmarsh-grass
Puccinellia maritima

HEIGHT To 30cm.
ECOLOGY & NATURAL HISTORY
Hairless, tufted perennial.
HABITAT Grows in middle and
upper levels of saltmarshes and
forms swards.
FLOWERS Borne in spike-like
heads, with spikelets carried on
branches, July to August; the
branches, 2–3 per node, are
mainly upright, not spreading.
FRUITS Small, dry nutlets.
LEAVES Grey-green and
often inrolled.

B&I STATUS Widespread
and locally common.
NW EUROPEAN STATUS
Widespread, north to S
Baltic shores.

Reflexed Saltmarsh-grass
Puccinellia distans

HEIGHT To 30cm.
**ECOLOGY & NATURAL
HISTORY** Hairless,
tufted perennial. Has
spread along salt-treated
roadside verges
inland.
HABITAT Grows
in upper levels of
saltmarshes, in coastal
saline grassland, and on
seawalls.
FLOWERS Borne in spike-
like heads, with spikelets
carried on
branches,
June to
August; the branches
spread and become
reflexed in maturity
and in fruit.
FRUITS Small, dry
nutlets.
LEAVES Grey-green and
often inrolled.

B&I STATUS Widespread
and locally common.
NW EUROPEAN STATUS
Scarce and local
throughout.

Borrer's Saltmarsh-grass
Puccinellia fasciculata

HEIGHT To 60cm.
ECOLOGY & NATURAL HISTORY Tough, hairless and tufted perennial.
HABITAT Brackish marshes and grassland, typically on or beside muddy margins of drying pools and ditches.
FLOWERS Borne in spike-like heads, with greenish white spikelets carried on stiff branches, June to August; the branches are spreading or upright, not reflexed.
FRUITS Small, dry nutlets.
LEAVES Grey-green and flat.

B&I STATUS Local, found mainly in S and E England.
NW EUROPEAN STATUS Scarce and local, mainly NW France and Low Countries.

Stiff Saltmarsh-grass
Puccinellia rupestris

HEIGHT To 35cm.
ECOLOGY & NATURAL HISTORY Tufted, spreading or prostrate annual.
HABITAT Bare, brackish mud, tracks and on and behind seawalls.
FLOWERS Borne in dense heads, with spikelets carried on stiff branches, June to August; the branches are spreading, not reflexed.
FRUITS Small, dry nutlets.
LEAVES Flat but with hooded tips.

B&I STATUS Local, found mainly in S England.
NW EUROPEAN STATUS Scarce, NW France only.

Marram *Ammophila arenaria*

HEIGHT To 1m.
ECOLOGY & NATURAL HISTORY
Perennial that stabilises shifting
sands by means of its underground
stems.
HABITAT Coastal sand dunes.
FLOWERS Borne in dense spikes,
with 1-flowered, straw-coloured
spikelets, July to August.
FRUITS Small, dry nutlets.
LEAVES Tough, grey-green,
inrolled and sharply pointed.

The cater-
pillars of a
moth called
the **Shore
Wainscot
*Mythimna
litoralis*** feed
only on the
leaves of
Marram.

Two pioneer grasses – **Sand Couch *Elytrigia juncea***
and **Lyme-grass *Leymus arenarius*** – are usually
the first to colonise sand on the seashore. Thereafter,
Marram is the dominant force in dune stabilisation.
Thriving in situations where it is routinely buried by
wind-blown sand, it grows through its grainy blanket
and its roots and stems bind the substrate. Sealing
its own fate, sooner or later Marram is out-competed
by other plants as mature dunes inland become more
heavily vegetated. Find out more about sand dunes on
pages 16–19.

B&I STATUS
Widespread and
common on suitable
coasts.
**NW EUROPEAN
STATUS** Widespread
on suitable coasts.

Sweet Vernal-grass
Anthoxanthum odoratum

HEIGHT To 50cm.
ECOLOGY & NATURAL HISTORY Tufted, downy perennial with a sweet smell of new-mown hay.
HABITAT Grows in dry grassland, usually on acid soils in sand dunes; widespread inland.
FLOWERS Borne in relatively dense spike-like clusters, 3–4cm long, of 3-flowered spikelets, each with 1 straight and 1 bent awn, April to July.
FRUITS Small, dry nutlets.
LEAVES Flat with blunt ligules.

B&I STATUS Widespread and locally common.
NW EUROPEAN STATUS Widespread and locally common.

Cock's-foot
Dactylis glomerata

HEIGHT To 1m.
ECOLOGY & NATURAL HISTORY Tufted, tussock-forming perennial.
HABITAT Sea cliffs, sand dunes and all types of grassland inland.
FLOWERS Borne in an inflorescence of long-stalked, dense and egg-shaped heads, June to July; the panicle spreads with maturity and then fancifully resembles a chicken's foot.
FRUITS Small, dry nutlets.
LEAVES Rough with slightly inrolled margins.

B&I STATUS Widespread and common.
NW EUROPEAN STATUS Widespread and common.

Early Hair-grass
Aira praecox

HEIGHT To 40cm.
ECOLOGY & NATURAL HISTORY Annual that forms small tufts.
HABITAT Dunes and clifftops on acid, sandy soils, in short vegetation; favours similar ground inland.
FLOWERS Borne in a spike-like inflorescence, May to July.
FRUITS Small, dry nutlets.
LEAVES Grey-green and wiry.

B&I STATUS Locally common.
NW EUROPEAN STATUS Widespread, north to S Scandinavia.

Grey Hair-grass
Corynephorus canescens

HEIGHT To 25cm.
ECOLOGY & NATURAL HISTORY Perennial that forms dense tufts.
HABITAT Dunes and sandy shingle, especially where lichens have colonised; also on sandy heaths inland.
FLOWERS Inflorescence of purplish spikelets, each with an orange awn, June to July.
FRUITS Small, dry nutlets.
LEAVES Stiff and hair-like.

B&I STATUS Very local.
NW EUROPEAN STATUS Local and scarce, mainly Low Countries to S Baltic shores.

Bulbous Foxtail
Alopecurus bulbosus

HEIGHT To 25cm.
ECOLOGY & NATURAL HISTORY Tufted, grey-green perennial with stems that are bulbous at the base.
HABITAT Grows in damp, coastal grassland.
FLOWERS Borne in cylindrical, purplish heads, 2–3cm long, the spikelets with long awns and blunt ligules, June to August.
FRUITS Small, dry nutlets.
LEAVES Narrow and smooth below.

B&I STATUS Locally common in S England and S Wales only.
NW EUROPEAN STATUS Local, mainly NW France and Low Countries.

Similar **Marsh Foxtail** *Alopecurus geniculatus* is larger with longer flowering heads (4–7cm); it roots at the nodes and is widespread in damp grassland.

Sea Fern-grass
Catapodium marinum

HEIGHT To 15cm.
ECOLOGY & NATURAL HISTORY Tough and wiry annual.
HABITAT Grows in dry grassland.
FLOWERS Borne in a branched, superficially fern-like inflorescence with short-stalked or unstalked spikelets, more or less in one plane, May to July.
FRUITS Nutlets.
LEAVES Narrow and wiry.

Similar **Fern-grass** *Catapodium rigidum* has a twice-pinnate inflorescence. Widespread in lowland Britain, especially near coasts.

B&I STATUS Locally common in the south.
NW EUROPEAN STATUS Scarce and local, mainly NW France and Belgium.

Hard-grass
Parapholis strigosa

HEIGHT To 30cm.
ECOLOGY & NATURAL HISTORY
Easily overlooked, slender annual.
HABITAT Upper levels of
saltmarshes and damp, bare
ground near the sea. Tolerates a
moderate degree of trampling,
hence sometimes found beside
paths and tracks.
FLOWERS Slender spike of closely
adpressed spikelets, June to
August.
FRUITS Nutlets.
LEAVES Grey-green,
narrow and flat.

B&I STATUS Widespread
and locally common.
NW EUROPEAN STATUS
Scarce and local, north
to S Scandinavia.

Curved Hard-grass
Parapholis incurva

HEIGHT To 10cm.
ECOLOGY & NATURAL HISTORY Tough and
distinctive annual, recalling a dwarf, arched
version of *P. strigosa*.
HABITAT Bare coastal ground including upper
levels of saltmarshes.
FLOWERS Borne in a curved, purplish
inflorescence of compact, closely-adpressed
spikelets, June to August.
FRUITS Nutlets.
LEAVES Grey-green and narrow, with an
inflated sheath.

B&I STATUS Scarce and
local, in S Britain only.
NW EUROPEAN STATUS
Scarce and local, mainly
N France.

Annual Beard-grass
Polypogon monspeliensis

HEIGHT To 70cm but occasionally miniature (less than 10cm).
ECOLOGY & NATURAL HISTORY Distinctive and often ephemeral annual. When found in botanically-stressful environments its stature is said to diminish with the years, plants becoming dwarfed before disappearing.
HABITAT Bare, grassy places near the sea, especially the drying margins of drainage channels.
FLOWERS Borne in a dense inflorescence with long awns, green at first, turning silky white later, partly shrouded by uppermost leaf at first, June to August.
FRUITS Dry nutlets.
LEAVES Flat and rough.

B&I STATUS Scarce and local, mainly coastal SE England.
NW EUROPEAN STATUS Scarce and local, NW France only.

Hare's-tail Grass
Lagurus ovatus

HEIGHT To 50cm.
ECOLOGY & NATURAL HISTORY Attractive and distinctive plant.
HABITAT Sand dunes.
FLOWERS Borne in egg-shaped heads that are softly hairy, June to August; the awns are bent halfway along length.
FRUITS Dry nutlets.
LEAVES Grey-green and hairy; sheaths on stem leaves are inflated.

B&I STATUS Naturalised and rare, mainly in S England.
NW EUROPEAN STATUS Scarce and local, NW France only.

Sand Cat's-tail
Phleum arenarium

HEIGHT To 15cm.
ECOLOGY & NATURAL HISTORY
Slender annual.
HABITAT Sand dunes and sandy
shingle.
FLOWERS Borne in elongate-ovoid
heads of spikelets, greenish white
maturing straw-coloured, May
to July.
FRUITS Nutlets.
LEAVES Narrow and flat with an
inflated sheath.

B&I STATUS Widespread
but local.
NW EUROPEAN STATUS
Widespread but local.

Sea Couch
Elytrigia atherica

HEIGHT To 1m.
ECOLOGY & NATURAL HISTORY
Tough, spreading and patch-
forming perennial.
HABITAT Grows in maritime
grassland, on upper reaches of
saltmarshes, beside brackish
creeks and on sea walls.
FLOWERS Borne in a stiff,
unbranched inflorescence with
many-flowered yellowish green
spikelets, June to August.
FRUITS Small, dry nutlets.
LEAVES Green with a sharp,
terminal point; initially flat but
inrolled when dry.

B&I STATUS Widespread
and locally common.
NW EUROPEAN STATUS
Locally common, mainly
NW France to Low
Countries.

Sand Couch
Elytrigia juncea

HEIGHT To 60cm.
ECOLOGY & NATURAL HISTORY Patch-forming, spreading perennial.
HABITAT Sandy shores, just above the strandline, ahead of Marram colonisation.
FLOWERS Borne in a stiff, unbranched inflorescence with widely-spaced spikelets, June to August.
FRUITS Nutlets.
LEAVES Grey-green, initially flat but inrolled when dry.

B&I STATUS Widespread and locally common.
NW EUROPEAN STATUS Local, mainly N France and Low Countries.

Similar **Early Sand-grass** *Mibora minima* is a contender for the smallest grass in the world. Its flower spikes are often just 1cm long; they are one-sided and usually tinged purple, February to April. Rare, in scattered locations from Lancashire to Dorset, in bare, coastal sandy ground.

Greater Quaking-grass
Briza maxima

HEIGHT To 60cm.
ECOLOGY & NATURAL HISTORY Distinctive tufted annual.
HABITAT Sand dunes, coastal grassland and track margins.
FLOWERS Clusters of overlapping spikelets, borne on pendant stalks, May to July.
FRUITS Nutlets.
LEAVES Green and 4–8mm wide.

B&I STATUS Introduced and naturalised in SW Britain.
NW EUROPEAN STATUS Local, mainly NW France.

Quaking-grass
Briza media

HEIGHT To 40cm.
ECOLOGY & NATURAL HISTORY Distinctive perennial.
HABITAT Grows in dry grassland, including sand dunes, usually on calcareous soils.
FLOWERS Borne in an open, inflorescence, the dangling spikelets resembling miniature hops or cones and carried on wiry stalks, June to September.
FRUITS Small, dry nutlets.
LEAVES Pale green and form loose tufts.

B&I STATUS Widespread and locally common.
NW EUROPEAN STATUS Widespread and locally common.

THE ISLES OF SCILLY – a botanical hotspot

Located 28 miles off the coast of Cornwall, the Isles of Scilly harbour a wealth of botanical treasures and a floral mix found nowhere else in our region. Influencing the assemblage of plants are the islands' geographical location, the moderating effect on the climate of being surrounded by the sea, and the history of human land use.

Understandably, many classic maritime species thrive around the islands' coastline, with habitats that include cliffs, maritime heaths, grassland and dunes. Plants such as Thrift *Armeria maritima* and Sea Campion *Silene uniflora* grow locally in profusion and can be found in the main section of this book. Adding spice to the botanical fusion, the archipelago's mild climate and geographical location mean that a handful of species from southern Europe and the Mediterranean region have their best (sometimes their only) British and Irish stations on Scilly. Plants such as Orange Bird's-foot *Ornithopus pinnatus*, Rough-fruited Buttercup *Ranunculus muricatus*, Smaller Tree-mallow *Malva multiflora* and Four-leaved Allseed *Polycarpon tetraphyllum* fall into this category and and can be found in the main section of the book.

Over the last century or so, bulb and cut-flower cultivation have been important for the local economy, with relatively small sheltered fields the norm and regular tilling standard practice. Although not as widespread as in the past, this continuing low-intensity agricultural land-use has ensured that so-called 'arable weeds' thrive far better on the islands than in mainland Britain. Species such as Corn Marigold *Glebionis segetum*, Small-flowered Catchfly *Silene gallica* and several species of ramping-fumitory *Fumaria* do well and also feature in the main section of this book.

Human impact on Scilly flora extends beyond agricultural influence with a horticultural dimension adding visual impact to the islands. Introductions from all round the world, including escapees from the Abbey Gardens on Tresco, often seem quite at home on the islands to the point where it can be hard for the untutored eye to distinguish introduced alien species from genuine natives. The effect may be pleasing to the human eye but in some situations, and with certain species, the exotics have turned into botanical 'thugs'. As a consequence, efforts are often needed to combat their spread because they can effectively exclude native flora and cause local extinctions, with a resulting loss of native biodiversity. Some of Scilly's exotic introductions are found elsewhere in southern Britain; an example is Hottentot-fig *Carpobrotus edulis*, which because of its wider occurrence is featured in the main section of the book.

For botanists interested in finding out more about Scilly's exotic plants, reference to Rosemary Parlow's *Discovering Isles of Scilly Wild Flowers* provides a good introduction. For a more exhaustive account, refer to *The New Flora of the Isles of Scilly* by Rosemary Parslow and Ian Bennallick. Some of the most regularly encountered species include: Tree Houseleek *Aeonium arboretum*; Bermuda Buttercup *Oxalis pes-caprae*; Giant Herb-Robert *Geranium maderense*; Wireplant *Muehlenbeckia complexa*; Purple Dewplant *Disphyma crassifolium*; Pale Dewplant *Drosanthemum floribundum*; Deltoid-leaved Dewplant *Oscularia deltoides*; Sickle-leaved Dewplant *Lampranthus falciformis*; Shrubby Dewplant *Ruschia caroli*; Common Purslane *Portulaca oleracea*; Giant Viper's-bugloss *Echium piniana*; Bear's-breech *Acanthis mollis*; Ake-ake *Olearia traversii*; Cineraria *Pericallis hybrida*; German-ivy *Delairea odorata*; Hedge Ragwort *Brachyglottis repanda*; Shrub Goldilocks *Chrysocoma coma-aurea*; Cape Daisy *Osteospermum jucundum*; African Lily *Agapanthus praecox*; Jersey Lily *Amaryllis belladonna*; New Zealand Flax *Phormium tenax*; Chilean-iris *Libertia formosa*; Blue Corn-lily *Aristea ecklonii*; Bugle-lily *Watsonia borbonica*; Red Corn-lily *Ixia campanulata*; Tubular Corn-lily *Ixia paniculata*; Spanish Iris *Iris xiphium*; Plain Harlequinflower *Sparaxis grandiflora*; Freesia *Freesia x hybrida*; and Eastern Gladiolus *Gladiolus communis*. A visual snapshot of some of the most iconic and eye-catching horticultural alien plants follows, to whet your appetite for more.

Giant Herb-Robert *Geranium maderense*

Purple Dewplant *Disphyma crassifolium*

Pale Dewplant
*Drosanthemum
floribundum*

Wireplant *Muehlenbeckia complexa*

Tree Houseleek
*Aeonium
arboretum*

Giant Viper's-bugloss *Echium piniana*

German-ivy *Delairea odorata*

Cape Daisy *Osteospermum jucundum*

Eastern Gladiolus *Gladiolus communis*

Bermuda Buttercup
Oxalis pes-caprae

Ake-ake *Olearia traversii*

ARCTIC AND ALPINE FLORA MEET THE COAST

The further north you travel in Europe, the more severe the climate becomes, particularly during the winter months. This has a profound influence on what grows where, with some surprises thrown into the mix. Predictably, as you head towards the Arctic circle you increasingly encounter tundra species growing at sea level. Perhaps more surprisingly companion plants sometimes include flowers that thrive on mountain tops in Scotland or further afield in the Alps. This is particularly true where soils have a calcareous influence through wind-blown shell sand or lime-rich bedrock. In Britain, outposts where Arctic and Alpine flora flourish at sea level are found on the northern Scottish coast, with an outlier at The Burren on the west coast of Ireland. Here are some interesting examples of Arctic and Alpine plant species regularly encountered near northern shores.

Moss Campion
Silene acaulis

HEIGHT Cushion-forming.
This charming perennial forms cushions of densely-packed wiry leaves. These are studded in June and July with pink flowers, which are 5-petalled and 9–12mm across.

Purple Saxifrage
Saxifraga oppositifolia

HEIGHT Creeping.
Growing on damp, shady rocks this mat-forming perennial has trailing stems, with small, dark green leaves carried in opposite pairs. In March and April, purple flowers appear, which are 10–15mm across.

Cloudberry
Rubus chamaemorus

HEIGHT To 20cm.
This creeping, downy perennial has rounded, palmately-lobed leaves and white flowers that are 15–25mm across with 5 white petals; these appear from June to August. The striking fruits are red at first, but ripen orange.

Mountain Avens
Dryas octopetala

HEIGHT To 6cm.
Favouring basic soils, this creeping perennial has flowers that are 3–4cm across with 8 or more white petals and masses of yellow stamens; the flowers appear in June and July, and face and follow the daily progress of the sun. The fruits have feathery plumes.

Dwarf Cornel
Cornus suecica

HEIGHT To 15cm.
This distinctive creeping perennial has umbels of small, purplish black flowers surrounded by 4 white bracts; they appear from June to August and are followed by bright red fruits. The oval leaves have 3 veins on either side of the midrib.

Field Fleawort
Tephroseris integrifolia ssp. *tundricola*

HEIGHT To 65cm.
This Arctic counterpart of South Stack and Field Fleaworts favours calcareous outcrops on the northern Scandinavian coast. Its yellow and orange flowers are borne in heads, 15–25mm across; they appear in open clusters from May to July. The oval, toothed leaves grow mainly as a basal rosette.

White Mountain Orchid
Pseudorchis straminea

HEIGHT To 20cm.
Look for spikes of tightly-packed yellowish flowers that appear in July. The species forms small colonies where conditions suit it, and often favours areas of sparsely-vegetated wind-blown sand. Its range includes coastal northern Scandinavia. Formerly treated as a subspecies of Small White Orchid *P. albida*, which occurs in northern Britain.

SEAWEEDS

Seaweeds are dominant seashore plants, found in a range of habitats from rocky shores to estuaries. Zonation among the group is usually obvious, each species having evolved to cope with differing periods of exposure to air, inundation by the sea, and tolerance of wave action. Some seaweeds are intertidal and can be discovered growing *in situ* while others live submerged but wash up on the strandline when dislodged by gales.

Seaweeds do not produce flowers, and reproduce by a process called alternation of generations: an asexual generation produces spores, the next produces sex cells. In some seaweed species, the two generations look identical but in others there are marked morphological differences. Unlike flowering plants, seaweeds lack proper roots, stems, leaves and a vascular system, which does not stop some species growing to a huge size. In common with flowering plants, seaweeds photosynthesise, harnessing sunlight energy using a green pigment called chlorophyll. In some species, chlorophyll's colour is masked by other pigments.

Modern seaweed classification recognises three superficially similar but unrelated groups, broadly categorised by colour. Green seaweeds are treated as true plants and their chlorophyll is not masked. Red seaweeds are also regarded as true plants and their green chlorophyll is masked by red or bluish pigments; the group includes chalky, coralline species. Brown seaweeds have least in common with flowering plants and their green chlorophyll is masked by brown pigments. Here is a selection of some commonly encountered species.

Channelled Wrack
Pelvetia canaliculata

LENGTH To 15cm.
This brown seaweed forms an obvious zone on upper shores of rocky coasts. The olive-brown and much-branched fronds have inrolled margins.

Spiral Wrack
Fucus spiralis

LENGTH To 35cm.
This brown seaweed grows attached to rocks on the upper shore. Its fronds branch regularly and typically twist in spiral fashion towards the tip; frond margins are not serrated and air-bladders are absent.

Non-flowering plants

Bladder Wrack
Fucus vesiculosus

LENGTH To 1m.
This tough brown seaweed grows on rocks on the middle shore. Its fronds are olive-brown or greenish brown and branch regularly; groups of 2 or 3 air-bladders are found along its length and spongy reproductive bodies occur at the frond tips.

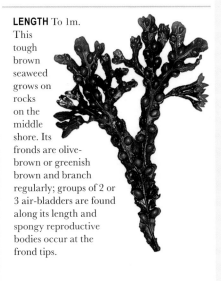

Serrated Wrack
Fucus serratus

LENGTH To 65cm.
This brown seaweed grows on rocks on the lower middle shore. Its fronds are greenish brown and flattened, with distinct midribs; they branch regularly and have serrated margins. Air-bladders are absent and reproductive bodies are found in pitted, swollen frond-tips.

Egg Wrack
Ascophyllum nodosum

LENGTH To 1.5m.
This brown seaweed grows in a zone between the upper and middle shores. The tough, leathery fronds branch regularly and are flattened towards the tips. Air-bladders occur along the length and note the sultana-like yellowish green reproductive bodies.

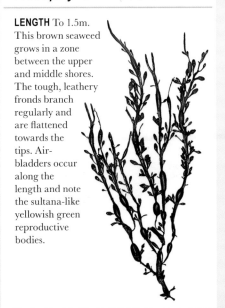

Thongweed
Himanthalia elongata

LENGTH To 2m.
This unusual brown seaweed starts life as a button-like structure growing attached to rocks on the lower shore. The frond arises from this and is olive-green, long, slightly flattened and strap-like, sometimes forking towards the tapering tip. Vast quantities of fronds are washed up on the shore after autumn storms.

Kelp
Laminaria digitata

LENGTH To 1m.
This impressive brown seaweed comprises a branched and tough holdfast, a flexible stipe and a broad blade, divided into strap-like fronds. It typically forms dense beds with only the floating frond exposed at most low tides. Plants are often washed up after winter gales.

Sugar Kelp
Saccharina latissima

LENGTH To 1.5m.
This distinctive brown seaweed grows on sheltered lower shores and in the past was harvested by crofters on the west coast of Scotland as a source of food. The frond comprises a stout stipe and strap-shaped blade with a crinkly margin.

Gutweed
Ulva spp.

LENGTH To 75cm.
An aptly named green seaweed which grows in sheltered estuaries, brackish lagoons and upper shore rock pools. The fronds comprise variably constricted, membranous tubes that inflate with oxygen in sunshine.

Sea Lettuce
Ulva spp.

LENGTH To 40cm.
This green membranous seaweed grows on extremely sheltered shores, and often in rock pools. It soon becomes tattered.

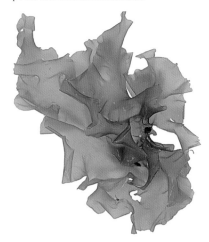

Velvet Horn
Codium tomentosum

LENGTH To 20cm.
This green seaweed grows on the mid- to lower shore. Its branching, greenish fronds end in rounded tips and its texture is rather felt-like.

Red Rags
Dilsea carnosa

LENGTH To 45cm.
A bright red seaweed which grows on the lower shore and among kelps. Its fronds are broad, flattened and elongate, and sometimes tear towards the tip.

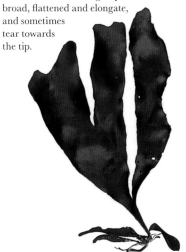

Pepper Dulse
Osmundea pinnatifida

LENGTH To 15cm.
A tufted, branched seaweed which sometimes forms dense mats. Its fronds are slender and purplish brown or olive; they are tough and rubbery.

Dulse
Palmaria palmata

LENGTH To 40cm.
This flat, reddish brown seaweed grows on rocks and the stipes of kelps. Its fronds are tough and membranous, and usually divided into finger-like lobes towards the tip.

Laver
Porphyra spp.

LENGTH To 50cm.
This membranous seaweed is represented by five superficially similar species. The fronds are thin and membranous, ranging from red or purple, to yellowish green. The fronds grow mainly attached to rock but some species are epiphytic on larger seaweeds.

Wrack Siphon Weed
Vertebrata lanosa

LENGTH To 10cm.
There are several superficially similar species but this one grows on the fronds of Egg Wrack. Its tufted-looking fronds comprises branched, segmented stems that collapse out of water. Previously known as *Polysiphonia lanosa*.

Coral Weed
Corallina officinalis

LENGTH To 6cm.
This atypical pinkish red seaweed has branched stems and calcified segments. It is common and widespread in rock pools on the middle shore.

Common Pale Paint Weed
Lithophyllum incrustans

LENGTH To 5cm.
This encrusting pinkish red seaweed forms flattish, calcified plates and you might be forgiven for failing to recognise it as a plant at all. It favours sheltered rocky shores and pools.

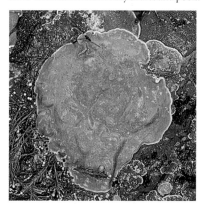

TERRESTRIAL NON-FLOWERING PLANTS

Terrestrial non-flowering plants range from single-celled algae, through mosses and horsetails, to complex ferns, plants with roots and a vascular system that transports food and water. Like flowering plants, they photosynthesise, trapping sunlight energy using pigments (including chlorophyll) and creating food. Unlike flowering plants, reproduction is primitive: they do not produce flowers or seeds but instead spores feature in their life-cycles.

Sandhill Screw-moss
Syntrichia ruraliformis

HEIGHT To 5cm.
This yellowish green moss forms dense and extensive patches in sand dunes. Its leaves are recurved, tapering and end in a thin point. The spore capsules are reddish, cylindrical and upright.

Whitish Feather-moss
Brachythecium albicans

HEIGHT Spreading.
Look for open carpets of the species on bare, sandy soil in dunes. The leaves are yellowish green, oval and pointed-tipped, and spore capsules are rarely seen.

Haircap mosses
Polytrichum spp.

HEIGHT To 10cm.
Superficially similar *Polytrichum* species are widespread, often forming carpets in damp dune slacks. The leaves are narrow and spreading, with the plants themselves resembling miniature conifer shoots.

Field Horsetail
Equisetum arvense

HEIGHT To 75cm.
This distinctive plant forms spreading, perennial patches in damp coastal grassland. The stems comprise sterile shoots that carry whorls of undivided branches. Fertile stems appear in early spring.

Variegated Horsetail
Equisetum variegatum

HEIGHT To 50cm, but sometimes prostrate.
This little-branched or unbranched perennial
has rough, ridged stems and sheaths at the
joints marked with black and white.
It is locally common in dune slacks.

Bracken
Pteridium aquilinum

HEIGHT Frond length to 2m.
This familiar fern carpets coastal slopes and
cliffs with dry, acid soils. At first the fronds are
compact with curled tips, and mature fronds
are green and are repeatedly divided 3-times.
Spore cases appear around the frond margins.

Hay-scented Buckler-fern
Dryopteris aemula

HEIGHT Frond length to 50cm.
This fern's
fronds smell
of hay when
crushed
and are
repeatedly
divided 3
times, with
pale brown
scales on
the stalk. It
favours west-
facing slopes.
Upturned
tips of
pinnules give
a crisped
appearance.

Sea Spleenwort
Asplenium marinum

HEIGHT Frond length to 30cm.
Tolerant of salt spray this is a classic maritime
fern, found in crevices and under cliff over-
hangs. The leathery, shiny fronds taper at
both ends and have broad, oblong lobes and
a green midrib.

Non-flowering plants

Lanceolate Spleenwort
Asplenium obovatum

HEIGHT Frond length to 30cm.
This fern usually grows within sight of the sea, on walls and rocky banks. The fronds are fresh green and do not taper towards the base, and the pinnae are often reflexed.

Polypody
Polypodium vulgare

HEIGHT Frond length to 50cm.
Damp, wooded valleys are home to this fern as well as damp dune slacks and coastal stone walls. The leathery fronds, which are carried on slender stalks, are dark green and divided simply.

Adder's-tongue
Ophioglossum vulgatum

HEIGHT To 10cm.
This distinctive and unusual fern grows in damp dune-slacks. Each plant has a single bright green, oval frond that is carried on a short stalk. The spores are borne on a tall fertile spike.

Dwarf Adder's-tongue
Ophioglossum azoricum

HEIGHT To 4cm.
Although similar to Adder's-tongue this species is much smaller and often has paired fronds. The spores are carried on a short fertile spike. It grows in short coastal grassland in western Britain.

Maidenhair Fern
Adiantum capillus-veneris

HEIGHT Frond length to 35cm.
Shady rock crevices and gullies, usually on calcareous rocks, are favoured sites for this delicate-looking fern. Its pendulous fronds comprise bright green, fan-shaped pinnae borne on a dark, wiry and divided stem.

Royal Fern
Osmunda regalis

HEIGHT Frond length to 3m.
This large and impressive fern grows on damp, shady sea cliffs and in dunes, mostly on acid soils. Its fronds are triangular overall, repeatedly divided 2 times into oblong lobes. The golden spores are carried on separate, central fertile fronds.

Jersey Fern
Anogramma leptophylla

HEIGHT Frond length to 8cm.
This delicate annual fern has fronds that are divided two times and resemble leaves of culinary flat parsley. It grows on bare banks and granite walls and in our region it is confined to Jersey.

Land Quillwort
Isoetes histrix

HEIGHT Leaf length to 8cm.
This atypical, tufted fern-relative has wiry, curved leaves that give the plant a superficial resemblance to a Thrift seedling. It grows in seasonally-drying hollows on the Lizard Peninsula in Cornwall, and the Channel Islands.

LICHENS

Lichens are intriguing 'partnership' organisms. They comprise a fungal body that creates structure and provides substrate attachment, and which is host to a photosynthesising partner, usually an alga but in some instances a cyanobacterium. Lichens are neither plants nor animals in the strict sense.

Cladonia spp.

HEIGHT Spreading.
Several *Cladonia* species are common in dunes. Some form intricate networks of wirewool-like, densely packed blue-grey or whitish strands. Some comprise scaly stalks topped with bright red spore-producing bodies, while others recall miniature stag's antlers.

Sea Ivory
Ramalina siliquosa

HEIGHT Length to 3cm.
Tolerant of salt spray, this tufted, branched lichen grows on coastal rocks and stone walls. Its branches are flattened and grey, and have disc-like spore-producing bodies.

Dogtooth Lichen
Peltigera canina

HEIGHT Spreading.
Look for this species in sand dunes where it forms dense mats, attached to the ground by root-like structures on the lower surface. Tooth-like reproductive structures appear on the upper surface.

Black Lichen
Lichina pygmaea

HEIGHT Encrusting.
Tolerating inundation by seawater, this patch-forming lichen grows on the middle shore in crevices and on rocks. It forms densely packed, branched and flattened dark brown tufts.

Tar Lichen
Verrucaria maura

HEIGHT Encrusting.
Tolerant of salt spray and occasional inundation by seawater this lichen grows on coastal rocks and stabilised shingle. Its surface is sooty black and cracked. At a glance, it could be mistaken for a patch of dried oil.

Orange Sea Lichen
Caloplaca marina

HEIGHT Encrusting.
This striking orange lichen forms irregular patches on rocks around high-water mark on the seashore. It tolerates salt spray and brief immersion in seawater.

Non-flowering plants

Yellow Scales
Xanthoria parietina

HEIGHT Spreading.
Although this bright orange-yellow lichen grows inland it is most spectacular on coasts. Its surface is wrinkled and slightly scaly, and it forms patches on rocks and walls.

The colourful, encrusting alga **Trentopohlia sp.** recalls a lichen and indeed it is one of the commonest symbionts in lichen partnerships. It is usually found forming encrusting patches that coat shady, damp rocks.

Map Lichen
Rhizocarpon geographicum

HEIGHT Spreading.
This rock-encrusting lichen has a yellowish surface etched with black spore-producing bodies. When two neighbouring colonies meet, boundaries become defined by black margins, creating a map-like appearance.

Golden Hair Lichen
Teloschistes flavicans

HEIGHT Width to 7cm.
This unmistakable lichen comprises a network of bright orange, interweaving strands that form a wirewool-like mass. It is restricted to coastal heaths and short, cliff-side vegetation in western Britain.

Crab's-eye Lichen *Ochrolechia parella*

HEIGHT Spreading.
Look for this encrusting, patch-forming lichen on walls and rocks. Its surface is greyish with a pale margin and clusters of raised, rounded and flat-topped spore-producing structures; these give rise to the lichen's English name.

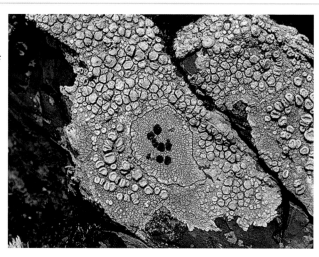

Black Shields
Tephromela atra

HEIGHT Encrusting.
Tolerating salt spray, this patch-forming species grows on rocks, at and just above the high-tide mark. Its knobbly surface is grey while the spore-producing structures are rounded and black with pale grey margins.

Anaptychia runcinata

HEIGHT Width to 10cm.
This cushion-forming lichen comprises overlapping, flattish, olive-brown leathery lobes. It grows on rocks and stone walls, usually within sight of the sea.

Non-flowering plants

FURTHER READING

BSBI Handbooks. A series of identification guides to selected plant groups or families. Botanical Society of Britain & Ireland.

Bunker, F.StP.D., Maggs, C.A., Brodie, J.A., & Bunker, A.R (2017). *Seaweeds of Britain and Ireland Second Edition*. Wild Nature Press/Princeton University Press.

Cole, S. & Waller, M. (2020). *Britain's Orchids: A field guide to the orchids of Great Britain and Ireland*. WILDGuides/Princeton University Press.

Field Studies Council FSC AIDGAP Guides to a wide range of taxa including Grasses, Mosses, Ferns and much more.

French, C.N. (2020). *A Flora of Cornwall*. Wheal Seton Press.

Harrap, A. & Harrap, S. (2009). *Orchids of Britain and Ireland: A Field and Site Guide*. Second edition. A&C Black.

Parker, S. (2016). *Wild Orchids of Wales: How, When and Where to Find Them*. First Nature.

Parslow, R. (2020). *Discovering Isles of Scilly Wild Flowers*. Parslow Press.

Parslow, R.E. & Bennallick, I.J. (2017). *The New Flora of the Isles of Scilly*. Parslow Press.

Poland, J. & Clement, E. (2019). *The Vegetative Key to the British Flora*. John Poland.

Preston, C.D., Pearman, D.A. & Dines, T.D. (2002). *New Atlas of the British and Irish Flora*. Oxford University Press.

Rich, T. & Jermy, A. (1998). *The Plant Crib*. Botanical Society of Britain & Ireland.

Rose, F. & O'Reilly, C. (2006). *The Wild Flower Key*. Frederick Warne.

Rose, F (1989). *Colour Identification Guide to the Grass, Sedges, Rushes and Ferns of the British Isles and north-western Europe*. Viking.

Smith, P.H. (2021). *Wildflowers of the Sefton Coast*. Lancashire and Cheshire Fauna Society.

Smith, R., Hodgson, B, & Ison, J. (eds.) (2016). *A New Flora of Devon*. The Devonshire Association for the Advancement of Science, Literature and the Arts.

Stace, C. (2019). *New Flora of the British Isles*, Fourth Edition. C&M Floristics.

Sterry, P.R. (2006). *Complete British Wild Flowers*. HarperCollins.

Streeter, D., Hart-Davies C., Hardcastle A., Cole F. & Harper L. (2009). *Collins Flower Guide*. HarperCollins.

USEFUL ADDRESSES

Botanical Society of Britain & Ireland (BSBI) bsbi.org

Field Studies Council (FSC) field-studies-council.org

The National Trust nationaltrust.org.uk

Plantlife plantlife.org.uk

The Royal Society for the Protection of Birds (RSPB) rspb.org.uk

The Wildlife Trusts wildlifetrusts.org

INDEX

Italicised page numbers refer to stand-alone photographs.